MAYA WARS

MAYA WARS

Ethnographic Accounts from Nineteenth-Century Yucatán

Edited by

Terry Rugeley

University of Oklahoma Press : Norman

ALSO BY TERRY RUGELEY

Yucatán's Maya Peasants and the Origins of the Caste War, 1800–1847 (Austin, 1996)

Of Wonders and Wise Men: Religion and Popular Cultures in Southeast Mexico, 1800–1876 (Austin, 2000)

LIBRARY OF CONGRESS CATALOGING-IN-PUBLICATION DATA

Rugeley, Terry, 1956–
Maya wars : ethnographic accounts from nineteenth-century Yucatán / Terry Rugeley.
p. cm
Includes bibliographical references and index.
ISBN 0-8061-3355-4 (alk. paper)
1. Mayas—Yucatán Peninsula—History—19th century—Sources. 2. Mayas —Wars 3. Yucatán (Mexico: State)—History—Caste War, 1847–1855—Sources. I. Title.
F1435.1.Y89 R84 2001
972'.6504   2001027355

1 2 3 4 5 6 7 8 9 10

Text design by Ellen Beeler

Contents

Illustrations

FIGURES

MAP

Acknowledgments

Innumerable people contributed to this book. First and foremost, I owe special thanks to the many archivists in Yucatán, Campeche, Mexico City, Belize, and the United States who aided me in my quest for the history of southeastern Mexico: like dragons, they guard treasures. Back home in Oklahoma, John Drayton, Jeff Burnham, Ross Hassig, and H. Wayne Morgan deserve special mention for their faith in and support for this project. The manuscript profited from Evelyn VandenDolder's rigorous copyediting and from the innumerable efforts of the University of Oklahoma Press's staff. I am deeply indebted to the many people of the Yucatán Peninsula, particularly in the town of Peto, who shared with me the living components of Maya culture. Eleuterio Poot Yah, Pastor Juan Pech, and Ismael May May provided outstanding instruction in the intricacies of the Maya language. David W. Walker and David G. LaFrance provided comments and suggestions that helped make this a better book. Finally, I thank my mother, Theresa Rugeley; my wife, Margarita; and my in-laws in Mérida, all of whom stood by me through many months of research and writing. If I have managed to capture on paper some part of what was a century of chaos, then much of the credit must go to these individuals.

Financial support for this project was provided by the American Philosophical Society, the Oklahoma Foundation for the Humanities, the University of Oklahoma Research Council, the Dean of the University of Oklahoma College of Arts and Sciences, and the University of Oklahoma Presidential Travel Fund.

Note on Orthography

The documents included in this book come from British, U.S., French, German, Maya, and Hispanic-Mexican authors and were written over a span of a hundred years. Needless to say, a project of this sort presents problems of orthography.

As much as possible, I tried to make the spelling of Maya words consistent with the modern orthography used in *El diccionario básico español-maya, maya-español,* by Ramón Bastarrachea et al. (Mérida: Maldonado Editores, 1992), the best codified and increasingly the most common system on the Yucatán Peninsula. The only exceptions were place names and last names that have retained traditional colonial spellings: for example, *h* instead of *j, c* instead of *k, u* instead of *w, th* instead of *t',* and *dz* instead of *ts*. The plural form of Maya words ending with a consonant is *-o'ob;* the plural form of Maya words ending with a vowel is *-'ob*.

All English words appear in modern U.S. spellings, and Spanish terms follow spellings of modern Spanish. Punctuation has been similarly modified to reflect modern usage. Some long paragraphs have been divided into two or more paragraphs to enhance readability. All translations from Spanish and Maya are my own.

Chronology

1812–14   Leaders of the *sanjuanista* movement organize Maya resistance to church taxation. Period of the Spanish Constitution. Padre Baeza writes his ethnography.

1821   Mexican independence.

1833   Federico de Waldeck begins his tour of Tabasco and Yucatán.

1839–40   Santiago Imán leads a revolt, which culminates in Yucatán's separation from Mexico.

1841–42   B. A. Norman visits Yucatán.

1842–43   Mexico's invasion of Yucatán ends in failure.

1846   U.S. armed forces invade Mexico. The Mexican War begins.

1847   The Caste War erupts on July 30 in the village of Tepich. *Batabs* are persecuted in northwestern Yucatán.

1848   Rebels realize maximum gains by May. Yucatecan army begins gradual recovery of lost territory. The Mexican War (with the United States) ends.

1849   Assassination of original rebel leaders Cecilio Chi and Jacinto Pat. Rebel leadership fragments among different lieutenants, including Venancio Pec and Florentino Chan.

1850   First known appearance of the Speaking Cross. The first *pacífico* peace treaty is signed in Chichanhá.

1852   Gen. Rómulo Díaz de la Vega occupies Chichanhá in April, striking a severe blow at rebel power in southeastern Yucatán and inaugurating a four-year lull in the Caste War.

1853   A second *pacífico* peace treaty is signed in Belize City.

1855   Marcelo Uc makes his journey to Mérida. Gradual renewal of Caste War hostilities. Venancio Puc emerges as the principal rebel leader.

1857   Missionary Richard Fletcher first visits Corozal in British Honduras (Belize). Rebels raid the town of Tekax.

1858   William Anderson meets with rebel leaders in Pucté. Rebels overrun Bacalar, occupying it for the next fifty years. José María Rosado is taken prisoner. Padre Amado Belizario Barreiro travels from Mérida to Flores, visiting Caste War refugee communities.

1860   José de los Angeles Loesa is taken prisoner by rebels.

1863   Beginning of French Empire in Yucatán. In Chan Santa Cruz, rebel leader Venancio Puc is assassinated, giving way to a triumvirate of Bonifacio Novelo, Crescencio Poot, and Bernabé Cen.

1865   José Demetrio Molino begins a two-year term as Indian Defense Attorney. A *pacífico* delegation travels to Mexico City to meet with Emperor Maximilian. A Yucatecan missionary initiative begins among *pacífico* communities.

1867   Fall of the French Empire. Hostilities erupt between Chan Santa Cruz and the *pacíficos*. John Carmichael visits Chan Santa Cruz. Richard Fletcher writes his ethnography in Corozal.

1868   Bonifacio Novelo dies.

1875   Bernabé Cen dies in combat.

1876   Porfirio Díaz's Revolt of Tuxtepec ends Mexican (and Yucatecan) political instability.

1879   Salvador Valenzuela visits Caste War refugee communities in the northern Petén.

1885   Crescencio Poot is assassinated.

1890   Ludovic Chambon visits Yucatán.

1898–1901 Gen. Ignacio Bravo occupies what will become the territory of Quintana Roo.

1910   Mexican Revolution.

1915   Gen. Salvador Alvarado brings the Mexican Revolution to Yucatán. Santiago Pacheco Cruz works with the revolutionary educational system.

MAYA WARS

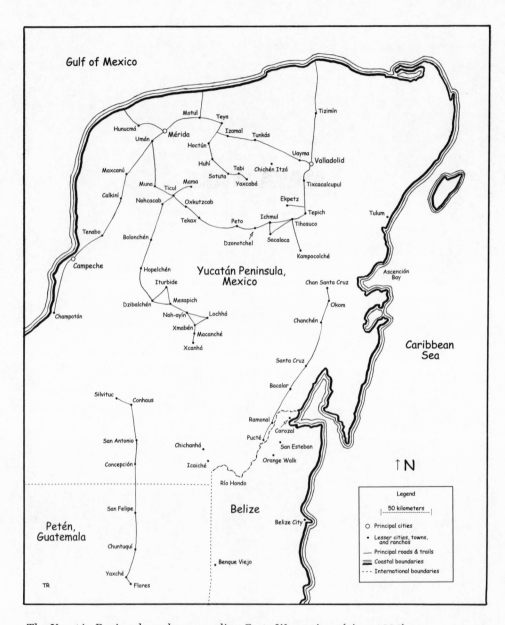

The Yucatán Peninsula and surrounding Caste War regions (circa 1864).

Introduction

In this book I hope to acquaint the reader with writings by and about the Mayas of the nineteenth-century Yucatán Peninsula. Some of the selections are well known to scholars; others, to my knowledge, have never been seen before, not even by specialists in the field. All of these selections, however, have something distinctive and important to say about a culture that has been in a constant state of evolution since long before the birth of Christ, and which remains an important component of life in southeast Mexico, Belize, and Guatemala.

This selection of writings concerning the nineteenth-century Yucatec Mayas appears in what can only be described as a lacuna of translated and published information on the subject. Such a gap becomes even more curious when compared with the abundance of such works in related fields. For example, published records of contact with North American Indian groups have become relatively common. Readers who are interested in the ethnohistory of the United States and Canada can find any number of such accounts, ranging from memoirs of explorers and expeditions to missionary chronicles, military reports, and even captivity narratives. Much the same is true for early Spanish contact with the great Mesoamerican and South American cultures, peoples such as the Aztec and Inca. Although these sources have their biases and distortions, they serve as windows into the lives and cultures of native civilizations. No such information, however, is available to the reader who is interested in the history of the Maya people. This ethnic group constitutes the third-largest body of native speakers (after Quechua and Nahuatl) in the Americas and includes more linguistic homogeneity than its larger counterparts.

The absence of edited and published ethnohistorical material becomes even more striking when we consider the historical importance of the people, the time, and the place. Yucatec Maya culture spanned what are today the Mexican states of Yucatán, Campeche, and Quintana Roo, with a significant presence in the state of Tabasco, northern Belize, and Guatemala. This macroregion was one of the more cohesive and less balkanized areas of Mexico following independence (1821). If the extent of the Yucatec Maya tongue had defined political geography, it would have resulted in the largest state in the early Mexican republic.

The Yucatec Maya region is even more significant because of the Caste War, the largest rural uprising in the history of nineteenth-century Mexico. This bloodletting began in 1847, continued for some twenty-five years, and then subsided into a highly successful Maya separatist movement that claimed most of what is now Quintana Roo until the early part of this century. The war brought international involvement, internal social changes, and messianic religious movements; generated much scholarly research; and captured the attention of the general public. However, we have little published material that allows us to read directly from contemporary sources regarding the nature of life before, during, and after this upheaval.

The protagonists and perspectives found in this book also have an importance that transcends the Maya region and even the nation of Mexico. The nineteenth century was a time when indigenous peoples throughout the world suffered from the creation and expansion of nation-states, the transition from public to private resources, the dramatic global dispersion of European peoples and culture, and a host of other stresses on preestablished ways of life. These themes run through the histories of the United States, Mexico, Canada, Australia, New Zealand, the Pacific Islands, Southeast Asia, Africa, and virtually all of Latin America. The Yucatec Maya story provides one singularly well illustrated example of an indigenous peasantry's attempt to cope with a world whose very foundation was shifting beneath their feet.

For all these reasons, I believe that an edited compilation of writings by and about the Yucatec Mayas is long overdue. A complete edition of all of the relevant letters, journals, reports, military dispatches, and newspaper articles would run into dozens of volumes and is probably impossible. Nevertheless, the selections contained herein include some of the era's richest and most descriptive writings and will provide the reader with a panorama of the people, the time, and the region that played such a critical role in modern Mesoamerican history.

THE DEEP PAST

The Maya peoples have a long and varied history, a brief review of which is needed to set the stage for the nineteenth century and its ethnographies. Preclassic Maya civilization first coalesced along riverbanks in what is now Belize and northern Guatemala around 1800 B.C. and continued in those areas until approximately A.D. 250. These simple settlements gradually increased in population and were influenced by the older and more sophisticated Olmec culture of Tabasco and southern Veracruz, from which they absorbed such innovations as jade working, the Mesoamerican calendar, glyph writing, and the cult of the jaguar.

Beginning around 500 B.C., the Maya settlements underwent a population expansion that continued for more than a millennium. Maya settlements extended over a large area, including what is now Yucatán, Tabasco, Chiapas, Belize, Guatemala, Honduras, and El Salvador. Material life was heavily based on the cultivation of corn, beans, and squash, supplemented with a wide variety of fruits, vegetables, and game.

Pre-Columbian Maya culture (i.e., pre-1492) reached its height in the Classic Period (roughly A.D. 150 to 650), a time during which art styles achieved their most innovative and refined stages, population densities reached their limits, and social stratifications attained their most complex states. The impetus for this development came from trade spinning off from Teotihuacán in central

Mexico, together with innovations in food production that allowed the Mayas to maintain high populations in the relatively fragile ecosystems of the rain forests. The Maya peoples never achieved political unification, but during the Classic Period powerful cities or supercenters, such as Tikal, Palenque, Dos Pilas, and Caracol, dominated the surrounding communities. The strongest centers lay along rivers that formed trade routes between the Gulf Coast and the Caribbean coast of Central America.

Between A.D. 650 and 900, Classic Maya civilization suffered a widespread collapse. Ceremonial construction halted, elite polities disappeared, and populations decreased precipitously. The decline of the great Maya centers was apparently caused by the collapse of Teotihuacán (beginning in A.D. 600), massive overpopulation, and a top-heavy social structure. Changing trade routes also played a role, as coastal navigation replaced the overland routes that had favored the Petén area.

The most dynamic area of Maya culture shifted to Yucatán, where the political landscape, energized by colonizations of Toltec peoples from central Mexico, witnessed the rise of powerful new centers, such as Mayapán and Chichén Itzá. Many of these centers rose over Classic Period sites, which, although never as spectacular as Tikal or Palenque, had managed to survive the collapse in better condition. Their Mexican overlords eventually dissolved into the gene pool of the numerically superior Mayas, and their language appears to have disappeared altogether. Nonetheless, these centers imparted key features to the Postclassic culture, including Toltec art styles, human-heart sacrifice, phallic worship, and the cult of the Plumed Serpent god, whose original name (Quetzalcoatl) was literally translated into Maya as K'u'uk'ul Kaan. Although they were economically and architecturally impressive, these centers were no more successful than their Guatemalan predecessors in establishing political unification (if indeed this was their goal). After various attempts to forge a political league, the Maya communities dissolved into generalized tribal warfare between 1441 and 1461, which was the condition in which the Spanish found them when they made their first incursions in the early sixteenth century.

After a handful of uncertain and unsuccessful early contacts, the Spanish conquest of the Maya peoples began in earnest in 1526, when Francisco de Montejo, a former officer of Hernán Cortés, launched the first full-scale invasion of the Yucatán Peninsula. The Mayas' fragmentation, however, made them difficult to conquer. Because the region lacked a centralized state, the Spanish could not strike at the top, as Cortés had done with the Aztecs in 1519 and as Francisco Pizarro later did with the Incas in 1532. After a year of failures, Montejo was forced to retreat to Tabasco. From there he spent the next twenty years organizing the gradual conquest of the Mayas, a project that was largely completed in 1546. Meanwhile, the Mayas of the Chiapas region fell to Diego de Mazariegos in the 1520s, while another Cortés lieutenant, Pedro de Alvarado, conquered the Guatemalan highlands between 1525 and 1530. The only remaining holdouts were the Itzá Mayas, who were based on an island in Lake Petén, now the city of Flores. Combining warfare with diplomacy, these Mayas managed to resist until 1697. The only unconquered peoples were the Lacandons, a fusion of Carib Indians and Yucatec Mayas, the latter of whom provided the dominant linguistic influence.

The three hundred years that followed witnessed the forging of the syncretic culture seen today in many parts of Mexico, Guatemala, and Belize. The stage for displaying all other cultural and economic features—the rural village—highlights this syncretism. Like most groups in pre-Columbian Mesoamerica, the Mayas had centered their daily life around the village, which they perceived as the intersection of the four cardinal points of the universe. The Spanish also adhered to the concept of city-as-civilization and, for reasons of exploitation and administrative efficiency, did everything in their power to keep the Mayas concentrated in established settlements. The new Maya towns, however, were centered around the village church. (The great churches seen today in rural Yucatán are largely seventeenth- and eighteenth-century constructions.) Families occupied urban lots known as *solares;* households often shared a single patio. The town remained the center of social life, although the need for fresh lands created the countervailing tendency of pushing people outward into faraway temporary fields and in many cases resulted in the formation of new settlements. The tension between these two forces—concentration and dispersal—continued well into the nineteenth century.

Village economic life also combined Maya and Spanish practices. During the nineteenth century most Maya families lived from *milpa* farming, or slash-and-burn agriculture. Virtually the only way to produce corn in Yucatán's rocky soil was to slash the vegetation, burn it when it was thoroughly dry, and leave seeds in small holes within the soil for the summer rains to germinate. Fields lost their fertility after two plantings and had to lie fallow for five to ten years. To this agricultural economy, the Mayas added metal tools brought by the Spanish. The most important of these was the machete; while adopting the long-bladed style common in other parts of Mexico, the Yucatec Mayas also used a smaller, hook-bladed version, which they called *loobché* or *coa.* Spanish metal pikes allowed the construction of artificial wells. Chickens, pigs, and even cattle assumed critical importance in the Mayas' daily diet. By the nineteenth century, most rural Maya men owned crude shotguns (*escopetas*), which they used to hunt deer, javelina, and other forest game.

Little by little, however, a commercial economy insinuated itself into these subsistence-oriented communities. Private estates, or haciendas, began to appear in the mid-seventeenth century; their growth continued unabated until the Mexican Revolution. Hacienda owners lured Mayas as permanent or part-time laborers, teaching them to tend cattle and horses. Cities also held new attractions and generated new forms of employment. Mérida's predominantly Maya suburbs encouraged the growth of artisans, including carpenters, shoemakers, black-

professional diversification

smiths, silversmiths, and several dozen others. Mayas living on the coast worked as fishermen, whereas others delivered mail or operated a sedan transportation service known as *koché*. Then as now, all villages boasted a team of masons known as *albañiles*. Although dependent on agriculture, the Mayas of the nineteenth century achieved some degree of professional diversification.

Tribal government and tribal identity did not exist among the Yucatec Mayas mainly because of colonialism's intense emphasis on village organization and the eradication of indigenous authority above that level. In political terms the most important colonial institution for the Mayas, as for many other native peoples in Mexico, was the *república de indígenas,* or town council. This organization consisted of nine or ten elected officials, usually prominent and perhaps even prosperous adult men, who bore the responsibility of managing village affairs. The chief of this body was the *batab,* a pre-Columbian term referring to the village headman, a role for which the Spanish used the generic term *cacique*. Those who served under him included an assistant or understudy known as the *teniente* (lieutenant), two upper officials (*alcaldes* or "mayors"), four lower officials (*regidores* or "representatives"), and a scribe, or *escribano,* a literate peasant who processed the Maya-language documents that the *república* produced and guarded. The *república* handled a wide range of village affairs and in general negotiated between the Maya villagers and their Spanish overlords. It kept village land titles, it oversaw wills and inheritance, it acted as a small claims court, it collected taxes and tribute, it encouraged church attendance, and it kept the peace by attending to the myriad affairs that were too small for the peninsula's handful of Spanish officials. The *repúblicas* played significant roles in the colonial era, and even though their powers diminished after Mexican independence (1821), they nonetheless remained important factors in the society. It would be the *batabs* of eastern Yucatán who organized the Caste War uprising of 1847. Several of the documents in this book are translations of Maya-language *república* documents from the early national period.

The religion of the villages was Catholicism, or at least a syncretized version of it. During the first 150 years of colonization, the Franciscans carried out most of the work of evangelization in Yucatán. They imparted to the Maya peasantry their basic doctrines of Christianity: God the Father, the death and resurrection of Christ, the tales of Genesis, the sacraments, the sanctity of the church, and the all-important redemptive powers of the cross. Each village acquired its *aj bolon pixan,* or patron saint, whose fiesta became the high moment of the ritual year. The Mayas adopted Spanish prayer sessions, such as the novenas, in their quest for protection and healing. Many of the old ways persisted, however. The four rain gods, or *cháaks,* retained their importance. The field gods (*balams,* or *yumtsilo'ob*) demanded routine offerings before and after any agricultural labors. The forest swarmed with supernatural denizens of pre-Hispanic vintage, and witchcraft and evil winds remained the curses of village life.

Despite a prolonged adjustment period that allowed many features of pre-Conquest Maya society to survive under Spanish rule, conflicts and friction continued throughout the colonial period. As in other parts of colonial Latin America, these struggles mostly fell into two categories. During first-stage revolts, native peoples tried to throw off the yoke of Spanish rule while it was still young and untested. Such uprisings normally took place within two decades of the initial conquest and found their leadership among the remaining elements of the traditional indigenous elite. Second-stage revolts occurred much later, usually in the second half of the eighteenth century, when the Spanish Bourbon reforms were beginning to uproot old folkways, centralize political authority, tighten previously inefficient tax systems, and stimulate the commercial economies of the Americas.

For the Yucatec Mayas, the early revolt came in 1548, when the still-influential Maya priesthood led an attempt to wipe out Spanish presence on the peninsula. The revolt failed and was suppressed savagely. For the next two hundred years, most resistance was of a daily, small-scale variety: minor episodes of violence, flight to the southern hinterlands, lack of enthusiasm for the Spanish language, and so forth. A noteworthy second-stage uprising took place in 1761 in the small village of Quisteil when local Mayas gathered under the leadership of a charismatic eccentric who called himself Jacinto Canek, a reference to the last of the independent kings of the Petén Mayas. The movement owed much to Canek's appeal to millenarian visions but also drew upon tensions associated with an increasingly commercial economy, such as taxes, land sales, and the high-handedness of Bourbon-era Spanish officials. This uprising also failed. Canek met a miserable fate of torture and execution in the plaza of Mérida. The repression of the revolt, however, made a lasting imprint on the memory of rural Mayas, and nearly a hundred years would pass before ideas of armed insurrection once more circulated in the region.

THE NINETEENTH CENTURY AND THE CASTE WAR

The Mayas have experienced many turbulent times, but as with other peoples of Mexico and Central America, few eras were as troubled as the nineteenth century. Struggles for independence, subsequent political and economic reforms, and a thirty-year period of almost constant civil war drastically shook a world that had grown comfortable during the colonial era. In few places were the changes so wrenching as in southeastern Mexico.

The Mayas of Yucatán entered the nineteenth century as the clear majority on the peninsula. Estimates vary, but they probably constituted about 80 percent of the total population of 350,000 to 500,000. The previous century of economic growth had greatly increased contact among the races. The three principal cities of the region—Mérida, Campeche, and Valladolid—were ethnically mixed. Creoles (Mexican-born Hispanics) also lived in all of the lesser

towns and in many of the smaller villages. As sugar cultivation grew in importance, the population increasingly shifted from the old colonial northwest to
towns in the southern and eastern regions, such as Tekax, Peto, and Tihosuco.

These developments, in turn, effected important changes for the Mayas.
They accelerated a long-term trend toward commercialization and Creole land
ownership. The change was gradual enough to allow the more prosperous
Mayas to participate. Some became *hacendados,* or owners of the commercial
estates known as *haciendas,* and even small-scale urban bourgeoisie. A privileged few became rich and a somewhat larger stratum became relatively comfortable. Most Mayas, however, remained independent peasants; a few worked
as resident laborers on haciendas as part of an institution known as *peonage.*
The Mayas in the east, particularly in the string of villages extending north-
ward from Bacalar to Valladolid, learned the intricacies and advantages of con-
traband, in this case English manufactured goods, such as textiles, perfumes,
and metalworks, smuggled into the country from British Honduras. The
increasing contact between Mayas and Hispanics also acquainted the eastern
peasantry with new ideas of what was politically possible.

The first significant change was the *sanjuanista* movement of 1812–14. Taking advantage of the collapse of royal authority in the wake of Napoleon's invasion of Spain, a small party of Liberal Creoles attempted to mobilize the
peasantry against that bulwark of colonial rule, the Catholic Church. By manipulating the colonial governor into abolishing peasant church taxes, the *san-
juanistas* galvanized Maya political consciousness and provoked a general,
albeit mostly peaceful and passive, resistance to virtually all taxes and authority. Regal authority returned in 1814 with the restoration of Ferdinand VII to
the Spanish throne, but the effects of this episode lingered in peasant consciousness, and the demand for tax reduction remained a permanent feature of
the political landscape for the next twenty-three years.

In the end, independence came to Yucatán without so much as a rifle shot.
The elimination of Spain, however, sparked an all-out competition for power
among various Creole factions. Like greater Mexico, Yucatán teetered back and
forth from federalism to centralism and later from liberalism to conservatism.
Such political terms often served as little more than pretexts for the interests of
local actors, who would change political affiliations if circumstances demanded
it. Virulent quarrels over state and municipal elections eventually embroiled
the Maya peasantry as well. The watershed was the revolution of Santiago
Imán, a Creole merchant, military officer, and property owner from the town of
Tizimín. In order to raise an army against the oppressive rule of central Mexico
(which badly needed Yucatecan men and supplies for its ill-fated wars to
reconquer Texas), Imán mobilized and armed the Mayas by promising one of
the things they wanted most: the abolition of church taxes. His revolt succeeded, and Yucatán briefly became an independent nation (1840–43, 1845–46,
and 1846–48). More importantly, the struggle gave the Mayas military and

organizational experience and raised a multifaceted welter of expectations that mostly centered around tax relief. The entire process was repeated in 1842–43, when Mexico attempted an invasion to reclaim its wayward province.

The triumph of the Imán revolt and the defeat of the Mexican army dramatically accelerated trends that had been underway since the late colonial years. One of these was the alienation of public lands. In order to reward officers, soldiers, and those who had financed the wars, the state granted them legal title to lands that were hitherto part of public domain. The largest of these grants went to priests, officers, and entrepreneurs; a plethora of smaller awards, however, was given to foot soldiers and average citizens. Even some of the Maya *batabs* applied, albeit unsuccessfully. The exact effect of this land alienation on Maya society has been debated: many *ejidos* (village common lands) remained intact, the issuance of specific land grants did not directly correspond with the timing of Caste War mobilization efforts, and demands for land restitution did not figure highly in the demands and correspondence of the rebels. Nevertheless, it is clear that a massive change in land usage was underway and that such a change accelerated significantly during the 1840s, heightening the tensions of the time.

The 1840s also saw a burst of politically motivated violence that touched all sectors of the society. Once the constraints of centralism were removed, Yucatecans threw themselves with gusto into elections—and into rebelling against the results of those elections, which were seldom fair or impartial. A wave of municipal uprisings followed the triumph of Santiago Imán as out-groups attempted to reverse their fortunes by seizing control of local Hispanic city councils (*ayuntamientos*), intimidating their rivals, and employing other less-than-parliamentary tactics. These feuds increasingly embroiled the local Maya peasants, who were recruited to work for the interests of their Hispanic patrons. A similar process took place within the military as local militias began to elect their own officers. By 1847 violence was a well-established reaction to losing at the polls.

The decades following independence, particularly those following the triumph of Santiago Imán, also witnessed increased pressures for the Maya elite. The *batabs* and *repúblicas* had previously served as linchpins for social stability, negotiating between the highs and lows of rural society. Their balancing act, however, proved difficult to maintain in an independent Mexico. Although they had traditionally been small-scale *haçendados,* entrepreneurs, and lesser men of property, the Maya elite found it difficult to compete as Hispanic Creoles poured into the sugar-producing zones in search of quick gains and a political sphere of their own. The business of the Maya town governments was increasingly limited to tax collection, while those taxes became ever more difficult to collect in the face of rising popular expectations for relief. The brunt of post-1821 political violence, which had been confined to non-Maya political actors, now turned on the Maya elite. The assassination of the *batab* and *república* of Tabi in January 1847, the sad consequence of yet another Yucatecan civil war, marked the first time in living memory that Maya officeholders had been murdered.

The Caste War of 1847 almost certainly began as another Creole revolution, in this case designed to support the interests of a politician named Miguel Barbachano and his various followers, who were particularly strong in the east and southeast. As always, the instigators relied on local Maya leaders to organize and equip supporters. The revolt was called off, but by this point a handful of Maya *batabs* had ideas of their own. Led by Jacinto Pat of Tihosuco and Cecilio Chi of nearby Tepich, the Mayas in the east gradually took up arms in what became a race war against local authorities between July and November 1847.

The uprising deeply frightened Yucatecan Creoles, who ever after exaggerated the success of the rebel forces. In reality, the Maya insurgents suffered from severe problems. Despite trade connections with British Honduras, most were poorly armed and supplied. The rebel forces lacked unity, training, and discipline; followers rallied behind *caudillos* (military or political leaders) who failed to coordinate their actions. Worst of all, the goals of the movement were never clear. The better-off and more sophisticated leaders probably aimed at political advantage, improved conditions, and local autonomy, and not at the extermination of the Spanish race, points clearly stated in some of the correspondence reproduced herein. In talking to the masses, however, the leadership used incendiary rhetoric that liberated long-simmering racial animosities. The eastern *batabs* had relatively little influence on Mayas living in the west. Moreover, the initial uprising lured disaffected non-Mayas, who hoped to use the war to settle scores with old enemies. These deep emotions, however, could not entirely compensate for real material weaknesses. Despite its initial success, the rebel initiative had overextended itself before the end of 1847, even though Creole panic and disorganization helped to conceal rebel weaknesses.

The Yucatecan state, reinforced with arms and supplies from Mexico, Spain, and the United States, managed to retake the initiative in May 1848 and gradually beat the rebels back into the forests in what is now the state of Quintana Roo. Defeated and demoralized, the surviving leaders created an oracle, the Speaking Cross, which preached absolute obedience and war to the death. Gradually a new organization took shape in a place that came to be called Chan Santa Cruz ("Little Holy Cross," which is now named Felipe Carrillo Puerto). An iron-willed individual named Venancio Puc governed this society from some undetermined date in the mid-1850s until his assassination at the hands of subordinate officers in 1863. After a brief period of chaos, a triumvirate arose: Bonifacio Novelo and Crescencio Poot (two of the original rebels), along with Bernabé Cen, whose origins and early involvement in the war remain unknown. Novelo died a natural death in May 1868, and Poot soon displaced Cen, who was killed in a raid in northern Yucatán in 1875. Poot himself was overthrown and murdered in 1885.

As early as 1853, three distinct groups of Mayas lived on the peninsula. The largest group comprised those who continued to live in the northern, western, and central areas controlled by the Yucatecan government. This group included independent villagers and, increasingly, war refugees who turned to life on the hacienda to provide a modicum of security. Many of these Mayas participated as *indios hidalgos*, a Maya ancillary military corps that performed such services as transporting supplies, clearing roads, constructing breastworks, and at times participating in armed combat.

From the 1870s onward, the peninsula's economic landscape was increasingly dominated by henequen, a maguey whose tough fibers provided the binder twine needed for the mechanization of the U.S. wheat industry. Village life declined dramatically in the henequen zone of the northwest, replaced by permanent peonage and temporary hacienda labor. The year 1869 witnessed the formal abolition of the *repúblicas de indígenas,* although the role of *batab* tended to survive at a less official level, with prosperous or semiprosperous Mayas continuing to mediate between Hispanic property owners and the mass of poor Mayas. In the more diversified regions of the south and east, however, villages conserved some of their *ejido* lands and independent spirit. Relations between non-Mayas and Mayas were characterized by patron-client relationships in which the latter sacrificed autonomy in favor of the protection and opportunity provided by the *yuum,* or master. The estates also isolated the Mayas from the rural church, which had previously functioned as one of their main social controls. Clerical discipline over education and marriage practices declined, although the Mayas' folk Catholicism remained as lively as ever. In fact, to attract and satisfy Maya workers, property owners had to internalize many features of village religion. They usually built a chapel with a patron saint, whose feast day served as the occasion for hacienda celebrations, just as the day of the *aj bolon pixan* had done, and still does, in towns and villages.

The second Maya group included the far more exotic and mysterious rebels of Chan Santa Cruz. These Mayas went through various factional conflicts and splintering, but they held out until they finally made peace with the Mexican revolutionary state in the 1920s and 1930s. Supplied with British arms, they controlled most of the region of Quintana Roo until a federal army occupation in 1898–1901 seized Chan Santa Cruz, forcing the true believers to carry on in outlying villages. Today the cult of the Speaking Cross survives as a subcult of Catholicism. Veneration of the temple in Felipe Carrillo Puerto is shared among organizations in five villages, the officers of which bear such military titles as *sargento* (sergeant) and *comandante* (commander).

The third Maya group comprised numerous refugees and former combatants who settled in what is now southern Campeche and made peace with the state in exchange for virtual autonomy. The so-called *pacíficos del sur* included Hispanics and even refugees from the Central American wars, but the dominant cultural influence was Mayan. Lacking the will and organization of Chan Santa

Cruz, the *pacíficos* never constituted a formidable military power but survived through a combination of subsistence, trade, and strategic alliances with the Mexican state. Toward the end of the nineteenth century, they increasingly supported themselves through chicle tapping; this new form of employment, together with the revolutionary land reforms, permanently altered the communities' social structures. Only two or three of the old *pacífico* settlements still exist, and they retain little of the original flavor of the settlements visited and described by Yucatecan missionaries in the 1860s.

NINETEENTH-CENTURY SOURCES

Fortunately for modern-day readers and scholars, even times as troubled as Mexico's early national period produce a wealth of publications and manuscripts that illuminate the lives, passions, and persuasions of everyday people. The primary documents come from Mayas themselves. People of Maya descent and culture entered into the economic life of the peninsula, adopting the legal mechanisms and record-keeping practices of the Spanish. Mayas left wills, bought and sold land and houses, signed contracts, gave power of attorney, contracted mortgages, filed protests, and bailed their friends and family out of jail. Through these means, they established an important presence in the notary archives found in Mérida. Notarial papers are particularly useful in tracing the lives of the more affluent and urbanized, but residents of smaller towns are also represented. Until the early nineteenth century, Maya-language papers of the *repúblicas de indígenas* were archived among these volumes. Scholars have recently analyzed them to reconstruct the lives of both the colonial and the national periods. After the 1840s Mayas continued to express opinions and exercise their rights through the written word, albeit mostly in Spanish translation. The Caste War generated a sizable corpus of Maya-language correspondence, some of which is reproduced in this book. Documents written by Mayas themselves often reveal common-sense concerns that contrast with the exotic otherness painted by their Hispanic and Anglo observers.

A vaster body of writings comes from Hispanics, Anglos, and Europeans who had the opportunity to witness nineteenth-century Maya culture firsthand. Among Creoles, one group that had extensive contact with Maya peoples was the priesthood. Syncretic Christianity pervaded both rural and urban life. The parish system remained a key form of spatial and social organization well into the twentieth century. By 1800 the Catholic missionary impulse had largely exhausted itself in Mesoamerica; crown authorities were phasing out "regular" orders, such as the Jesuits (banished in 1767) or the far more important Franciscans (secularized in 1820).[1] The dominant force in religious administration, therefore, was the secular order, the hierarchy of priests who tended to village

---

1. These orders were known as "regular" because they lived by special rules or, in Latin, *regulae*.

affairs. These clergymen had vast experience with their Maya parishioners. Most rural priests spoke the Maya language, and many of the successful *curas,* or pastors, served in the same parish for twenty years or more. When the Caste War began, both church and state called on priests to negotiate with the rebels or to administer remote settlements. The bulk of their correspondence is preserved in the Archivo Histórico de la Arquidiócesis de Yucatán in Mérida, although the prolific church writings turn up in other archives as well. These heterogeneous collections also include correspondence and petitions from Maya rebels and parishioners. Maya refugees in Belize felt the evangelical influence of Methodist missionaries, who left an important, though hitherto unexamined, body of writings on their experiences among the Mayas. I have included some of the more revealing selections in this book.

A considerable body of ethnographic materials comes from the civil and military officials of the nineteenth century. These administrators were less patient with Maya cultural differences than were their religious counterparts. Nevertheless, the dogged legalism of nineteenth-century Hispanics ensured that wills dictated by Mayas entered the notarial records and that news of goings-on in remote villages filtered back to Mérida. Even accounts of military slash-and-burn operations, such as Gen. Rómulo Díaz de la Vega's 1852 march to Chichanhá, contain useful clues to how Maya peasants reacted to the debacles of war and the impossible stress of finding themselves between two armies.

The accounts of foreign travelers also help to shape what we know about a specific time and place. The late nineteenth and early twentieth centuries witnessed an explosion of interest in the Maya area. Initially visitors came as private individuals: the gentleman archaeologist, the compulsive traveler, and so forth. Later both Europe and the United States sent professional researchers into the field to map ruins, study languages, and explore folkways. The most important research initiative was the Carnegie Project, a complex multidisciplinary program designed to cover archaeology, ethnology, geology, linguistics, and botany. The project was curiously lacking in historical depth, but it did result in what is undoubtedly the most important body of ethnographic writings on the Maya peoples, namely, the various works of Robert Redfield, Alfonso Villa Rojas, and Margaret Park Redfield. I have made no attempt to excerpt from their monumental works, such as *Chan Kom: A Maya Village, The Maya of East-Central Quintana Roo,* or *The Folk Culture of Yucatan;* readers interested in further study should consult them as indispensable ethnographic texts. Less known, however, and included herein, are important contemporary works by Karl Sapper, a German geologist; the British archaeologist Thomas Gann; and Santiago Pacheco Cruz, a schoolteacher with extensive experience in rural Yucatán, who joined in the wave of ethnographic interest in the 1920s and 1930s. Pacheco Cruz's description of rural folkways was written after the Mexican Revolution had spread throughout the peninsula but was, in fact, a reminiscence of his nineteenth-century childhood in Tinum in the state of

Campeche. His account concludes this book with an appreciative description of rural ceremonies and celebrations.

To represent the Yucatecan past, I chose documents that cover a wide range of themes and perspectives. The selection criteria varied. First, I was drawn to writings that attempt a comprehensive profile of Maya culture. This group includes the ethnographies of Padre Baeza, Richard Fletcher, and Thomas Gann. Second, in order to restore the Maya voice to our knowledge of the nineteenth-century experience, I included documents of the *repúblicas de indígenas,* correspondence of the Caste War leaders, and the wills, court testimonies, and petitions of Yucatán's peasantry. Third, I added papers that provide vivid accounts of the Caste War. Composed chiefly of military reports and captivity narratives, these documents paint an indelible portrait of the militarized Maya society, which, for more than fifty years, resisted subjugation by both the state of Yucatán and the nation of Mexico. This group also includes entries that detail the lives and travails of Mayas and Hispanics who fled to remote areas to escape the violence of the Caste War. Fourth, I punctuated the foregoing material with brief documents that illuminate ethnographic details not found elsewhere: a flowery letter to the emperor of Mexico, rumors of flying serpents, the Maya method of guarding money, and many other cultural tidbits that do not deserve to languish, unread, in a mound of obscure paperwork known only by a handful of specialists.

Though compelling, these writings are not without biases and distortions. Writing involves power. Historians impose an interpretation on people of the past; anthropologists do the same for the peoples they study, placing greater emphasis here or there, choosing between emic and etic readings, and so forth. The men who wrote the accounts in this book were no exceptions. Bias in ethnographic reporting is inevitable. Although it cannot be eliminated, readers can become aware of the prejudices and predispositions.

The roots of distortion were varied. Many of the authors presented herein held some degree of power over the Maya peasants and rebels they met. For more than three centuries, village priests imposed religious doctrines and social norms and could enforce those impositions with punishments. The Catholic priests whose memoirs and correspondence appear in this book often took an exaggerated interest in the Maya religious, medical, and family practices that were at odds with Christian teachings. Foreign travelers enjoyed the support of local officials and property owners, who were usually willing to lend Indian labor and resources to visitors. Travelers often viewed the Maya peasantry from the perspective of someone who benefited from their exploitation. Once the Caste War began, the rebels and refugees generated by the conflict required the support (explicit or tacit) of political authorities in Belize, Guatemala, and Campeche, as well as the advantage of trade with those states. Correspondence to and from such authorities was therefore strongly conditioned by considerations of tactical benefit and a preoccupation with assessing military strength. Later archaeologists, such as Thomas Gann, came searching for the remains of a long-vanished culture. They were naturally sensitive to evidence of cultural continuity between the ancient Mayas and the villagers they met in the 1910s and 1920s. Their passion, however, became their vice: these early-twentieth-century academics tended to exalt twentieth-century Mayas as untouched remnants of a pre-Columbian past, a distortion that ignored centuries of historical experience and change.

These writings thus suffer from cumulative biases that distill into a variety of pejoratives regarding the Mayas: barbarous, superstitious, idolatrous, phlegmatic, isolated, atavistic, and opposed to innovation and progress. One wishes that the Mayas themselves had made a greater attempt to record their own culture and experiences. A gender bias also exists: Men authored the vast bulk of surviving nineteenth-century texts, and the few women who did write were mostly Hispanic.

Despite these shortcomings, I think that the nineteenth- and early-twentieth-century texts reproduced in this book constitute essential documents for historian and anthropologist alike. They have the advantage of being of the time and place. Their authors wrote during crucial moments in the history of southeastern Mexico; for that reason alone, their words merit consideration. In addition, men such as Padre Baeza, Richard Fletcher, and Santiago Pacheco Cruz were keen observers and recorded many details that are still valid for Maya ethnography. Their writings offer a cumulative ethnographic picture that has few rivals in the literature of nineteenth-century Mexico and Guatemala. Without further delay, we now turn to the past, as told through the words of the men and women who lived it.

I

THE PREWAR YEARS

The first section of this book consists of documents drawn from the years 1800–47, the half century that preceded the Caste War. The stresses of the age have been well documented, both in the foregoing introduction and in the historical literature. It is important to remember, however, that it was also a time of optimism and of a society's growing consciousness of itself and its peculiarities. The break with Spain led Hispanics to question who they themselves were and who were the Maya peasantry around them. For the first time foreign travelers began to enter Yucatán, and they returned with the first descriptive writings produced by non-Hispanics. The early decades of independent Mexico offered a place for the indigenous peasantry. Maya town councils continued to play an administrative role, and more than a few Mayas managed to succeed in the growing commercial economy. The following selection offers some of the better descriptive writings as well as documents produced by the Mayas themselves.

1

"What Three Centuries of Experience Teaches"

The Report of José Bartolomé del Granado Baeza

José Bartolomé del Granado Baeza (1742–1830) served as cura, *or pastor, of the parish of Yaxcabá, located in the center of Yucatán, for more than thirty years. In 1813, in response to a thirty-six-point questionnaire from the bishop, he composed the following description of the Maya peoples under his supervision.*[1] *Although the questionnaire itself does not survive, its content can usually be inferred from Baeza's responses. This document is often cited in the original Spanish text. The only attempt at an English translation has been a highly modified version published in 1921.*[2]

Baeza's ethnography is included here for several reasons. First, it offers a broad (if incomplete) view of Maya culture from the perspective of a longtime observer. Second, the text provides observations on language, material culture, work habits, religious customs and beliefs, culturally related personality traits, and relations between poorer and more affluent Mayas. Third, the document illustrates Baeza's own preconceptions and concerns. The text was written during the years when Mexico struggled for independence from Spain (1810–21). This struggle had a enlivening effect on Maya political consciousness, encouraging the Mayas to assert themselves before such traditional authorities as village priests. Preoccupation over this change in attitude recurs throughout Baeza's text, as do certain denigrative views regarding his Maya parishioners.

1. My parish of Yaxcabá consists of five villages and 15 haciendas and ranchos, whose inhabitants total 8,591, namely 70 Spanish-Americans, 850 mestizos, 7,442 Indians, and 229 *pardos* or mulattos.[3] There is no one of European origin or pure Negro.

---

1. Several Spanish-language versions of this text are available, the most important being the 1845 version that appeared in *El registro yucateco*, 165–78. In 1989, in *La revista de la Universidad Autónoma de Yucatán* 168: 52–63, Rodolfo Ruz Menéndez published a corrected and more complete version based on his access to copies of the original document from the Archivo General de las Indias in Spain. My translation follows the Menéndez version.

2. See Santiago Méndez et al., "Report on the Maya Indians of Yucatan," *Indian Notes and Monographs* 9, no. 3 (1921): 136–226.

3. The term *mestizo* refers to a Spanish-Indian mixture, *pardo* to a black-Indian mixture, and *mulatto* to a Spanish-black mixture.

2. The mestizos come from a mixture of Europeans or Americans with Yucatecan Indians; and the mulattos, the mixture of these two castes with African Negroes. I have no information in all the province of Yucatán of any Negro from the Philippines.

3. The Indians, mestizos, and *pardos* of this province generally speak the Maya language. Here in Yucatán there are few Indians who understand Spanish, and this only in common, trivial matters. For this reason, when Christian doctrine is taught to them in Spanish, they do not understand enough to reap the benefit of the sacraments, unless it is taught to them jointly in their own tongue.

4. They show little love for their wives and children, and it can be said of them that they are *sine affectione*,[4] as Saint Paul said of the Gentiles. By reason of my position as pastor, for more than 45 years I have attended them during their final illnesses, and very rarely have I seen tears shed over the death of parents, children, spouses, or relatives. Much more commonly I have seen them with their eyes dry and serene in all circumstances. Usually their children have no education other than what is provided by the *curas* and ministers, the *maestros de capilla*, and the *fiscales de doctrina*[5] at the door of the church, or in the main houses of the haciendas and ranchos, where they are to gather at 8:00 A.M. every morning to learn Christian doctrine. Moreover, there are some parents who, through lack of Christian spirit, refuse to send their children, and it is necessary to force them with punishments. Generally they dedicate themselves to agriculture or manufacturing such simple items as *petates*, mats, cases, baskets, wickerwork, henequen sacks, *mecapales*,[6] straw hats, and so forth. Rare indeed is the individual who takes up other mechanical or liberal arts.

5. Many Indians show a marked affection for the Europeans and Americans[7] from whom they have received no injury. But they look with hatred and disdain on those who they believe have done them wrong. Such were the *encomenderos*,[8] to whom they paid tribute while receiving no benefit in return, as well as those whom they served by order of the government, to the detriment of their own interests.

6. The wise dispositions of the Cortes[9] have done away with these two powerful grievances, abolishing tribute and personal services and firmly prohibiting with strictest penalties the abuse and poor treatment the Indians suf-

---

4. "Without affection."

5. A *cura* was a village priest. The *maestro de capilla* was a Maya church assistant who was responsible for the cleaning and upkeep of the building. The *fiscal de doctrina* oversaw the teaching of catechism for Indian children.

6. A *petate* is a straw mat used for covering the earthen floor of a hut. A *mecapal* is a form of apron worn by Maya laborers.

7. I.e., Creoles, or Spaniards born in the Americas.

8. Recipients of *encomienda*, or tribute.

9. The governing body that established a Spanish constitution in 1812 during the temporary absence of a king.

fered. It seems to be that this has proven sufficient to win them over and reconcile them.

7. Although many Indians know how to read and write, they seldom do so, either because they are naturally slow and clumsy in both skills or because there is little written in their language. Or else it is because of something that is absolutely certain, that the entire household is always busy. When they do write, it is on our own form of paper and not on leaves or tree bark.

8. Just as the Maya language is short on terms for intellectual and spiritual matters, so too it is quite rich in material and mechanical terms. For this reason it is the most common language in all villages, even among Spanish Americans, and much more among the lower classes. Even in the city of Mérida and the villa of Valladolid, among the better class of people it can still be called highly common since they are weaned on it, for their wet nurses are Indians or lower-class individuals who know no other tongue. This is the first reason that the Indians speak no Spanish: because they never hear a language other than their own. The second reason is that Spanish is difficult for them to pronounce when not taken in with mother's milk, as experience has shown with foreigners of different nations and with African *bozales*[10] who have settled in this region. They learn Maya more rapidly than Spanish, and for this reason, when some Indians try to speak the latter, they do so with many barbarisms, except for those who have applied themselves, with good effect, to formal study. For these reasons and for their natural limitations, I think it would be very difficult to introduce Spanish among them as a common practice.

9. The virtues that up to now have prevailed among the Indians have been humility and patience as well as submission and respect toward authorities, at least while the fear of punishment was over them. Avarice is virtually unknown, for they are content muddling through life; few aspire to riches. They are frugal, as I will explain in article 17. Many of them are kind, generous, and compassionate, devoted to the crucified Christ and Holy Mary, whose rosary they say, and to other saints. They frequently observe the sacraments; this is especially true of women, whose presence I have been able to count by the hundreds. They pass a blameless life, and this includes not only those who began to take the sacraments in their youth, but also those who after a debauched life became devotees of God.

10. The vast majority of the Indians are superstitious. During my first fifteen years in this parish, this problem kept me busy; but after whippings and imprisonments, exemplary punishments that I imposed on offenders in accordance with superior orders, the superstitions have subsided over the following fifteen years and only occasionally does one hear of such things.

The most common form of fortune-telling is through a piece of crystal called a *saastun*, that is, a clear, transparent stone: through it, they say, they can see

---

10. The term *bozal* referred to a black slave born in Africa.

dden objects and identify the cause of diseases. What I have come to understand about this is that there have been some who, through a pact with the
devil, have indeed told fortunes with the *saastun*; but more commonly those
who use it are simply imposters and thereby gain reputations among their
people. Consulted and given gifts, they lead lives of leisure, and with their
tricks and artifices, lead the ignorant and the simpletons to believe that they
have foretold things that they secretly arranged in advance. I can give this
example, which is fairly common: they lead a sick man to believe that by
means of the *saastun* they have determined that some evildoer has put a spell
on him, and that in order to identify the spell or its author, it is necessary to
keep watch for three nights.

For this event they prepare *aguardiente* or *pitarrilla,* food, and lit candles.[11]
During those three nights, they drink and carry on to their satisfaction; while
the others are asleep or not paying attention, they bury in or near the house a
wax doll with a pin through the part corresponding to the patient's physical
pain. Finally, when everyone wakes up, they launch into their divinations with
the *saastun* and go directly to the place where they buried the doll. They take
it out in front of everyone and lead them to believe that this has caused the
spell. Later they effect the cure with the first herbs they happen to find, and if
by chance the patient does recover, they win a grand reputation among the
ignorant. It also happens that they may secretly learn that prior to his illness
the patient has had a quarrel with someone; in such case, they persuade him
that through the *saastun* they have learned that said person is in fact the cause
of the evil. Some three or four years ago a vagrant tried this, but a God-fearing
Indian woman denounced him to me. When he had confessed his sin, I applied
the appropriate punishment, and I have not known him to return since.

The most common of their superstitious ceremonies are as follows. The first
is the incantation, with certain terms that I have not been able to persuade
them to explain to me. But I have certain indications that in them they mention
illnesses and the winds that they believe cause them. The only thing that they
have told me is that over a sick person they pray the Our Father, the Hail Mary,
and the Creed, whereas some use the prayer to Saint Anthony found in the
Mexican manual. The second is called *keex,* or "change," and it boils down to
the following. Around the house of the patient they hang certain foods and
drinks intended for the *yumkimil,* meaning "Death" or "the Lord of Death," by
which means they hope to save the patient's life. The third is to hang gourds
with a drink known as *sak ja'* under beehives so that the bees do not abandon
the hive, or so that they produce much honey, or so that their owners do not
fall ill.

I know nothing of any wizards or magicians. In this village that I have

---

11. *Aguardiente* is a crude rum made from cane sugar; *pitarrilla* is a beer made from tree bark
and was common in rural villages.

administered for more than 40 years, the only such thing has been an old man who, on death's door, told me that he was accustomed to transform himself through diabolical arts. Here, too, a girl of ten or twelve told me that she had been carried off by witches, changed into a bird, and taken along in their nightly travels, and that one night they perched over the rectory where I live, some two leagues from her own house. It is likely that she was impressed by stories of witches, which they commonly tell, and that she dreamed it with such a vividness that the impression seemed real.

What is certain is that in the present day one hears little of sorcerers, and pretenders are more common that the real thing. Nor have there been authenticated cases of spells or curses; those instances reported to me have turned out to be natural illnesses or else pretenses with the aim of slandering their enemies. It also seems to me that some falsely cultivate for themselves the reputation of wizard in order to intimidate the rest.

11. In this parish there are catechisms of Christian doctrine written in the same Maya language used throughout the province and approved by the bishops.

12. A practice that now seems to me quite rare in the entire bishopric is idolatry, something that in another era created a cult to the devil through various figures of clay or stone. What does survive today is something the Indians call *tich'*, which is to say "oblation" or "sacrifice" and which is popularly called "mass of the *milpa*" because it is an imitation of the true mass and takes the following form. Over a spit or *tapezco* made with equal plates, which serves them as a table, they place a wild turkey, in whose beak the man born to the role of priest[12] pours *pitarrilla* (one of the drinks which I will discuss in article 18). Then they kill it, and the assistants take it to be cooked while beneath the earth they bake several huge loaves of corn bread that they call *kanlajun tas [waaj]*, meaning "fourteen tortillas or crusts," streaked with beans, something whose meaning they have not explained to me. After cooking everything they place it on the table, along with various gourds of *pitarrilla*. Then the priest approaches and lights an incense made of copal.

Some of those who reported this and some of the main offenders and their accomplices have assured me that they begin by invoking the three Divine Persons, and that they pray the Credo, and that taking the *pitarrilla* like a bishop, they sprinkle it to the four winds, invoking the four Pabajtunes, who are the lords or keepers of the rain. Next, approaching the table, they raise up one of the gourds, and to solemnize the event, they take it to the mouth. To close the event everyone eats and drinks to his satisfaction, while the sponsor of the event is the most favored and carries away a significant portion to his house.

A *mayordomo*[13] of a hacienda, some 80 years old, questioned as to who

---

12. The *h-men,* or Maya shaman, often learned the trade from his father. This is presumably what Baeza refers to when he says *nace de sacerdote,* or "born of a priest."

13. The *mayordomo* functioned as the hacienda's foreman.

were these Pabajtunes, told me that the red Pabajtun, who sits in the east, is Santo Domingo. The white, seated in the south, is San Gabriel. The black, seated in the west, is San Diego, and the yellow one, who is also called "Xcanlcox" and is seated in the middle,[14] is Santa María Magdalena. He also confessed to me that, in fact, the *pitarrilla* is *yáax ja'*, meaning "first water" or "first liquor," because it was said to have been the first liquor that God made, and that God the Father used it when saying the first mass, and that after rising to Heaven with the Most Holy Mary, he left the four saints to oversee the rains.

With the punishments that I mentioned in article 10, I have managed to control this. Nor does there seem to me to be a better way. The problem lies in finding someone to report them because the first thing that they tell the participants is that they are to reveal nothing, not even during confession. But with God's help I have managed to set things right through preaching the divine word, and there has been no lack of God-fearing people who inform. The Yucatecan Indians are normally very simple and of limited understanding and are governed more by emotion than by reason. At the same time, they are quite cowardly and afraid, and for this reason the only effective remedy that exists, and which has existed, to hold them to their responsibilities is punishment by whipping, applied with kindness, discretion, and prudence. Many wise and pious men who have skillfully governed them have realized this. It is what three centuries of experience teaches. And they themselves confess it when they repeat the adage: *Je' masewale' ma' táan u yubik t'aan tu xikin, wa má tu paach,* meaning "The Indian doesn't hear through his ears, but through his backside." An unfortunate tendency, the truth being that it is necessary to treat them like children to keep them Christian! If on top of everything they manage to shake off the fear of whipping, which is now and has always been even among them the most common punishment and the only thing that restrains them, I think that their piety and religion would soon end, along with their respect and obedience to legitimate authorities.

I was in the act of writing this when three *doctrina*[15] teachers came to me, saying that very few children attend catechism because their parents will not permit it and saying that they can no longer be punished or compelled. Some two weeks ago a boy challenged his own father, threatening to strike him because he came to the defense of his wife, whom he [the boy] was abusing. Many fail to respect even the magistrates. The love and respect that they show me for always treating them with kindness and for having spent on them and their churches all that remains to me from the church rents—it seems that it has all turned to hatred and alienation, and among them there has been no shortage of those who say that by demanding church rents I am robbing them,

---

14. Baeza uses the term *mediodía,* meaning "noon," presumably as a way of saying "center" or "north."

15. *Doctrina* referred to classes of Catholic doctrine.

along with everyone else. Even though they know perfectly well that it is the only income I have to pay my three companions, who are so necessary for good administration, and that in the past month there has not been enough to pay them. To see such terrible beginnings, I fear that diabolical sacrifices and other superstitions will return soon and with great force, like a torrent that has long been suppressed.

13. If we compare the moral and political condition of these same Indians in the first century after conversion to their current condition, it seems to me that there has been notable improvement since I see them better grounded in faith and good habits. They are as cultured as their natural simplicity permits and will be more so if the Cortes, which has liberated them from the slavery and oppression in which they were found, issues as I hope the wise laws needed to preserve in them the righteous fear of punishment.

14. In their marriages I know of no arrangements other than the wife going to live with her in-laws or the husband with his in-laws. The latter is more common since the episcopal decrees have prohibited the wife from living with the father-in-law because of the unfortunate results that experience has frequently shown, namely, the father- or brother-in-law abusing her. To guarantee the betrothal, they are accustomed to sending *arras,* or a bride-price, of little value to the bride's parents. There is no custom of the intended husband lending any services.

15. Their most common illnesses are seasonal. In part of the summer and all of the autumn, when fresh foods abound, so too abound diarrhea and vomiting. In the winter there are fierce attacks of constipation, rheumatism, croup, and pains in the side because, after laboring over the fire, they expose themselves to cold airs, and they wet themselves with splatterings of water. Ordinarily they use no other cure than to bleed themselves and to drink sour *pozole,*[16] boiled lemonade, or something known as *xkantumbub,* which is said to be a sanguinary herb. They use neither vomiting nor purgatives, nor have I seen anything worth mentioning among those whom they call *yerbateros.*[17] There are no thermal baths in this country.[18] On repeated occasions experience has shown me that an amalgam of wild boar's tooth in a lime solution, uncooked and taken with a bit of water at room temperature, is a highly efficient remedy for pains of the side. In the 30 years and five months that I have worked in this parish, its number of residents has nearly doubled.

16. In order to recognize the seasons of the year, they have no calendar other than our own because they no longer remember their ancient calendars. As a result of hearing the church bells, they know well the hours of the day and night, more or less, and with the Spanish names of one, two, three, etc. They

---

16. A beverage made from freshly boiled corn.

17. A *yerbatero* is a person who cures with herbal remedies.

18. There were thermal baths, however, in one remote part of the bishopric of Yucatán. The town of Teapa in southern Tabasco has thermal baths that are still worth a visit.

rest from early evening until about 4:00 in the morning; they work from sunup to sundown.[19]

17. Ordinarily they prepare two meals: one at daybreak and the other at two or three in the afternoon. If they are going to work their fields, after a breakfast of tortillas and *atole*,[20] they carry with them a flask of *pozole,* which they make from pure corn cooked for a long time and dissolved in water, to refresh themselves at noon. When the sun sets they abandon their work and return to their houses to prepare the second meal. Their most common foods are beans or parboiled herbs. They only eat meat when they buy beef or pork on Sunday, to be eaten that same day, or when by chance they happen to kill some wild animal. Almost always these are very simple dishes. When the poor cannot afford special meals, they content themselves with tortillas, chile, and a gourd of *pozole* or *atole.* Even the most prosperous Indians ordinarily have only a single dish. It is certain that all of them are very given to eating, but this comes as a result of their hard work. When they work for entire weeks in the Spanish houses or in the rectory for the stipulated salary,[21] they and their wives prepare three meals. When there is no shortage of food, a silver *real*'s worth of food is enough to feed one person for a week.[22]

18. They know no fermented drink other than *pitarrilla,* which they call *balche',* which is the name of a plant whose cutting they place in a mixture with honey and water with no other ingredient. After it has fermented, it becomes highly intoxicating. Experience has taught that this drink is healthy and that it purges the bladder of noxious humors. They are very partial toward it and also to *aguardiente.*

19. It seems to me that among them there remain no bad habits or inclinations to worship the moon, nor even a memory of such.

20. Nor does it seem to me that they maintain any of the customs of their primitive forefathers, nor do they have information or any tradition of how they came to inhabit this land.

21. I have never heard that in their burials or in their duels they use any unusual ceremony.

22. Among them there is no shortage of those who know how to carry out their obligations faithfully and know how to keep their word and their promises, but it seems to me that more numerous are those who are unreliable. The

---

19. The version of *El registro yucateco* renders this paragraph as the response to a separate question, whereas the Menéndez edition groups it with answer 15. The former seems to be more correct because the paragraph clearly deals with separate and distinct subject matter, and the Menéndez edition omits an answer 16 altogether. For that reason, I have followed the *Registro* edition.

20. *Atole* is a drink made of dried cornmeal dissolved in water.

21. The exact phrase here is *por el estipendio tasado.* Recent reforms had established set wages for Indian labor, wages that the rural *curas* were under pressure to observe; hence, Baeza's insertion.

22. A *real* is a coin worth one-eighth of a peso.

exception being the promises they make to the sacred images: they carry these out faithfully and with devotion.

23. They lie easily, something that I attribute more to their limited capacities than to malice. They know that lying is forbidden, and I know of no one who has a mistaken opinion on this point.

24. Next to lying, their main vices are the lasciviousness of both sexes and drunkenness among the men. But to tell the truth, it seems to me that these vices are not permitted to dominate as they do among other classes of people, perhaps because they are always busy with their work. It is commonly said that they are inclined to steal, but ordinarily their thefts are petty.

25. Well-to-do Indians readily lend a hand to one another, and usually they will do so with the other classes when they are certain that they will not be cheated.

26. The stony ground of this country prevents the use of the plow. The farmer's work boils down to slashing the overgrowth, burning it as summer approaches, planting the corn and beans when the rains fall, which is in May or June, fencing off the plantings, and chopping out the weeds. In order to expand their operations, prosperous Indians hire day laborers, or *jornaleros,* at good wages, whether in silver or in kind below its daily price.[23] This is particularly true during times of scarcity, like now. When a *carga*[24] of corn costs 12 *reales,* they pay their workers four *reales,* and they feed them well while invoking the following maxim, "This is the sweat of my brothers, and it would not be right that they pay too much for their food." They routinely work in their fields or in the common lands of the village, and when they work on someone else's land, they pay five *cargas* of corn or ten *reales* in silver for every 100 *mecates,* retaining the right to work the land for a second and third year. A *mecate* is 24 square *varas.*[25]

If they live on a hacienda they are called *luneros.* In exchange for the land they occupy, for the fields they work for their own consumption, and for the water (should the owner of the hacienda supply it), they provide a day of service on Monday or a silver *real.*[26] The normal practice is to work twenty *mecates* of *milpa rosa* and twenty of *caña* or ten of one and ten of the other, according to the varying circumstances of the haciendas. *Milpa rosa* is overgrown land, whereas *milpa caña* consists of the stalks of corn from the previous year, stalks

---

23. By paying in kind "below the daily price" (*a menor precio del corriente*), the prosperous Maya paid his workers a greater quantity than was owed, thus allowing the worker to resell the surplus at a profit. Here is an arbitrary example: If he owed the worker ten pesos, and each bushel of corn was worth one peso on the market, the owner could pay the worker as if each bushel were worth a half-peso, making the total pay twenty bushels. It saved the owner the trouble of having to produce cash wages before he sold his own crop.

24. A *carga* is the equivalent of forty-five pounds.

25. A *vara* is the equivalent of approximately .835 meter.

26. The term *lunero* comes from the word *lunes,* or "Monday." The resident peon originally worked for the estate owner on Monday in exchange for access to estate land and came to be identified by his day of labor.

that they beat down in order to burn. In good years the going price of a *carga* is two *reales,* and when they sell in anticipation of a harvest, they usually do so for half that amount. But if the purchaser lacks skill, they have the habit of not supplying all the corn that he purchased.

27. The Yucatecan Indian does not seem to me cruel or irascible. The most common punishment, and virtually the only one used among them, is the whip; and when they understand the reason, they harbor no grudge, nor do they take it as an insult.

28. Among them there is no inclination to human sacrifice.

29. Even among the most savage of Indians this inclination is not found, nor in this land has there been an example of such for one or two centuries. Their sacrifices are limited to what I have described in articles 10 and 12. They neither cremate cadavers nor offer them food but rather bury them in cemeteries according to the rites of the holy church.

30. In my parish there are no rich men of any class, only those of modest prosperity, those who have gained some security: the Indians through agriculture, and the others through commerce.[27]

31. The *caciques,* [who are] Indian leaders and past officials, lead normal lives like the rest. They practice agriculture on their own or by hired labor, which they pay at normal wages. They commit no outrages upon the others, nor do they demand unpaid service from them. The other Indians respect them.

32. Before the publication of last year's November 13 decree, the Indians, men as well as women, lent personal service to the *curas* and the Spanish Americans in exchange for the salary stipulated by the *arancel.*[28] Men's service normally boiled down to cutting firewood for the kitchen or carrying fodder for the horses. Beyond these chores, in the rectories there were one or two who were to prepare and serve at the table or to do specific errands, and another to care for the orchard and horses. The women's service consisted of cooking and grinding the corn and making the tortillas, which are the normal bread of the province. Those who were personal servants took care of the plantings, or else cut wood, or else gathered salt from the salt pools. These services have come to an end.

33. Some Indians show a talent for music and use the instruments as the Spanish do,[29] although not with the same skill. Some have good lungs and a good voice; they sing in the choirs of the villages, although none of them know the solfège. They still use some of the songs of their language for celebrations and public dances, and they accompany them with a small rustic flute and

---

27. At this point Menéndez (p. 60) reports that Baeza inserts the following footnote, which is omitted in the *Registro* version: "In almost all the villages of the province the same thing happens, and of more than 500,000 Indians that we know of, there would hardly be 20,000 who have two shirts of *patí,* and this constitutes their wardrobe and finery." As explained in Baeza's note to article 36 below, *patí* was an indigenous, handwoven fabric.

28. The *arancel* was a list of set prices for religious services.

29. Here Baeza says *los americanos,* although the implication is clearly to Hispanic Americans, or Creoles.

something known as a *mitote*. This latter is made of solid wood of a rounded shape like a column and is usually about a yard long and a third or so in diameter; it has a large mouth, almost from end to end, through which the entire center has been hollowed out until it reaches the thickness of a board. On the side opposite the mouth, they cut two long rectangular wings, which begin at opposite ends and meet in the middle, divided only by a single cut of the saw. To play it they place the *mitote* mouth down over the ground and with the wings on top. They strike these with two short sticks whose ends have been covered with a leathery resin that makes them bounce in order to not muffle or muddy the sound. This instrument carries a deep reverberation, an echo that resonates through the ground with a continuous *vé, vé, vé* and is so strong that I have heard it from as far as twelve miles away.[30]

The Indians have used this instrument since pagan times and even now are accustomed to using it for the idolatries. They say that its name is *tankul*, not *tunk'ul*, as is said now. *Tankul* has two meanings: "before the idol" and "now we worship." It seems to me that this is quite literally the winged instrument that the prophet Isaiah mentions in chapter 18, which begins, *Ve terra symbalo alarum,* which some sacred writers apply to the discovery and conquest of these Indians.[31] But they have really known nothing of that *symbalo alarum* because they have never heard of the *mitote* or *tankul,* nor of its principal use. These days it is customary in the solemn church functions to accompany the ringing of bells with one or more *mitotes,* bugles, trumpets, and flageolets to draw the attention of the village.

34. The Yucatecan Indians are by nature cowardly and fearful, and there is no memory of them having once been outstanding warriors; nor scholars since they are so primitive and slow to understand that they do not reason quickly, and even in trivial matters, it frequently happens that after explaining something to them clearly and vividly, they do it the opposite way. They have such poor memories that despite attending catechism daily, and from age six or seven to 12 or 14, very many never learn it completely, even though the catechism is so brief that it can be recited in a quarter of an hour, more or less. So we have to content ourselves with their learning and understanding the minimum necessary to receive the fruit of the sacraments. It is certain that some who have applied themselves to study have gotten some middling advantage from it, but they seem to me to be only those who, by color or physiognomy, give some evidence of other races in their heritage.

35. Those who do not run from catechism and the preaching of the Gospel share the Catholic ideas of eternity, reward and punishment, final justice, Heaven, Purgatory, and Hell.

---

30. Baeza's estimate of the *tunk'ul*'s carrying power strikes me as exaggerated.

31. "Woe to the land, the winged cymbal, which is beyond the rivers of Ethiopia" (Isa. 18:1). This is the translation given in the 1609 Douay English version of the Bible. More recent translations render this as "the land of whirring wings," apparently a reference to locusts.

36. The dress that Indian men normally use in public consists of a shirt like ours of woven cloth, with wide pants stretching to the knee or perhaps to the calf cut from the same cloth;[32] a white belt or perhaps of colors; a handkerchief and straw hat; and perhaps leather-soled sandals made with *mecate* rope.[33] When they go to work in the fields, they strip off their clothes and wear only a cloth apron and a handkerchief fixed to the waist at opposite ends, hat, and sandals.

The women wear the same white cloth. Their dress consists of a long petticoat that reaches to the ankles and a wide, square *hipil* with a cutoff collar. At the top corners it has two smaller openings for the arms, which remain covered up to the shoulders. This *hipil* goes over the petticoat and is bordered at the edge. They cover their head and part of their cheeks and arms with a strip of the same cloth and go barefoot, except for the few who wear shoes. This is how they come to church, with a certainly homespun simplicity. In their home they wear only the petticoat since the heat of this country is excessive, and they are always working, and the cooking fires are almost always lit within the homes. The clothing I have described usually has a blue or pink border. *Mestiza* and *parda* women use the same outfit and usually make it from linen, with a border of thread, spiral, or silk.

---

32. At this point Menéndez (p. 62) reports that Baeza inserts the following footnote, which is omitted in the *Registro* version: "The cloth which they use for their dress is *patí*, a beautiful fabric which the Indians make from cotton, which is harvested in abundance in the *partidos* of Valladolid, Tihosuco, and Tizimín, but only for use within the peninsula. They work without hand looms and with utter indolence, for which reason they produce scarcely a yard per day even when they work from sunup to sundown. Some *curas* and other well-intentioned individuals have tried to introduce hand looms. But those who have put money in such projects have lost all their investment, with nothing whatsoever to show for it."

33. *Milpa* farmers use a special rope to measure the size of a *mecate*. With typical peasant thriftiness, they recycled used rope for sandal cords.

2

The Work of the Maya Town Councils

No collection of writings by or about the Mayas of the nineteenth cen-
tury would be complete without a few sample documents produced
by the repúblicas de indígenas, *or Maya town councils, which oper-*
ated from the early colonial period to the year 1869. Abundant in the
colonial era, Maya-language documents began to decline in both pro-
duction and retention after independence. Nevertheless, enough sur-
vive to paint a portrait of Maya life that differs markedly from the one
drawn by Spanish priests. Rather than depicting the rural Mayas as
superstitious and intractable, these papers reveal that rural villagers
were methodical, orderly, and concerned about the operation of
public affairs. The following text provides a selection of four brief
documents that capture the repúblicas *in some of their more repre-*
sentative activities.

MEASURING LAND BOUNDARIES

In the first of these four selections, we find the república *of Uayma*
carrying out one of its most important tasks: supervising a boundary
survey intended to mark the line separating village communal lands
from nearby commercial properties. The stone markers to which the
república refers are known in Spanish as mojoneros *and in Maya as*
multuno'ob. *Note that the* república *members walked the distance of*
these boundaries with the subdelegado, *the regional official respon-*
sible for the survey.[1]

Act of Measurement, Uayma, 9 August 1804
  On this day we, along with the other villagers, have gone as [part of] a commission that was given to our greatly esteemed and beloved *subdelegado*[2] by

---

1. The source of the following material is Archivo General del Estado de Yucatán (Mérida), Poder
Ejecutivo Box 174, Ayuntamientos, "Testimonio de mensura de las tierras que corresponden al
pueblo de Uayma," various dates.

2. The *subdelegado* was a political official whose power encompassed a *partido,* an administrative territory consisting of a head town and surrounding municipalities. Originally charged with
tax collection, the *subdelegados* assumed other administrative responsibilities during the first
three decades of the nineteenth century, duties that included overseeing the appointment of
Maya officials. After 1835 the *subdelegados* lost power to the office of *jefe político* and reverted
to the exclusive role of tax collection.

señor Governor Don Benito Pérez so that [the former can] deliver to us a just measurement. The road that is its boundary stretches to Palib to the stone marker of Petcah. In the same fashion, the end of the boundary extends to the stone of Chumpahi, to the great stone marker of Chioplé, to the great stone marker of Cuch'ul, [and] to the great stone marker of the village of Uayma.

Our esteemed *subdelegado* proceeded to walk. He went to the north in a straight line running to the stone marker for some distance and the village of Chocholá, which reached to the great stone marker of Chocholá, where begins the village of San Antonio Subul. The path goes from the north for some distance to the village of Tzabtun in a straight line of markers. On the other side of its limits is [the village of] Xyaxmultun; the great stone marker of Tzabtun is where it begins; and the village of Nocac. [This boundary] goes to the north for some distance to the village of Tzalam Kancab. On the other side of the boundary is the great stone marker Cross of Stone, the stone marker of Ycicil. It goes north for some distance to Nocac. On the other side of that boundary [is] the stone marker of Chich . . . there begins the land of Pop. [This boundary] goes north to the village of Chich. On the other side of its boundary [is] the great stone marker of Chak Petcah [and] the great stone marker of Uayma.

We testify that the measurement has been completed by the esteemed *subdelegado* señor Don Ignacio Rivas, the commissioned Don Joaquín Rosado, [and] witness Don Manuel García; and that Don José de Arce pays the cost in its entirety to the honored magistrates, and [that the measurements are] as they should be from this date forward, and we sign,[3]

Don Bernardino Ts'ul, *Gobernador*[4]	Sebastián Ku, *Regidor*
Manuel Hau, *Teniente*	Andrés Chan, *Regidor*
Pascual Ku, *Alcalde*	Mateo Canché, *Regidor*
Pedro Nahuat, *Alcalde*	Santiago Ba, *Regidor*

José Ek
Bernardino Ac
Domingo Ku
Fernando Ku
Tomás Ku
Manuel Ku, *Escribano*

PROVIDING A RECEIPT FOR CHURCH REMODELING

The Maya repúblicas *of the early national period had to cooperate closely with the local religious hierarchy, seeing to both the good*

---

3. Two copies of this document exist, each with a slightly different set of signatories, evidently a problem that occurred in the reproduction. I have followed the original, which includes the scribe Manuel Ku. The original document does not appear among the papers of the Uayma land dispute.

4. The term *gobernador,* or "governor," was occasionally used to designate a *batab,* but this practice became relatively rare after 1821.

repair of the church and the faithful attendance of the peasant parishioners. In this brief document, the town council of Sacalaca testifies that a local Maya artisan received the appropriate payment for his services. The local Catholic Church had a complicated relationship with its Maya flock, but, as illustrated here, it was also an employer.[5]

Sacalaca, 24 September 1815

We, the *batab, teniente, alcaldes, regidores,* and *escribano,* here in the village of Sacalaca of the Assumption of Saint Mary the Virgin: . . . we state the truth and verify what was paid to Gabriel Cituk by our beloved *cura, bachiller* Don Bacilio Mansanilla.[6] It happens that he made a window for the sacristy; its price was two pesos and six *reales.*[7] It happens that he fashioned a beam, two pesos and one half-peso. It happens that he repaired the ceiling, two pesos; and he refashioned the cross beam, for which he was paid six reales. The total money paid to Gabriel Cituk for his work was eight pesos. That is how it happened. He was paid by our esteemed *cura bachiller.* Thus we here swear this testimony to be the truth, and we sign below.

Don Leonardo Chuc, *Batab*   Francisco Pisté and Martín Ek, *Alcaldes*
Nicolás Tsul, *Teniente*   Tomás Ek and Yldefonso Sulu, *Regidores*
Francisco Cituk, *Escribano*

HANDING OVER TAX COLLECTIONS

From the state's point of view, one of the most critical functions of the Maya batabs and repúblicas was the collection of peasant taxes. In fact, their knowledge of the Maya language and people made them virtually the only individuals capable of such a task. Tax grievances grew during the late colonial and early national periods and served as one of the motivating forces behind the Caste War. The Maya elites of the villages, however, struggled with the process throughout the 1820s, 1830s, and 1840s. In this document, the república of Hoctún testifies to its timely delivery of state taxes in 1822.[8]

---

5. The source of the following material is Archivo Histórico de la Arquidiócesis de Yucatán (Mérida), Decretos y Oficios, microfilm roll 96, 24 September 1815.

6. A *bachiller,* indicating that he had completed a course of study beyond that of *primeras letras,* or basic education.

7. A peso was worth eight *reales.*

8. The source of the following material is Archivo General del Estado de Yucatán (Mérida), Poder Ejecutivo Box 1, Ayuntamientos, I, 36, 24 August 1825.

We, the *batab, alcaldes, regidores,* and *escribano* here at the village of the beloved patron saint San Miguel Archangel, give [our] true testimony as to the payment, which the men counted, of the roster of the Christmas contributions [given] to Rafael Moguel in the year 1822. . . . Furthermore, [we give the list of] those who are dead and those who are exempted from payment.[9] This is the truth; we sign below here at the village of Hoctún on 24 August 1829.

Pablo Kan, *Batab*

Antonio Can, *Teniente*

Vicente Kuyoc, *Escribano*

SUBMITTING NOMINATIONS FOR THE OFFICE OF *BATAB*

Maya public offices were in some ways democratic affairs. Details of the nineteenth-century electoral process are unclear largely because of the lack of village-level records. It appears that Mayas selected their own nominees for office (with the first of three names being their favorite), although lower offices and possibly that of batab involved some form of popular election. Final approval, however, lay in the hands of Hispanic officials, to whom letters such as the following were addressed.[10]

Ekpetz, 28 November 1830

We, the *alcalde, regidores,* and *escribano* of this village, have carried out the election, just as our esteemed *subdelegado* instructed, in order that we, the officials, [may] consider three men of the greatest respect and virtue. Below are their names . . . the esteemed Don Justo Ic, the esteemed Don Francisco Tsul, and Don Matías Kawil. [We do this] so that, of the worthy men selected, one of these three may in the end be appointed to the *república*.

Feliz María Aké, *Teniente*	Urbano Catzim, *Regidor*
Francisco Catzim, *Alcalde*	Teodoro Yc, *Regidor*
Juan Nepomuceno Tuyú, *Alcalde*	Feliciano Kinil, *Regidor*
	Alejandro Balam, *Regidor*
Agustín Tzuc, *Escribano*	

9. Tax exemptions were granted for several reasons, such as widowhood, destitution, or the hereditary status of *hidalgo,* or Maya noble. The title *hidalgo* originally referred to a Spanish nobleman but was subsequently granted to Mayas who had cooperated during the conquest of Yucatán. *Hidalgo* status, however, had declined in importance by the beginning of the nineteenth century. It was later revived as an honorific title conferred upon Maya peasants who performed ancillary services during the Caste War.

10. The source of the following material is Archivo General del Estado de Yucatán (Mérida), Poder Ejecutivo, Empleos, Ekpetz, 28 November 1830.

3

"Intellectual Barbarism"

Federico de Waldeck Visits Yucatán

Few nineteenth-century travelers to Yucatán enjoyed as unusual a life as that of Juan Federico Maximiliano, Barón de Waldeck, a Prague-born (1766) painter, lithographer, and compulsive traveler. Few travelers also saw as much at such critical moments. In 1799 Waldeck journeyed with the French troops to Egypt. After traveling through East Africa, northwestern Sudan's Dongola Desert, Madagascar, and the Indian Ocean, he made his first visit to the Americas shortly after 1815, when he toured Chile and Guatemala. After a trip to London in 1822, he returned to Mexico two years later, this time to the capital, where he worked as an engineer for the British mining company Minas de Tlalpujahua. Quickly tiring of the routine, he departed once more in 1830 to sketch the archaeological ruins of Palenque in Chiapas. In 1833, the year of the worldwide cholera epidemic, Waldeck crossed through Tabasco into Yucatán, where he remained until 1835, traveling, sketching, and satisfying his restless curiosity. Thereafter Waldeck spent most of his life in Europe, producing highly stylized lithographs and composing memoirs and historical studies. He died in 1875 at the incredible age of 110.

Waldeck presents a perspective that is very different from that of Baeza (see chapter 1). A child of the French Enlightenment, Waldeck cast a dim eye on what he regarded as superstition, backwardness, or bureaucracy. Waldeck, who is most interesting when he is disparaging, displays considerable racism in his writings but nevertheless opens windows to the places and times of his journeys. Much of his memoir revolves around city life or archaeological explorations. Waldeck, however, also included sundry observations on Maya life. The following excerpts from his 1837 published account describe Maya reactions to a lunar eclipse, Maya ways of guarding money, and miscellaneous topics, such as chewing gum and courtship.

AN ECLIPSE IN CAMPECHE[1]

Here we see an element of superstition that will give some idea of the state of intellectual barbarism in which these people still howl. On June 21, near 2:00 in the morning, I was awakened by a strange noise, which made me fear that the city was being attacked by the faction from Mérida. I did not take long to realize that it was something equally tragic. There was a superstition to which the ancient Indians of Mexico subscribed, that when an eclipse of the sun or moon occurred, one of these two astral bodies was imprisoning the other. In order to drive off the aggressor before it devoured its adversary, they would shoot arrows toward the sky. . . . Nor was this all. To put an end to the celestial duel, the Indians would make their slaves and their dogs cry out, beating them while they themselves let out the same frightful howls.

The spectacle that I beheld on June 21 was nothing short of a repetition of that ridiculous scene. There was an eclipse of the moon, and the Indians of Campeche did all in their power to liberate this unfortunate asteroid from the embrace of its enemy; only now, skyrockets replaced arrows, as if to show that the Yucatecans of today are no strangers to the advances of civilization. Here we see what an ignorant and despotic clergy has made of the peoples conquered by Spanish arms.

ON GUARDING MONEY[2]

When the Indians have only a few *reales,* they place them in their ears; but when they have accumulated a significant amount, they hang it in a purse made from broad pantaloons wrapped around their waists. Some hide it in a cotton belt, which they carry with them. The women wrap their money in the sleeves of their shirts. The *kuspaches,* or Indian runners or porters, carry, hung at their side, a small pouch similar to that used by the Scottish highlanders. This pouch, made from the skin of a tiger and decorated with the animal's tail, serves to carry the letters entrusted to them, along with their tiny fortune of silver coins. In order to guard the triggers of their decrepit rifles from the rain, hunters wrap the weapons in tiger skin, the tail of which hangs like a cord down the length of their thighs. In the province of Chiapas they use the pelts of the *mirmecófagos didáctilos* for this same purpose.[3]

The Indian is quite miserly and buries his money in the ground; since only objects of little value are sold, [he] collect[s] only *pesetas, reales,* and *medios.* Prior to the most recent drought, money was so scarce, owing to the Indians'

---

1. The source of the following material is Federico de Waldeck, *Viaje pintoresco y arqueológico a la provincia de Yucatán (América central) durante los años 1834 y 1836,* trans. Manuel Mestre Ghigliazze (Mérida: Compañía Tipográfica Yucateca, S.A., 1930; orig. 1837), 29–30.

2. The source of the following material is Waldeck, *Viaje pintoresco,* 100–101.

3. The *mirmecófagos didáctilos* is the two-toed anteater.

tendency to hoard it, that to change a peso cost a *medio real,* that is, about one-sixteenth of the former's value. But hunger obliged these savages to dig up their tiny treasures in order to buy food, and now in the plaza the small coins are more common than the large ones. Silver hidden for many years has returned to circulation and soon went to the United States in exchange for the corn that was shipped from that nation. There are as many metal species as before, but said abundance of coins will probably not last long because little by little the money disappears and a new deficit is felt.

SUNDRY OBSERVATIONS[4]

The natives of the West Indies are in the habit of chewing a rather expensive substance, betel.[5] Here this gum has an equivalent, which the mestizos and Indian women chew as well. Said natural product is called *cha'* in Maya and *sicte'* in Spanish. It is nothing more than the resinous pulp of the *zapote,* which makes *cha'* relatively expensive. The Indians imagine that the use of this gum keeps them from losing their teeth. I can easily believe this because, white and tough, it only softens with heat, and chewing it with force cleans the teeth and leaves the mouth with an aromatic perfume that is quite agreeable. . . .

The Indians have an altogether singular manner of expressing their amorous desires, and one must be initiated in the secrets of this language in order to understand its signals. In the streets, along the roads, and under the doors of coaches, Indians of both sexes are often seen in deep conversation; sometimes it goes on for whole hours, and the passerby who does not grasp the veiled intention of this long and intimate exchange is likely to wonder what they are talking about. On various occasions I myself have been quite intrigued by these interminable conversations, and this is what someone quite knowledgeable in the ways of Indians explained to me one day.

When the talk has to do with nothing more than matters of family and friends, the two parties remain steadfast on their feet, not leaning against the wall or gesturing with more than their arms. When it concerns matters of the heart, the man leans against some nearby object, and while he talks, the woman carelessly swings one of her feet from left to right but without being too obvious. If the woman likes what the Indian says and accepts his proposition, she now begins to play with her foot, and at this point it can be guessed how the conversation will end. When the young woman is not inclined to let herself be seduced by the blandishments of the gentleman, she notifies him through her voice and her foot, keeping her head raised and immobile and laughing at

---

4. The source of the following material is Waldeck, *Viaje pintoresco,* 106–7.

5. The betel palm, which is actually native to Southeast Asia, produces a nut commonly chewed for its flavor and as a digestive aid. At the time of Waldeck's writing, the West Indies was filling with Asian contract laborers, who brought the betel habit with them.

every word of the frustrated suitor. This matter of expressing their desires has something candid and modest, which has always seemed to me preferable to the refinements of seduction used by lovers in civilized countries.

Because the greater part of the Indians and the women of the villages go barefoot on good roads, carrying their sandals (*alpargatas*) to reserve for use in the cities, it happens that here they acquire an extraordinary dexterity in the use of their feet. The women never stoop to recover something that has fallen to the floor; with their toes they can pick up fruit, a piece of firewood, and even a coin, while they carry a full basket over their heads. I have seen men who picked up rocks in the same manner and threw them with incredible skill. Virtually all the Indians are ambidextrous; they can manage a hatchet or machete in either hand with equal skill. With his savage instincts, his profound ignorance, his great agility, [and] his well-developed physical faculties, the native of this land is the living transition between monkey and man.

4

Bulls, Beehives, and Silver Coins

Executing a Maya Will

What did a Maya of the early nineteenth-century own? This brief document is excerpted from the 1834 will of José María Uc, a relatively prosperous individual from the town of Tunkás. It offers a representative selection of what constituted material wealth in those days: land, cattle, debts, icons, furniture, and knickknacks. The only common estate item not found here is a house. Uc's total estate was valued at 735 pesos, which placed him in the higher registers of Maya wealth. Of that total, approximately 70 pesos were used to cover debts, burial fees, and masses for his soul; another 30 pesos paid the legal fees for executing the will. Following the common practice of the time, the estate was divided equally among the remaining heirs: approximately 212 pesos apiece to his widow and two sons.

As with the documents of the repúblicas, the will of José María Uc shows a dimension of Maya life that was not often captured in Hispanic ethnographies. Rather than dwelling upon features that seemed exotic and alien, the will depicts a people involved in the practicalities of daily life: acquiring material wealth, working within the legal framework, and learning to survive, and even to prosper, under terms largely imposed by the dominant Hispanic culture.[1]

44 branded cattle, $5 apiece	$220.0[2]
9 branded bulls, $5 apiece	45.0
13 plots of land throughout the countryside, $2 apiece	26.0
2 mules, totaling $60	60.0
2 gelded horses, $10 apiece	20.0
3 mares, $10 apiece	30.0
1 colt, $5	5.0
63 beehives, $1^{1}/_{2}$ reales apiece	$11.6^{1}/_{2}$
29 more beehives, at $14^{1}/_{2}$ reales	$1.6^{1}/_{2}$

---

1. The source of the following material is Archivo General del Estado de Yucatán (Mérida), Fondo Justicio, Civil, 1834.

2. From left to right, the monetary units divided by decimals are as follows: peso and *real* (an eighth of a peso).

1 chain with reliquary, $15	15.0
1 rosary with case, $8	8.0
1 pair of earrings, $4	4.0
1 silver spoon, 3 reales	0.3
1 lance, 12 reales	1.4
1 dagger, $2	2.0
1 rifle, broken, $2	2.0
1 pair of spurs, 6 reales	0.6
1 cauldron, 28 reales	3.4
3 cushions and 1 bed, 4 reales	0.4
2 tables and 1 chest, 10 reales	1.2
1 "bath"[3] with grinding stone, 4 reales	0.4
2 jugs and 1 glass bottle, 4 reales	0.4
1 ring and 1 brush, 2 reales	0.2
Assorted strips of tanned leather, 12 reales	1.4
3 yokes, 6 sacks, and 1 cord, 9 reales	1.1
1 saddle, $2	2.0
1 leather jacket, 4 reales	0.4
$34, 6 reales owed by Antonio Yupit	34.6
$235, 3 reales from the estate of his father, Nicolás Uc	235.3
Total	$735.0

---

3. The term *baño,* or "bath," apparently refers to the large bowl-shaped stones in which corn was ground.

5

"A State of Listless Bondage"

B. A. Norman Visits Yucatán

*B. A. Norman was a New Orleans book dealer, traveler, and gentle-
man archaeologist who, inspired by the writings of John Lloyd
Stephens, visited the Yucatán Peninsula between December 1841
and April 1842, shortly after Yucatán's separation from Mexico. A
pithy writer and keen observer, Norman also carried a good deal of
cultural baggage, including a dislike for the Catholic Church and for
traditional Spanish institutions in general. Norman visited Mérida,
Chichén Itzá, Campeche, and various small towns in between. He
also composed what is apparently the first English guide to Maya
grammar and vocabulary, which he appended to the text published
in 1843.*

*The following is a selection of his observations on the Maya
peoples and the conditions of life in rural villages and estates. A citizen of the slave-holding state of Louisiana, Norman was particularly interested in capturing the essence of a way of life that did not
legally enslave the Mayas, but which, in practice, confined them to
doing menial jobs for Hispanics. He was also fascinated by the way
that the Mayas' passive resistance to such a system penetrated their
personalities and culture, making them both cooperative and
intractable.*

FIRST CONTACT WITH THE MAYAS[1]

[Upon] returning to our lodgings we met a *calesa*,[2] preceded by two Indians
with lanterns tinkling small bells, followed by four Indian soldiers armed with
muskets. The carriage contained a priest, who was going to administer holy
unction. The people, as is the universal custom here, knelt as he passed. To
obviate a similar necessity, we retreated into the nearest house, thereby escap-
ing a charge of heresy and the unpleasantness of coming into contact with
muddy streets.

---

1. The source of the following material is B. A. Norman, *Rambles in Yucatan; or, Notes of Travel
Through the Peninsula, Including a Visit to the Remarkable Ruins of Chi-Chen, Kabah, Zayi, and
Uxmal* (New York: J. & H. G. Langley, 1843), 30–31.

2. A type of light carriage.

A stranger, on his first arrival in this country, is at a loss where to place the Indian in the scale of social life. He seems clean and well dressed, mingling with the whites, and without distinction. To have Indian blood is no reproach, and family groups, in many cases, show this most palpably. It is not unusual to hear mothers threaten to send their children home to their respective fathers whenever their rudeness requires chiding. The Indian, however, performs the menial labor of the country, and there is an appearance of apathy in his looks and actions, which seems to carry with it the signs of a broken or at least a sub-dued spirit resting upon him in a melancholy vision, a dreamy remembrance, of better days. For, say what we please of him, he is the humble descendant of a once great and powerful people—the "children of the sun," who were lords of that soil on which their offspring are now held in humiliating vassalage.

SOME GENERAL OBSERVATIONS[3]

The dress of the Indian is of the simplest kind. His food principally consists of corn which is prepared by parboiling and crushing on a stone by means of a roller. When ready, it is made into balls and, after being mixed with water, is ready to be eaten. Corn is broken in the same way and made into cakes called *tortillas,* which are the favorite food of all classes of society in this province. The wages for Indian service are from one to four dollars per month, the largest portion of which, in very many cases, is expended for candles and other offer-ings to their chosen saint.

In general, these Indians are extremely mild and inoffensive. Drinking is their most decided vice; but even this, as we have already remarked, cannot be called a prevailing one. They are a listless rather than indolent race and never "think for the morrow." They have quite an amiable expression in their coun-tenances, and their mode of conversation is pleasing. Their features remind one of those of the Asiatic [race] more than of any other. Their stature is short and thick-set, having but little resemblance to that of the North American Indian.

We looked in vain for their pastimes—they have none, except those con-nected with the church. They seldom dance or sing.[4] They are wholly under the surveillance of the priests and are the most zealous devotees to their rites and ceremonies. Their hours of leisure are passed in their hammocks or else in silently squatting about the corners of the streets. Though they wear the *outside* show of freedom, they have not even as much liberty as the most abject vassal of the Middle Ages. They are literally degraded to the position of serfs. They are always in debt and are consequently at the mercy of their creditors, who, by the law of this country, have lien upon their services until their debts are can-celed. This, together with the absence of nearly all the ordinary encourage-

---

3. The source of the following material is Norman, *Rambles in Yucatan,* 70–72.

4. An obvious mistake because songs and dances abound in the culture of the rural Mayas.

ments to exertion common in a colder climate and among a more progressive people, conspires to keep the Indian Yucatecos in a state of listless bondage, which they endure without a murmur, and we may add from our own observation, without much positive suffering. Legalized slavery, as it is well known, does not exist in any part of Mexico.

ON THE HACIENDA CHICHÉN ITZÁ[5]

This (Sunday) has been a lovely day so far as nature was concerned. Nothing but the continuation of the dancing and the wild music, interrupted at times by the revelry of drunken Indians, could be heard, except [for] the services at the church by the same actors! At vespers, the principal officiate was so drunk that he dropped the incense-cup and broke it all to pieces. Unfortunately for his dignity, it fell upon my foot, [whereupon] I was so vexed that I trundled the old reprobate most unceremoniously out of the sanctuary and performed the ceremony myself, as well as I knew how, and dismissed the congregation. If the pope has any gratitude, he will send me a cardinal's hat, at least, for this interference.

There are about eighty Indians attached to this estate. Their wages are one dollar per month and a sack of corn, which contains about two bushels, worth here from thirty-seven and a half to fifty cents per sack, but the amount of wages varies in different parts of the country. In some sections laborers are employed by the job—so much for cutting down wood, the work being measured out; so much for planting an acre, and in the same way, for taking in the crops, [etc.], the prices of which are regulated by custom—but they are all under as abject bondage at present as if they had been born slaves. Their wages, low as they are—owing to the few wants of these people—more than cover their necessary expenses; but the taxes and the feasts of the church absorb all the surplus. I have known an Indian to expend his month's pay and all he was possessed of besides in the purchase of candles and trinkets for a single festival day, the former to burn before and the latter to decorate his tutelar saint.

They are permitted to build their huts on the lands of the estate without cost. Among those I visited, the best were miserable enough, consisting merely of poles driven perpendicularly into the ground to support a thatched roof. Although plenty of soil is allowed them, they cultivate nothing for themselves. Everything around them indicates indolence and squalid poverty.

A VISIT TO YAXCABÁ AND TABI[6]

Having concluded my visit at Chi-Chen [i.e., Chichén Itzá] and my curiosity being fully satisfied, I was ready at an early hour to continue my journey

---

5. The source of the following material is Norman, *Rambles in Yucatan,* 131–33.
6. The source of the following material is Norman, *Rambles in Yucatan,* 134–37.

westward. The Indians, to the number of fifty or sixty, had collected to witness our departure. They had been very civil to us during our stay, and, to express our acknowledgments, I knew no better way than to make them a few presents, with which they appeared to be highly pleased. We took leave of our kind host and hostess with regret. They had taken great pains to make my state comfortable among them, and I shall always remember them with gratitude.

By eight o'clock we were out of sight of castles and palaces and buried in the thick woods of the country. Our route lay over a narrow, stony path through the small Indian town of Pisté to Yaxcabá—a distance of about nine leagues—where we arrived at two o'clock, rode up to the Casa-real,[7] and dismounted in the square. The church occupied one side of it, and public offices and dwellings the others. The square is spacious and comprises nearly the whole town. Many of the houses are uninhabited and going to ruin. It had rained heavily during the morning, and the rooms of the Casa-real, as usual, did not present a very favorable aspect to the wet and fatigued traveler. However, we got our horses taken care of and succeeded in obtaining a tolerable breakfast.

By five o'clock the inhabitants began to leave their hammocks and made their way to the Casa-real, knowing, apparently by instinct or some faculty peculiar to the inhabitants of small towns, that strangers had arrived. In this instance, we were glad to see them, for we were sadly in want of a dry place to rest. They offered to do everything for us. We told them our wants by showing them the rooms of the Casa-real. They promised to get others, appeared glad to serve us, and treated us with great politeness. Off they started, as we supposed, to fit us out for the night, and that is the last we ever saw of them. This is mentioned merely to show a marked characteristic of the people. A stranger with a sanguine temperament in this province must suffer!

We were obliged, as usual, to depend upon ourselves for quarters; and, after much research and disturbing the quiet of many poor old women in their hammocks, we found a store-house, in which we became somewhat comfortably accommodated for the night. Shortly after sunrise on the following morning, we continued our journey to Tabi, a distance of two leagues. At this place we spent an hour in visiting a *cenote*,[8] one of the most celebrated in the country. It had been the scene of some *miracle*, the particulars of which we were unable to learn, and is therefore held in much reverence by the Indians. The circumference is about fifty feet, and it is about seventy feet to the surface of the water from the top of the ground. The water is said to be about a hundred feet deep and has a subterraneous channel, the extent of which is unknown. In the absence of all rivers in this country, these watering-places, or natural wells, seem to be one of the most striking gifts of God's beneficence. Near this chapel

---

7. A public building which, among other functions, served as an inn for travelers.

8. A Spanish adaptation of the Maya word *ts'ono'ot*, referring to the limestone sinkholes common throughout the peninsula. Norman mangles this term into *sonato*. I have used the modern spelling.

is a tree of the mamey species, peculiar to the province, of extraordinary dimensions, growing apparently out of a solid rock.

This town is principally inhabited by Indians. The few whites here, as is usual in many other places, principally maintain themselves by selling small articles, cotton cloth, and liquors to the Indians. Save a church, there were no public buildings in this place. No animation or purpose was to be seen among these listless Indians, who, in that as in other particulars, resembled all of their race whom I had yet seen.

6

A Case of Winged Serpents

Folk Belief vs. Officialdom

Maya folk beliefs at times collided with the worldview of officialdom. In few documents was this more evident than in the following correspondence. This 1842 letter from the office of the Yucatecan governor to the mayor of Tixcacalcupul concerns the purported appearance of winged serpents in Santa Cruz, a rancho or small hacienda located outside of town.[1] The author refers to other correspondence on this matter, none of which, unfortunately, has survived. Nevertheless, the letter illustrates how urban and rural worldviews clashed at times, and how elements of Maya folk culture were capable of sparking popular enthusiasm.

The winged serpent was and remains an important part of the oral literature of rural Yucatán. This mythical creature probably represents a folkloric remnant of K'u'uk'ul Kaan, or Plumed Serpent, a key component of state ideology during the Maya Postclassic period (A.D. 900–1521). This and other elements of that ideology changed their meaning as Spanish colonialism gradually eroded the Maya ruling-class power, but they survived in popular narratives and served as the basis of wondrous apparitions. For a modern-day version of the winged serpent motif, see "La culebra alada" in Roldán Peniche Barrera's Relatos mayas *(Mérida: Editorial Raices, 1980), 9–10.[2]*

From the imagination, always eager for the marvelous and unusual, come those tales of winged serpents, which arrive from time to time to excite the gullibility of the vulgar, who, through their ignorance, are disposed to believe in such fantasies.

In order to obtain reliable information in hopes of dispelling the rumors that are now rampant—rumors regarding the serpent that appeared on the rancho

---

1. At the time of the winged serpent rumors, Santa Cruz was a property that consisted of forty-four resident workers, all of Maya surname, divided into nine households. Usage of terms such as *rancho* and *hacienda* was not always precise or consistent, and we find Santa Cruz described as both.

2. The source of the following material is Archivo General del Estado de Yucatán (Mérida), Libros Complementarios del Fondo Poder Ejecutivo, Correspondencia de los Gobernadores, Book 13, 25 June 1842, 61.

Santa Cruz on May 13 past—I wrote to Padre Don Eusebio García Rejón with regard to your letter of June 14.[3] But I observe from the tenor of your letter that the individuals who, on this and other occasions, have testified to various apparitions of certain winged serpents in the *cenotes* near that village suffer from that vice.[4] It is necessary that you make the people understand that their stories of such wonders do not merit belief because the supposed winged serpents do not exist in the natural world, and that until now they are only encountered in fables and in the stories of carriage drivers.

To quiet these false rumors, born of the credulity of the rabble and the malice of those who hope to entertain themselves at the rabble's expense, the government has ordered a full report on the supposed apparition on rancho Santa Cruz. It is hoped that, armed with this report, you will persuade everyone that the whole affair has been nothing more than a hoax, just like the other apparitions mentioned in your letter. Accordingly, you must find a way to expose these enchantments, and [the people of Tixcacalcupul] must learn to disregard those stories that certain individuals are accustomed to spinning in order to make fun of popular credulity.

---

3. Padre Don Eusebio García Rejón was the longtime *cura* of Tixcacalcupul. He had the misfortune of being in town during the outbreak of the Caste War and was murdered by the rebels, one of only three or four priests to perish this way.

4. *Aquel vicio.* It is not clear to which vice the author refers: gullibility, hucksterism, or some other vice mentioned in the now-lost related correspondence.

II

THE CASTE WAR

With the eruption of the Caste War in 1847, life changed dramatically for the Yucatec Mayas, especially those who fought on the side of the rebels. This section begins with a series of letters in which the original insurgent leaders present their views on the conflict's origins. A series of captivity narratives follows, depicting the mixture of religious beliefs, personal loyalties, and military readiness that formed the basis of the rebel society of Chan Santa Cruz from 1850 onward. The section concludes with some of the better analyses of how Maya peasants managed to create a highly effective military force with a minimum of resources.

7

"The Whites Began It"

Jacinto Pat's Letter on the Origins of the Caste War

One of the original leaders of the Caste War rebels, Jacinto Pat was a successful and propertied Maya from the town of Tihosuco, which today is part of Quintana Roo. The date of his birth is unknown, but Pat was already a married adult by 1828. He owned at least one hacienda (Culumpich) and a rancho (Panabá). By 1841 Pat was serving as batab *for the town of Tihosuco. He apparently became involved in an abortive, Hispanic-led political uprising in Tihosuco in 1843 and filed a claim for private title to public lands in that same year, a claim which was never ratified. Growing political violence and racial tension eventually led Pat into war against the Hispanics who had once mobilized local Mayas to assist them in Hispanic political revolts.*

On 18 February 1848, Jacinto Pat wrote the following letter to John Kingdom and Edward Rhys, two of his contacts in Belize. The letter contains several interesting points. First, Pat was already speaking of a peninsular division and a separate southeastern state before the signing and subsequent collapse of a peace treaty in Tzucacab[1] in April 1848. Second, he identifies taxes as the underlying cause of the rebellion. Written to trusted associates, Pat's letter provides one of the few clues to the Maya leaders' initial perceptions regarding the struggle's aims.[2]

Cenil, 18 February 1848

After receiving your honorable letter, I have examined its content, and immediately I have informed the other leaders and officers of my troops and all who are gathered with me to agree with what you say. It would be well if the lands of Yucatán were divided as you suggest to me because we are already tired of seeing so much death. For that reason we want peace, without being at war. It is because the whites began it, because what we want is liberty and not oppression, because before we were subjugated with the many contributions and taxes [*pagos*] that they imposed upon us. I for my part am very pleased

---

1. Tzucacab is a town fourteen kilometers southeast of Peto, located on the road to Tekax.

2. The source of the following material is Archives of Belize (Belmopan), Record 28, 18 February 1848, 220.

with what you say in your note. I only warn you and urge you that, without the division of lands in this state, it will be necessary to come . . . as I suppose the commissioned individuals will then see.[3] I hope that this process[4] will be paid for by the whites and not by us Indians since it was they who began [the war.] One other point concerns arms. I am not asking that they disarm us nor that we disarm them, but rather that each side retain its own arms.

Jacinto Pat, Commander

---

3. At this point, part of the original manuscript is damaged. The general idea, however, appears to be that any individuals commissioned as representatives of the Yucatecan government would find negotiations impossible if they did not accept Pat's basic condition: the division of the peninsula.

4. I.e., the work of a commission to be appointed to divide the peninsula.

8

"Through Fire and Blood"

Cecilio Chi's Letter to John Fancourt

Jacinto Pat's main partner in this conflict was Cecilio Chi, batab *of the nearby community of Tepich. Little is known of Chi's prewar history. In the 1830s he lived in Tihosuco and may have been related to Pat through marriage. He served as a military recruiter and peasant leader during the Yucatecan civil wars in the 1840s and had only recently become* batab *of Tepich when the Caste War erupted. Chi's historical reputation for ferocity may have been justified, or it may reflect that he had fewer options than his wealthier and geographically better-positioned partner: Chi commanded the northern forces of the Caste War and had less access to Belizean arms and supplies.*

The following correspondence, which was written on 23 April 1849, may not have been Chi's letter. Legend has it that he died in early 1849, murdered by his secretary, who was having an affair with Chi's wife. There is little doubt, however, that this letter reflects the ideas and attitudes of Chi's officers, its probable authors. Among its distinguishing features, the letter links the war to real historical events: Santiago Imán's unfulfilled promise of tax abolition and the political violence encouraged by Hispanic leaders, such as Domingo Barret, who rebelled against the state government in December 1846. The letter also captures an increasingly religious overtone to the Mayas' perception of their own struggle. We should, however, bear in mind that Chi's closing salutation—"God and liberty" (Dios y libertad)—was a standard feature of official correspondence in pre-Reform (pre-1855) Mexico, not a Maya innovation.[1]

Tepich

The war presented by the Spaniards against the Indians originated in a breach of faith committed by the citizen Don Santiago Imán. In the year thirty-nine, he declared war against the Superior Government of Mexico, alleging as a reason for doing so that it was with a view of liberating the Indians from the payment of contributions. After this war was won by the Indians, the same

---

1. The source of the following material is Archives of Belize (Belmopan), Record 28, 23 April 1849, 223.

citizen continued to levy contributions as usual, thus proving himself not to be a man of honor, having forfeited his word with the natives. But the hour has arrived when Christ and his divine mother have given courage to make war against the whites, as we had no money to pay such exactions as the Government thought proper to decree.

Don Domingo Barret sent troops under Don Santiago Méndez with orders to put every Indian, big and little, to death; to execute such an order, every white in this peninsula would be destroyed, as it has pleased God and good fortune that a much greater portion of them than of the Indians [have died].[2] Through God and his divine mother, however, we pity them and are willing to adopt the recommendation of the Superior Government of Belize, and at his suggestion, divide Yucatán for the sake of our wives and children. We are no cowards but have deemed it best to divide it in consideration of our children, as we wish to do away with the payment of all contributions and will not pay more than the whites.

For this reason, we request the Superior Government of Belize to send a commissioner in his name, duly authorized to divide Yucatán, pledging our word of honor to abide by his decision. We also beg of him to send a letter to the Captain General of the Capital of Mérida, recommending to him to enter into such a treaty with us as being the best method of settling our differences. We are Indians, but if he is not disposed to agree to this proposition, we are prepared to proceed through fire and blood to liberate ourselves from the payment of any contributions as long as we live.

God and Liberty,

Cecilio Chi, General

Venancio Pec, Commandant of Arms

José Atanacio Espada, Commissioner General & Commander of the Troops

---

2. Barret and Méndez were prominent Campeche politicians, although the actions attributed to them here are highly improbable. The accusations undoubtedly reflect a folk perception of political events.

9

"They Kill the Poor Indians As They Kill Animals"

Jacinto Pat's Letter to Modesto Méndez

By mid-1848 the Maya forces led by Jacinto Pat were beginning to disintegrate. Anxious for support, Pat began to cast around for potential allies. One possibility was Modesto Méndez, the corregidor, *or chief official, of the Petén, the northern district of Guatemala directly adjacent to Yucatán. The region was heavily Yucatecan in culture; the indigenous inhabitants spoke Maya, and many Yucatecan refugees had fled to the area after the Caste War erupted. Moreover, Pat himself had a small group of supporters in some of the northernmost villages.[1]*

*This letter, which was written on 11 July 1848, resembles Pat's other writings on the origins of the Caste War. He underscores once more the importance of tax grievances in the popular consciousness. In this letter, however, Pat goes beyond the familiar head taxes to church and state taxes (known as "contributions") and points to regional import/export duties (*alcabalas*) and local sales and property taxes (*arbitrios*) as equally onerous. Pat also takes special care to downplay the conflict as a race war, emphasizing that the Yucatec Mayas were perfectly capable of coexisting with Hispanics who treated them fairly. The original Maya version of this letter cannot be found in the archives; only the Spanish rendering survives. The English translation is my own.[2]*

My grand and respected sir:

I received your respectable and honored letter dated 31 May, in which you inform me that all those under your command enjoy peace and tranquility and do not pay the *medio* [*real*] contribution, to whom you should say that I am happy to know that a paternal government rules them.

With great respect I wish to inform you that here in Yucatán we suffer the evils and harms of the Spanish. They kill the poor Indians as they kill animals, but not all the Spanish; they who did so were well known, whether great or

---

1. For details on Pat's southern connections, see Terry Rugeley, "The Caste War in Guatemala," *Saastun* 3 (December 1997): 67–96.

2. The source of the following material is Archivo General de Centroamérica (Guatemala City), Legajo B28543, Expediente 279, 11 July 1848.

small. For this cause the eastern Indians and all their companions in Yucatán rose up, but they did no harm to all the Spanish, only to those who were cruel to the Indians. Furthermore, for some time they have paid contributions but received poor treatment.

Now, Sir, all that has ended, and it has been publicized that the *medio* contribution no longer be paid, neither for the Spanish nor for the Indians; that they will only pay three *reales* for baptism and ten *reales* for marriages, the Indians as much as the Spaniards. This is the liberty that the poor Indians of Yucatán were seeking. It is not a rebellion, as the Spanish say and write it; they [themselves] rose up, killing the poor Indians over the contribution. And not only the contribution, but also for the *alcabalas*,[3] [for] municipal taxes on corn, beans, chile, salt, all foodstuffs, and the slaughter of cattle and pigs. The poor Indian paid all this even when not right.[4] Even from here I can say it so that your grand and respectable person may know.

God and Liberty, Jacinto Pat[5]

---

3. *Alcabalas* were local sales taxes.

4. . . . *aunque no fuera su tiempo:* literally, "although not yet his time."

5. *Dios y libertad,* or "God and Liberty," was the conventional closing for official communications in Mexico and Yucatán prior to the disestablishment of the Catholic Church. As shown here, Maya peasants learned and adopted the practice.

10

One Hundred Blows or Death

Venancio Pec's Letter to Modesto Méndez

Jacinto Pat was assassinated in early 1850, apparently at the behest of lieutenants who were disgruntled about sustained losses and Pat's attempt to impose war taxes upon the soldiers. One of these lieutenants was Venancio Pec. Pec was born in 1810, was married to Candelaria Batún, and had two children. Even though he lived in Chichimilá in the early 1840s, he apparently functioned as the batab *of nearby Dzitnup. All other aspects of this individual's prewar life remain a mystery.*

After Pat's death, Pec became one of the most important southern chiefs. His forces were based in the town of Chichanhá along the Yucatán-Guatemala border. Like Pat, he discovered that economic allies were imperative to his survival, and he resumed Pat's diplomatic overtures to authorities in the Petén. On 23 September 1850, he sent the following letter to Modesto Méndez from Chichanhá. This document is noteworthy for its vivid depiction of justice among the rebel chiefs.[1]

In the name of God and the Holy Mother, señor Modesto Méndez, whose respectable person is found in the city of Petén: My señor, I have no other motive in writing to your respectable person than to learn if my vassals can travel and come to that city to carry out certain things they need to do, because they are afraid that harm will come to them since I have not written even once to your honored person. We know well that the city of Petén is under a different government, and for that reason [my men] are afraid to come to that city in search of things they need. And by the same token, I need some things, and I will entrust them to bring me whatever it may be. I hope that your respectable person will allow it, and I ask that you answer this letter so that I may know, by God and his Holy Mother.

Although the Spaniards are saying that they have already finished us, we trust in God that they will never finish us. We lack nothing in the way of food, even if the war lasts for ten years. They do not frighten us; they are dying of

---

1. The source of the following material is Archivo General de Centroamérica (Guatemala City), Legajo B28551, Expediente 135, 23 September 1850.

hunger because they no longer have Indians to make *milpas* for them to maintain them. In the same way, I say to your respectable person that if your subjects wish to come and sell anything, they should come without fear of harm or injury, because if I come to know that anyone has harmed a Spaniard, I will punish him with 100 blows or will kill him; absolutely no one has orders to do harm. I have no more to say. By the true God concluding with your honorable person, I kiss your right hand all the days of my life and bow my head before your respectable person, José Venancio Pec.

11

Looking for Hope

Pedro Ek's Letter to Manuel Nahuat

*Certainly the most exotic feature of the Caste War was the Speaking
Cross, the oracle that emerged to rally the Maya rebels in their worst
hour, sometime around late 1849 or early 1850. This letter was written on 17 March 1851 by a rebel military commander to one of the
guardians of the Speaking Cross. It nicely captures several features
of the emerging separatist society oriented around the cross and its
community, Chan Santa Cruz. On one hand, the document features
the elaborately ceremonial language used in much of the Maya correspondence. On the other hand, it includes references to the extraordinary piety associated with the cross and items related to it, such
as the candles and even the candle drippings. The original Maya
document is no longer extant. This translation is based on the Spanish version, which is filed in the Archivo Histórico de la Defensa
Nacional in Mexico City.*[1]

Yakaltsul, 17 March 1851

To my very beloved patrón, Don Manuel Nahuat, his honor being in Chan
Santa Cruz:

Sir, I have no other motive in writing to your respectability than [to send]
the money of Our Lord, the money that I am giving to my family, nine pesos,
and Sgt. Don Victoriano Durán is the one who carries it. Also I am sending to
you there a *real* and a half in the name of the Lord so that you do me the
charity of selling me one of his bodies,[2] a candle, and a rosary for my José
Guadalupe Ek, and so that you do me the charity of giving me some of the candle drippings of Our Lord to distribute among the families since many are
requesting them. Furthermore, may you do me the charity, in the name of the
Lord, of sending me the teachings that Our Lord has given. Also may it please
you to sell me another candle of Our Lord since that which you sold me has
been used.

Pedro Regalado Ek, Commander

---

1. The source of the following material is Archivo Histórico de la Defensa Nacional (Mexico
City), xi/481.3/3257, 17 March 1851.

2. The original text says *cuerpo,* which may mean "physical body" or "military corps." Because
the *cuerpo* is being sold, however, it may refer to an icon, possibly a cross or even a candle.

12

"Rejoicing among All the Inhabitants"

Rómulo Díaz de la Vega Enters Chichanhá

Gen. Rómulo Díaz de la Vega was born in Mexico City in 1804. He enjoyed close ties to the caudillo *and eleven-times president Antonio López de Santa Anna and built an impressive record of service during the Mexican-American War. Sent to Yucatán in June 1851 to direct the Caste War counterinsurgency, he devised a successful strategy that culminated in broad sweeps of rebel territories in the southeast a year later. Thereafter, the general spent most of his time involved in Yucatecan political intrigues. He became military governor of the region and later served a very brief term as interim president of Mexico. Díaz de la Vega was recalled in late 1854 at the height of his power to assist Santa Anna in his fight against the liberal revolt of Ayutla. He never returned.*

The following account describes the struggle for military and political control of the southeastern frontier in May 1852, a low point in rebel fortunes. In December 1850, rebel captain Angelino Itzá had signed the first of the Caste War's pacífico *treaties, whereby rebels agreed to lay down their arms in exchange for virtual autonomy. The treaty was arranged by none other than Col. Modesto Méndez, the* corregidor *of Guatemala's Petén district. Itzá's enraged superiors raided Chichanhá soon afterward, punished the would-be peace faction, and reestablished their own authority. Díaz de la Vega's forces arrived in April to restore the peace faction to power. The general's report includes some interesting details on the hazards of Caste War service, such as frequent mosquito-borne illness, and on the legal formalism that prevailed in Mexican villages, even those in the grips of civil war.*[1]

On the 3rd day of April I arrived in Chichanhá where, as anticipated, I found the column under the command of Col. Cirilio Baqueiro, now headed by Col. Rómulo Baqueiro because the former had unfortunately fallen sick during the early days of the campaign. In places such as Cacao and Agua Blanca,

---

1. The source of the following material is Archivo Histórico de la Defensa Nacional (Mexico City), xi/481.3/3300, 11 May 1852

located along the banks of the Rio Hondo, which divides Mexico from the British possession of Honduras, a column had been positioned according to my orders that was to proceed under the orders of Col. Patricio O'Horán and which, owing to a serious illness of that officer, was led by Lt. Col. Andres O. Maldonado.

This officer, together with Col. Baqueiro, had taken Chichanhá on 17 March past. When I tried to enter, I was met with a fierce resistance from the garrison that the rebels had positioned there; because of the conclusion of the above-mentioned treaty, their attention has been drawn to that place.[2] Our soldiers gloriously overcame this resistance, taking many Indian lives while suffering casualties of our own. The same enemy garrison had forced the inhabitants to flee their houses as our troops were arriving so that when we entered, the village was completely deserted.

In the process I ordered parties out in all directions, as much to follow the rebels into their hidden lairs within the woods as to gather up the fugitive inhabitants of Chichanhá. They carried out my intentions because, after gathering some, they later set them free so that these might go out and invite their companions to return, as indeed they did. And I am pleased to have returned almost all of these inhabitants to their old homes. Because there was a sufficient number of these, I ordered that they proceed with the election of a magistrate, a *cacique,* and a *media república,*[3] as the laws of the state dictate that they must do, and this order was carried out with the greatest order and solemnity. The elected officials took their oaths and were placed in possession of their respective offices, which caused great satisfaction and rejoicing among all the inhabitants.

---

2. The mentioned treaty was a peace treaty signed by rebel captain Angelino Itzá of Chichanhá and negotiated by Col. Modesto Méndez, the *corregidor,* or governor, of the Petén, Guatemala's northernmost district.

3. It is not clear what Díaz de la Vega meant by a *media república.* Either he was simply referring to a *república de indígenas,* or he preferred the creation of a smaller version of the same, which normally included eight or nine individuals.

13

"Nothing More Than Imposters"

The Captivity Narrative of José María Echeverría

Virtually nothing is known about Sgt. José María Echeverría, the source of the following information. Taken prisoner by rebels in the sixth year of the Caste War (1853), he was spared because of his ability to read and write, a proficiency that was greatly prized by an insurgent army that needed skilled intelligentsia. Echeverría remained a prisoner among the rebels until 1856, when he fled and made his way to his hometown of Huhí, where he was interrogated by the jefe político of Izamal.

Echeverría's testimony provides one of the few glimpses into rebel society between the death of Jacinto Pat in 1850 and the fall of Bacalar in 1858. His story reveals that Zacarías May was the main chief at that time, which means that Venancio Puc did not rise to power until the mid-1850s; if so, his ascendancy was probably related to his advocacy of the successful policy of conducting periodic raids into Yucatecan territory. Echeverría corroborates the heavy drinking that other visitors reported as common among the rebel chiefs. He also offers some surprising testimony that Chan Santa Cruz may have contained more Hispanics than Mayas in the mid-1850s; most of them were probably deserters from the army. Finally, his narrative includes the somewhat comic account of two priests (or perhaps imposters) who hoped to win the sympathies of the rebels but were thrown out when they overstayed their welcome.[1]

In compliance with Your Excellency's orders, Sgt. José María Echeverría, who fled from the general headquarters, which the Indian rebels call Chan Santa Cruz, presented himself before the magistrate of Huhí, his home, as was previously communicated.[2] I was eager to discover why he had made this journey

---

1. The source of the following material is Archivo General del Estado de Yucatán (Mérida), Poder Ejecutivo 65, Gobernación, Jefatura Política de Izamal, 8 November 1856.

2. Huhí was indeed Echeverría's home. The 1832 census lists him among boys ages 1–15; see Archivo General del Estado de Yucatán (Mérida), Poder Ejecutivo Box 5, Censos y Padrones, Volume III, Expediente 3, 18 December 1832. Echeverría would thus be between ages 24 and 39 at the time of his testimony. He does not, however, appear in the 1849 census, suggesting that he may have already been drafted into the army; see Archivo General del Estado de Yucatán (Mérida), Poder Ejecutivo Box 73, Censos y Padrones, "Pueblo de Huhí," 2 April 1849.

and to carry out Your Excellency's instructions regarding the war. Moreover, I wanted to know about the Indians' current resources, their plans, and their inclinations, as I assumed that this individual knew something about such details because I had learned that he had served as secretary to Zacarías May, the first chief of the rebels, and had remained at his side for two years.

I conducted an extensive questioning, which revealed that in April 1853 he had departed from Bacalar as part of the force that was being relieved. After a four days' march, Echeverría was taken prisoner by a party of Indians who, by order of Zacarías May, had taken up positions outside that town. This happened because they saw him traveling with three other companions who were quite ill; these latter were cruelly assassinated, but the Indians spared Echeverría's life when the aforementioned May discovered that he knew how to write. From then until the 2nd of October just past, May kept him by his side. At that moment, taking advantage of the fact that May [and] his companions—officers as well as soldiers—had fallen into a drunken stupor, and led by an Indian who knew the region well, he managed to escape. After wandering for a few days, he presented himself in Lochhá, the main headquarters of the currently pacified Indians. From there he passed through various towns until he came to his home. . . .

He says that the aforementioned Zacarías May is the first chief of the rebels. Chan Santa Cruz, which is May's usual place of residence, has some 200 Indians and more than 200 whites, all armed with good rifles. At the same time, another hundred live in a rancho called Sahcabchén, and there are a few more on ranchos whose names he does not remember. May maintains a lightly manned canton on the Pucté River to protect the commerce that the rebels conduct there with those from Belize.[3] Some [merchants] belong to the British flag, but it is actually a Frenchman who is the main supplier of gunpowder, and last August he sold them nine *arrobas*.[4] He states that upon heading out from Chan Santa Cruz the soldiers carried only two cartridges apiece, the majority of them using sharpened pieces of wood because there was no lead [for bullets].

The white soldiers had one of their own race as their chief; he kept himself in a headquarters separate from that of the Indians, and Echeverría did not manage to learn his name, only that he is reddish complexioned. The chief officer of May is Crescencio Poot. Echeverría was never able to hear the councils that took place among the chiefs, nor could he be present at their gatherings; he only heard them repeat the hope that they eventually had to triumph. He can give no information on the names of the white deserters from our ranks who have unexpectedly bolstered the rebels, with whom they jointly carry on the war and with whom they coordinate all their movements. Echeverría assures

---

3. Echeverría really means at a place called Pucté along the Río Hondo, which separates modern-day Quintana Roo from Belize. See the narrative of Capt. Anderson in the next chapter for details on the rebel redoubt in Pucté.

4. An *arroba* is a weight measurement equal to about twenty-five pounds.

that they consider as irreconcilable enemies those who break from their ranks and maintain communication with the whites since the signing of a peace treaty with the government. For this reason anyone from Chichanhá, from Lochhá, or their dependencies who happens to fall into the power of commander May is invariably assassinated. And the people from those places, by way of reprisal, do the same to those who come from Chan Santa Cruz and its dependencies.

Similarly, Echeverría says that although he was kept as the secretary of the aforementioned May, he was nothing more than one of his servants and was used to tabulate the articles and items that the Indians carried off in their raids. Another white—because he knew how to write in Maya—was used to keep military communications, writing and answering dispatches that came from other places and communicating the orders of the chief. Finally, [he reports that] he only made two trips with Zacarías May to Pucté on the Hondo River and that, during his captivity, he never left on any other occasion.

Echeverría reports an incident that is worth calling to the attention of Your Excellency. He says that at the end of April last year [i.e., 1855], two priests appeared at the headquarters in Chan Santa Cruz and that as an entourage, they brought two assistants to carry their baggage, men who spoke the Maya language. The chiefs and other inhabitants of that place received them without any great show of affection and for accommodations gave them a house behind the church and brought them food. Those priests preached in English, at least as far as Echeverría was able to tell, and said two masses there. After eight days Crescencio Poot declared before chief May that they should be thrown out because they were nothing more than imposters who went around deceiving people, and in fact, this was verified. They were then forced to leave without any assistance for their transportation from those parts. Echeverría adds that this year the harvest of corn, beans, and other vegetables has been outstanding.

14

"They Expressed Themselves Much Delighted"

William Anderson's Meeting with Rebel Maya Leaders

The early months of 1858 constituted a pivotal moment in the history of the Caste War. Emboldened by chronic infighting among the political classes in Mérida and Campeche and by the rebel authority now firmly established in Chan Santa Cruz, the rebel Mayas began a series of raids, which culminated in the seizure of Bacalar in March. Some weeks before then, Capt. William Anderson traveled from British Honduras to a river outpost known as Pucté to confer with the rebel chiefs regarding problems along the Belizean-Yucatecan border: raids, harassment of river travelers, and the problematic relationship between the rebels and the mahogany companies.

Anderson's letter to Belize superintendent Frederick Seymour provides a geographical description that is valid today, although the Pucté of his time was a small military outpost, whereas a nearby town with the same name is a relatively recent creation. More importantly, his description captures several features of southeastern rebel society. Anderson also reveals what the British perceived as the difference in attitude between Mayas and Hispanics.[1]

Belize, Honduras, 15th February 1858

Sir,

I last had the honor to address you from the "Corozal" on the 7th instant, informing you of my intention to start [the] next morning for Pucté, the Indian encampment on the Spanish side and about forty miles from the mouth of the Río Hondo. I arrived there on the morning of the 9th instant and found that the Indians had left on their return to "Santa Cruz" somewhat suddenly, in consequence of a rumor that a strong Mexican force had marched to intercept them, at which they expressed themselves much delighted and seemed quite confident as to the result in the event of an encounter.

The Indian encampment at Pucté was situated on the top of a hill about forty feet high but commanded by a much higher hill, immediately in the rear. From this encampment they had outposts, of which that on the Santa Cruz road

---

1. The source of the following material is British Foreign Office, 15 February 1858 (from Bancroft Library microfilm, University of California at Berkeley).

was the most important. They had also a line of pickets along the bank of the river on the Spanish side which furnished sentries below Douglas, a distance of about three miles. A strong party, it would appear, marched overland as far as down the river at Ramonal, about eleven miles, making prisoners of a Spaniard named Alpuche,[2] his family, and servants, in all about eleven persons, whom they took to Pucté and who were subsequently ransomed by the Spaniards [who were] at Cocos on the English side. They also captured a bungay[3] and dory belonging to Alpuche; the latter has been left at Cocos for sale.

The Indians came to Pucté for the sole purpose of procuring gunpowder, which they obtain from various parties residing [on] the River Hondo, New River, Corozal, and Belize, giving in exchange horses, mules, poultry, hammocks and various other articles. They sometimes purchase dry goods, but on the last occasion, they would only take powder or money, the latter enabling them to purchase the much coveted article in Belize.

The Indians were well armed with muskets, bayonets, swords, and in some cases with pistols. From their encampment and general appearance about it, as well the information I received respecting them, I should say that there could not have been less than 1,500 men, the majority of whom were armed.

One of the Indian chiefs, of whom there were three, came across to Douglas on the English side, saw W. Cherrington (Mr. Mosey's foreman), expressed his regret at the conduct of people last year, and said they wished to be on terms of friendship with the English.

According to the statement of some of the people residing at Cocos, the Indians took away about 85 kegs of powder; but on examining that part of their chapel at Pucté which served as a store for powder, and judging from the marks on the uprights of the building, which were said to indicate the quantity stored, I should estimate it at about 150 kegs or more.

The Indians brought their Santa Cruz with them, which they consulted on all occasions of importance.

The following conversation among the Indian chiefs was overheard by a man named Vito Ramos[4] living at Douglas, and I mention it here to show the value they set upon the means of procuring powder and the restraint it would seem to impose upon their propensity to pilfer. Zacarías May, one of the Indian chiefs, proposed that Corozal, San Esteban, and Orange Walk should be pillaged and burnt, but he was overruled by the other chiefs, who said "if we do so, how shall we be able to procure powder to withstand the Spaniards, and if we lose our friendship with the English, how shall we get powder?"

The Indians on the occasion of their recent visit to Pucté, although they came across to the British side in very large numbers, committed no excesses

---

2. That is, a Yucatecan Hispanic. The British in Belize used the generic term "Spaniard," which included Mexicans.

3. A small type of boat used on the Belize rivers.

4. The original manuscript records this individual's name as "Bito."

and always left their arms behind them; still their presence unsettled the minds of the mahogany [laborers], they having to work at some distance from their houses, which with their families, are left entirely unprotected and at the mercy of the Indians. Venancio Puc was the patron or headman, also the padre, and had charge of the Santa Cruz. Dionicio Zapata and Eleandro Santos were the fighting chiefs, and Zachariah May was the *comandante*. The Indians stated that they intend to return to Pucté in May next for the purpose of trading.

On returning by the river, I visited Chac and St. Helena at the former place; there was a guard of three men, who were very civil. I mentioned that there had been several breaches of international law committed at various times by the guard at Chac; the sergeant replied that he had only short[ly] arrived there, but that he had not stopped any craft and admitted the free navigation of the Hondo. . . .

From the Mexican commissioner at St. Helena, I met with a very different reception, his tone and manner being most uncourteous. He considered that he was perfectly justified in stopping and searching crafts as they passed up the river, [even] upon my telling him that it was a flagrant breach of international law. He replied that he had his orders and would obey them and that he would continue to stop and search crafts proceeding up the river.

15

"Not as a Prisoner but as One of the Family"

The Captivity Narrative of José María Rosado

Captivity narratives constitute a special genre within the North American literary landscape. Accounts of life among Indians provide important ethnographic details, although they occasionally veer off into fiction. The Caste War gave birth to a similar, though hitherto unexplored, genre for Latin America. Probably the most important of these narratives was the story of José María Rosado.

Rosado was a Yucatecan living in the town of Bacalar, near the border between present-day Belize and Quintana Roo. This community grew up around an eighteenth-century Spanish fortress of the same name; by the time of the Caste War, it served as a place of trade (both legal and illegal) between Yucatecans and Belizeans and as a center for logging interests along the border. Caste War rebels seized the town in 1848, lost it the following year, and recaptured it in February 1858, retaining possession until the arrival of the Mexican federal army in March 1901. José María Rosado was a witness to and participant in some of these events. Captured when Maya rebels overran Bacalar for the second time, he lived as a captive among them for several months but was eventually ransomed. Rosado later became a citizen of Belize.

Fifty-seven years later, in 1915, he composed this memoir of his experiences as a captive in Chan Santa Cruz. It is impossible not to wonder about the accuracy of a text purporting to describe the experiences of an eleven-year-old boy after nearly six decades. It seems doubtful that he would have remembered in such detail the names of all the individuals mentioned in his account, fragments of conversations, or the number of soldiers besieging Bacalar. Printed information on the history of the Caste War was available in Rosado's lifetime, and it is probable that Rosado drew upon much of this published material to structure his own memoir. A Refugee of the War of the Castes, however, still includes many intriguing details of life among the rebel Mayas, including methods of discipline, means of supplying soldiers, religious practices, the leadership's negotiating style, and the considerable, if unofficial, influence enjoyed by the wives of the top generals. The subheadings of this text are Rosado's own. The selection reproduced below, however, omits Rosado's two concluding sections describing his later life in Belize.[1]

My father was the son of a Spaniard in the Spanish Army stationed in the Canary Islands and came to Yucatán sent by the King of Spain with the troops long before the Independence of Mexico. He was married in Bacalar while on garrison, he had several children, who nearly all followed the military career, also their children, who held high ranks; one was the Governor of Yucatán for several years. I was born in Bacalar [on] 19th March 1847. [I]n June 1848 the town was besieged by a large number of rebellious armed Indians, and after several days of hard fighting (in which the commander of the troops, my uncle, died from seven wounds), the town was captured by the Indians, and the greater part of the inhabitants, including my Father and family, took refuge in this Colony.[2]

The Year 1854

I remember the year 1854. I had just started going to school when an epidemic of cholera broke out; the schools had to be closed. [W]ith only one Doctor belonging to the garrison and poorly supplied with drugs, a great number of the inhabitants, including the soldiers, died.

The Capture of Bacalar

The Indians continued periodically attacking the town, choosing the early hours of morning before dawn; but [the town] being well defended by entrenchments built of high and thick walls with several forts, they were easily repulsed and waited for several days and retracted to the wilderness. [B]ut they watched their opportunity in 1858, with a very small garrison and unsupported by the Mérida Government with all the State of Yucatán in a revolutionary state of different political parties, and rebelled against the Federal Government of Mexico. [T]hey again besieged the town with about 4000 strong against 100 mostly sick and demoralized soldiers to defend it; the town surrendered on the 26th of February.

I will remember that morning: about 2 o'clock, my dear Mother came into the room where my two brothers and myself slept and woke us up saying, "[T]he Indians have captured the town and our home is surrounded; dress quickly and come into the oratory, where we will all meet and pray." One of

---

1. The source of the following material is Richard Buhler, ed., "A Refugee of the War of the Castes Makes Belize His Home: The Memoirs of J. M. Rosado" (Belize: Belize Institute for Social Research and Action, 1970).

2. I.e., Belize. Rosado's account suggests that his family fled in 1848 but returned when the town was retaken by Hispanics in 1849.

the rooms was furnished with an altar with a large crucifix in the center and several wood carved, oil painted, well dressed statues of the Blessed Virgin, St. Joseph, St. Joaquín, St. Ann, and other Saints. When dressing I heard very sharp discharges of musketry and someone shouting from every side. Meeting my Mother with three of my sisters, three brothers, a nurse, and two servants, we all knelt before the altar; my Mother started reciting the holy rosary. The noise was so great, with hammering of the doors outside by the Indians with their guns and machetes, that my Mother had to get up, telling us, "[A]ll remain here. I will go to a window to speak to the Indians and to ask them to spare our lives." As soon as my Mother went out, all of us followed her. Before doing so I got near a corner of the altar and took from one of [the] Saints (I think St. Anthony) a very small statue of the Infant Jesus, which was seated on a book held by the Saint, and saying with great devotion, "[M]y infant Jesus, you will be my protector. I place my life in your hands; save me," and placed it in my trousers' pocket.

When my Mother got close to a window—built in regular Spanish style, which I saw in Havana; high [and] projecting out with strong iron bars; two shutters, each having a small shutter cut out from the top [as a] sort of lookout or ventilator—she knocked to call attention, and an Indian said, "[O]pen the door." [M]y mother said, "[B]ring one of your chiefs to speak with me." Another Indian said, "I am the *Comandante;* before you open, tell me if there are any armed men inside and how many." My Mother said, "I am only a woman with seven children and the female servants; my husband is out of town with one of his sons." My Mother opened one half of the door, and the captain with his guards (12 soldiers) came in. [S]hutting the door behind him, [he] said, "I will search the house, and if I find no men nor arms, you will be protected with your children; but you will open all your trunks and conceal nothing of value, and after I help myself, I will allow my soldiers to take the balance." The captain searched all the house, took all my Mother's jewelry and the money she had; then the soldiers took all the clothing, including some ornaments in the oratorio. Then the captain told my Mother, "I will go and consult my chiefs. I will leave my guard to protect you till my return; no one will harm you."

The captain returned about 9 o'clock a.m. and led us to the *cabildo* (town hall), and there all the prisoners, women and children, were gathered and supplied with provisions. All the men were made prisoners and put to demolish all fortifications and the greater part of the stone buildings, leaving intact four and the church, which is a beautiful, large, stone, arched-roof building. I may here state that my Father was *jefe político* (Mayor) of the town and was at his sugar ranch, along with one of my brothers, and therefore escaped capture. A good many of the families had cleared out of town on hearing a few days previously of the Indians' coming; some also escaped the same night.

Blake's Attempt to Ransom the Captives

A few days after the fall of the town, Mr. James Hume Blake, a prominent gentleman, arrived from Corozal during the night and was present at a conference held by all the chiefs headed by the Tatich, the Generalissimo.[3] Mr. Blake made a speech pleading for the lives of all the prisoners, offering to pay a sum for their ransom. After a long discussion in which the majority of the chiefs were in favor of accepting the offer, the Tatich announced that, if Mr. Blake would pay at once $10,000 Mexican dollars as a ransom for only the women and children, they would be handed over immediately; but unfortunately, Mr. Blake only had half that amount with him and proposed to hand it over for half of the women and children and be allowed to return in 3 days time with the balance of the money. Again after a long consultation and being nearly drunk, having swallowed a good many bottles of strong aniseed,[4] they became very noisy and violent, and all cried out, "10,000 dollars this very moment, or Mr. Blake better clear out at once if he wishes to keep his head on his shoulder." Mr. Blake, to avoid danger, had to go on board his boat and clear out. The next day he sent a messenger, but he was not allowed to approach the shore, and the chiefs continued their debauchery, followed by the soldiers.

Slaughter of the Captives

On the 3rd of March one of the Generals who was half sober came into the *cabildo,* selected 4 boys and 2 girls, took them to his quarters, examined them, and after being satisfied that they could read and write (although very little), I being one of the lucky number, he called his captain and told him, "[L]ook after these children; do not let them leave this room, and do not starve them." That same night all the prisoners—men, women, and children (with the exception of the 6 selected)—were securely tied by both arms, each led by a soldier carrying a sharp machete in his hand, marched to the cholera cemetery, and killed. Only one of the men prisoners managed to escape. I met him in the Colony, and he related to me that he was ahead of all the others and, arriving at the cemetery, his Indian, in striking him for the first time, the machete cut the rope, and his left arm got loose before the Indian got time to strike him again. [H]e turned round quickly and gave him a severe kick in the stomach, knocking him to the ground. The prisoner rushed to the bush and escaped, making the Hondo the second day and on the third day arrived in Corozal with a wounded arm in such a bad state that it had to be cut off to save his life.

---

3. The term *noj tatich,* or "great father," was reserved for the head general, who communicated directly with the Speaking Cross. A more idiomatic translation might be "leader."

4. *Anís* is an anise-flavored liquor still produced in Yucatán.

Rosado's Captivity

On the 4th of March the six selected children were divided, the 2 girls for the Tatich and the 4 boys one to each General. I had the good luck to fall into the good hands of Gral. Leonardo Santos, 3rd in command, stern, tall, of fair complexion, about 30 years of age, married, and with four children. The Tatich and the other 3 generals were also married and have children. When we were examined, an old half-blind man placed an old Latin grammar first in my hands and then in each of the other 5, and I was asked to read, which neither I nor any of the others could do well; and I got frightened, but I opened the book at random and recited the Christian doctrine and some prayers, which we all had learned at school. Then I was asked to write my name with a pencil; all the others did the same. The General said "mabob,"[5] good. "This has saved you from the machete, as we will now take you to our Santo Kaaj (Holy City) to teach our children; but nothing will save you if any of you ever attempts to escape."

We arrived at the General's country residence, a ranch with a large corn and peas field, and there met [the] General's wife with his children, delighted to see each other. There were about 25 Indians with their families looking after the crop of corn. For the next three days after our arrival, a continuous feast was kept, dancing and singing day and night with plenty to eat, pigs and poultry and game cooked in large quantities. A very large wooden trough [contained] a beverage made of fermented *palma real* (the tender part of cabbage trees, having the appearance of light lager, pleasant to taste but intoxicating if freely indulged in). The head steward took care that the women and children were sparingly served.

After the feast all the men started to work in the field. Under a very large sapodilla tree, a well erected shrine was kept in which there was a large wooden Cross ornamented with bright colored ribbon and flowers and light black wax candles burning every day. There I placed my small statue of the Infant Jesus. After the burning of the fields in preparing for the sowing of corn and peas, which takes place immediately after the first May showers, the General and his family started for the Santo Kaaj (Holy City of Santa Cruz). The night before starting, I went to take my little holy statue to carry with me, but to my surprise and great grief, it had disappeared from where I had put it and seen it every day. I said nothing to the others but kept the sadness to myself.

The General's house was a large building of stone wall with thatched roof with a hall and six rooms, covered verandah all around, a very large yard behind, well shaded with trees, [with] a portion fenced and kept as a fruit orchard and flower garden. There was a very deep, well constructed well, which supplied the house and neighbors with drinking water. In the front there was a large stone-wall enclosure with stone benches all around paved with

---

5. I.e., *ma'alob*.

stone and cement. This place was used for evening meetings and dancing during the May Santa Cruz fiestas.

The General's wife was a fat mestiza, once a prisoner in Bacalar in a house of one of my aunts, serving as a nurse, where she said she was well treated. Her name was Marcelina but called by the General and his children "Mama Mach." She seemed kind to me and said in gratitude for my aunt's good treatment she would see that I did not suffer during my stay with them. One day she asked me what was the matter, if I felt sick, as she noticed that since our arrival I looked very sad and down hearted. Suddenly she exclaimed, "[W]hat a bad memory I have. I meant to have told you from the day we arrived that I brought your little Infant Jesus. I took it from the shrine the evening before we left the country, thinking you would forget it." She went to bring it and handed it to me. I pressed it to my heart and thanked her, saying, "[F]orgive me, I have lost you; but you now return to me, and I hope forever." With Mama Mach's permission, I stood the little statue on her little altar where she had a decorated wooden cross, often lighting wax candles and placing flowers there. The rosary was there recited two or three times a week with singing in honor of the cross. To these functions all the family and some of the privileged neighbors came.

The children consisted of a boy seven years old, tall and thin, like his father—his name was Ceferino but called "Cef"—[and] a girl ten years old called "Nana." Both children had [a] clear complexion with greenish eyes, good dispositions, and smiling faces. These two children were my scholars for five months—teaching them to read and write for two hours in the morning and two in the evening for five days in the week, and one hour every Saturday for teaching the ordinary prayers.

Chan Santa Cruz

A large church was being built by the prisoners taken from the towns captured from time to time. There were about 30 masons, stone breakers, and lime and clay mixers. They were fed by the four Generals, each taking a week's turn. It was finished before I left. An old Indian called "Tat Naz" (Nazario) was in charge and acted as a priest (under the control of the Tatich). He led the prayers and rosary. The four Generals and all their officers met once a week here to hear the word and the command of the Sta. Cruz, who spoke through the mouth of Tat Naz' son in a fine tin whistle, always at midnight behind a curtain near the altar, all in darkness. Only the Generals and Officers were allowed in, the soldiers and women waiting outside to hear through one of the Generals what the orders were from the Cross.

A captain of General Santos once related to me what took place at one of these meetings. After closing the doors and extinguishing the light, the Tatich called out the names of the Generals and Officers who were present. Any absentees from the previous meeting had to give a satisfactory reason, and if the reason was not approved by the Tatich, the offender was ordered to send a quantity of corn to headquarters (the Tatich's house) next day. Then a small brass bugle sounded, a loud noise like the flapping of a large bird was heard, [and] the congregation all went flat on their faces, striking their breasts, saying, "[W]e believe in the Santa Cruz, who will talk to us." Then the cross, or rather Tat Naz' son, started in a sharp whistling voice, saying, "[M]y people and beloved chiefs, I have just now returned from a long excursion through the capital and principal military guarded towns of Yucatán. They are all in a state of revolt against Mexico, fighting between themselves for the Governorship of Mérida, all forgetting that the Maya race is still existing. [N]ow is our best time to wake them up and show them we don't forget them. My beloved chiefs, it is now a month since you returned from the victorious entry and capture of Bacalar, and as you are well rested, it is time to think of moving again. I therefore command my dear Tatich Don Venancio Puc, my Generalissimo, to prepare with his Generals a march to be made a week from now to attack and capture the City of Valladolid. I will be with them to direct them and make a victory for them." The gathering all shouted three times, *Viva la Santísima Cruz y nuestro Tatich.*[6] Then all dispersed.

The next day a grand meeting of all the officers and soldiers took place at the plaza of *Chi qui whik* in front of the General's (Don Pantaleón Zapata) house and arranged that the second General, Don Crescencio Poot, would take command of the expedition, assisted by the third General, Don Leandro Santos; and the fourth General, Don Bonifacio Novelo, was to follow as a reserve, leaving the first general to guard the Santa Kaaj (Holy City) and to place patrol communication between the city and the expedition. All the women were ordered to prepare a certain amount of *totopostes,* baked, thin, round corn cakes about 7 inches in diameter, strung in rolls of 20 each; and a quantity of boiled, dry, ground red pepper wrapped in corn trash, rolls of about 2 ounces each. This is the army rations, and if kept dry, [they] can be used at all times.

This expedition returned in about 4 weeks very unsuccessful, having lost about 200 men owing to visiting a large rancho where extensive distilling of *anisado*[7] was going on and which was too freely indulged in for several days. The Valladolid garrison attacked them, and they were driven back by a detachment of cavalry for some distance and dispersed. It took the Indians fully two weeks before they all arrived and found their homes. At the first meeting after their arrival, the Santa Cruz ordered that all the delinquents, including Generals and Officers, be then and there whipped. During the whipping all cried, "[M]ea culpa, I won't do it again."

Some time after a captain was ordered to be killed, macheted, for running away with another man's wife. All baptisms and marriages are performed by Tata Naz, the former to infants using the prescribed words and pouring water

---

6. "Long live the Most Holy Cross and our leader!"

7. I.e., *anís.*

on their heads, the latter [by] simply saying in Maya, *[Y]o te caso en el nombre de la Santa Cruz, amen.*[8] The greatest crimes punished by death were blasphemy against the Santa Cruz and meddling with another man's wife. Once a prisoner, a musician, was killed for telling some of the Indians not to take the cross for God, being only an instrument of torture and death of the only true God. At another meeting my General Leandro Santos was drunk, and when the Cross was talking, shouted, "Stop talking Brulio (Tata Naz' son, who acted for the Cross); we have enough of sorcery." He was immediately whipped and put under arrest. The next day he was taken by Tatich and the other three Generals and made to pay 2 bags of corn and was cautioned if such an offence was committed again, immediate death would follow.

These severe punishments kept the faith in many of the ignorant and fear and silence in the unbelievers. Of course, such religion was nothing but idolatry, as they would not allow any priests to remain among them but [were] always ready to kill them and burn their churches. The Indians were given to the feeding [of] souls (*janal pixan*), placing food on the graves of their relatives who had recently died and eating, drinking, and dancing before the corpses were buried.[9] Unfortunately this is done not only by the Indians but by some of the so-called civilized people of Yucatán.

Belizean Traders

During my nine months captivity in Santa Cruz, many traders had visited the town, coming from Corozal bringing salt, gun powder, shot, and other goods, which they sold to the chiefs. The soldiers were not allowed to buy anything direct but only through the chiefs. Amongst the traders there was one named Trejo, who became very friendly and intimate with the chiefs. He was well known to my father, having met him several times in Belize and Corozal. He reported having seen me several times, and I remember having seen him on a visit in the General's house, but I did not know that he was acquainted with my father, although he had mentioned it privately to the General's wife.

One day Mr. Trejo made his appearance with a parcel in his hand, and I was called to the hall, and my two pupils followed me. He then addressed himself to the General and his wife saying, "With your permission, I now hand the parcel to my little friend. It has been sent from his father in Belize." He shook my hand and gave it to me. I thanked him and said, "Tell my father that I thank him very much for remembering me, that I am quite well and happy where I am, as I am well treated, not as a prisoner but as one of the family of the General and his wife, and I don't know how to thank them"; and in proof of my gratitude, I now handed the parcel to the General's wife for her son's use. Both

---

8. "I marry you in the name of the Cross, amen."

9. Becoming increasingly commercialized in cities, *janal pixan,* or "food of the dead," remains an important part of rural life in Yucatán.

she and her husband seem[ed] much astonished at my generosity and refused to accept it but finally did so after my insisting and seeing that I was very much in earnest. The parcel contained a boy's complete suit of clothes, felt hat, boots, handkerchiefs, comb, brush, and a small flute. My friend was delighted with the outfit, and his joy was so great that he danced and sang for a long time. He afterwards told me, "I cannot think what made you part with your father's present. Nothing in the world could make me act as you have done. I have nothing to give you in return but *Dios botik tech*, which means 'God will reward you.'"[10] Mr. Trejo returned to Belize and a few weeks later paid another visit, [t]his time bringing me another parcel from my father, but which contained sweets and chocolate. These I also handed to my protectress, who shared them amongst all in the house, including myself.

One morning early in November, the General took me aside and said, "I have very important news for you. Mr. Lara (another traveler) arrived from Belize last night and gave me a letter from our friend Mr. Trejo, who could not come himself on account of illness. He says he has appointed Mr. Lara to act for him to carry out and fulfill his part of an agreement between myself and Mr. Trejo, and as Mr. Lara has handed me my Captain's receipt in fulfillment of Mr. Trejo's part, it now only remains for me to do my part. [B]efore doing it I have first to obtain the approval of Santa Cruz, but as you do not know or understand what I am telling you, I shall briefly explain.

"Mr. Trejo in his first visit was authorized by your father in Belize to sound me out first in a very quiet way and privately about the possibility of obtaining your freedom and allowing you to return to your father in Belize. Such an unusual and sudden proposition shocked me very much at first and caused me great anxiety, as I could not decide nor entertain such a serious and risky matter involving perhaps the immediate end of your life. I told Mr. Trejo that had any other person approached me on this subject, I would have immediately denounced him as a conspirator and traitor, with death and a fair trial afterwards. As he is a good friend, however, and for your life's sake, I told him to be cautious and not to utter a word to anyone else, and in a week after thinking the matter over, I would give him an answer.

"That night I had a very long consultation with my wife, and after a great discussion, we decided I should speak privately first with the chief, Tatich; and if I could get his consent, then I would try to influence my two friends, the Generals, in my favor; and that my wife, who is willing to do all in her power to save you, would do the same with the wives of the chief and the two Generals." Such news made me feel like the possibility of flying in the air and transporting myself to Belize and embracing my father. The next day the General and his wife started their work on my behalf, and from that night on, my prayers to the Infant Jesus for help were strong, and my little pupils and the General's wife joined me.

------

10. Literally, "God pays you."

The General again called me aside and told me, "I have to congratulate you on our success, for which you have to thank my wife; for without her intercession, it could not have been done, as I had three very strong opposers, the other three generals, who were always my strong enemies; but they have been convinced by the other three on my side and their wives. Everything is arranged, but as a matter of formality and to make it clear to the soldiers and the people, we have to go through some things tonight at twelve o'clock. You have to appear before the Santa Cruz, who will speak to you and ask you if you wish to go to your father. You will answer that you are well treated here and that you do not wish to leave us. You will likely be whipped, but you will gain your freedom."

At the appointed time, the General took me to the church, as he had said. The usual large gathering of soldiers was outside and Generals and officers inside. A few minutes after arrival the lights were put out, and I heard in the darkness a sound as if a storm was drawing near, and then a loud whistling voice started saying, "There is no fear of our enemy attacking us, as they have failed in their several attempts to organize an expedition against us. They are too disunited politically, fighting amongst themselves, and the present time is fitting for us to move and let the white faces know that the Mayas are very much alive."

After a good deal of preaching about drunkenness, gambling, and women, three young officers were whipped, each receiving 25 strong lashes, for interfering with the wives of soldiers. Then he advanced towards me saying, "You young white face prisoner, listen to me! Our beloved General Don Leandro Santos, in whose custody you are, has pleaded for your freedom, asking us to allow you to return to your father, who is in the English territory of Belize. Now tell me with all truth, '[D]o you wish to go? or do you wish to remain?'" My reply through the General, who was holding my hand, was as he had instructed me: "I wish to remain with you; I do not wish to go, as I am well treated by General Don Leandro Santos." Then the Cross said in a very loud angry voice, "You have not told the truth. I know the sentiments of your heart, that you are anxious to go to your father. You will be allowed to go to your father, but now you will be punished for telling a lie and trying to deceive me."

I was taken by a soldier and received two lashes, during which I screamed for mercy. When I returned with the General to the house, I met his wife and my two little pupils waiting for me, and they said, "We are very sorry for the whipping, but it is all over now; and although we are losing you, we are very glad that you are now feeling happy, knowing you will soon join your father in Belize. Let us all kneel before the Infant Jesus and thank Him for having saved your life and will now return you to your family in Belize." My back was blistered and burned me. I was put to bed, and warm hog lard was applied to my back with a feather.

Next day I was feeling well and happy, and the flogging [was] forgotten. Two days later [then], Mr. Lara was ready to start, and the General's wife got my baggage fixed. It consisted of small straw *pattakae* containing a thick twilled sheet, grass twine hammock, two trousers, two shirts, and a pair of sandals with leather soles and rope fastenings, all made in the city of Santa Cruz. She had asked me to leave with her my little statue of the Infant Jesus, as she said I could easily get another in Belize. I consented to her request.

After a very affectionate *adios* to the General, his wife, and my two pupils, thanking them for their kindness and care of me, I was on mule back with my *pattakae*[11] and in company with Mr. Lara, also on mule back, and an escort of six foot soldiers in charge of a sergeant. [O]n a cold rainy morning, November 20th, 1858, we started on our journey to Bacalar, which we reached after a week's traveling through incessant cold rains and over muddy roads. I had told Mr. Lara that I wanted to visit the ruins of Bacalar and see the place where my mother and other prisoners were massacred. He said that upon our arrival he would ask for permission to do this, but upon our arrival one night after dark, the sergeant in charge of us said that his instructions from the General in Santa Cruz were to see us direct, without any stop in town, to our boat ready waiting for us at the beach. Therefore, we had to obey orders, and we embarked at once in a good-sized open canoe with a canvas awning. We started at about nine o'clock, Mr. Lara and myself as passengers and a crew consisting of two oarsmen and one man at the rudder. We crossed the lagoon, and by six the next morning, we arrived in the Hondo River at the landing in English territory. *Deo gratias.* There Mr. Trejo had his residence and was awaiting us.

---

11. The term *pattakae* is probably Rosado's corruption of the Spanish term *petaca,* meaning "a small leather suitcase."

16

"A Mouthful of Bruised Peppers"

The Captivity Narrative of José de los Angeles Loesa

*Yucatecans who fled to Belize from 1847 onward continued to main-
tain social and economic ties with their mother country but also
with the Maya rebels of Chan Santa Cruz. The relationship was
always ambiguous. Exiles soon recognized the value of trade with
both Chan Santa Cruz and the pacífico communities; however, they
also recognized that both of these forces, especially the former, were
mercurial and potentially dangerous.*

*Some idea of the complex and changing relationship between the
exiles and the rebels comes from the testimony of José de los Angeles Loesa, a Hispanic Yucatecan exile who made his living by trading with the new masters of eastern Yucatán. His account of 26
August 1861 touches on economic life along the border; the unpre-
dictable nature of political conditions; the rebel obsession with
obtaining gunpowder; the capricious dictates of the Speaking Cross;
the iron-fisted rule of Chan Santa Cruz's chief general, Venancio
Puc; and the essentially opportunistic nature of Yucatecan expatriots,
such as Loesa himself.[1]*

I, José de los Angeles Loesa of Corozal, in the Northern District of the settlement of British Honduras, a trader, do solemnly and sincerely declare that I
was taken prisoner by the Indians of Santa Cruz on the 8th day of December
last past.[2] I was going from Bolonchén to X-Noh Akal to buy hogs. There were
in company with me Juan Loesa, Agustín Medina, Bonifacio Poot, Dámaso
May, and Ambrosio Medina. We had eleven hundred dollars in money and
three hundred dollars worth of goods. The Indians met us at about four miles
from X-Noh Akal. My companions were before; I was last in the path in which
we were walking. I saw them kill Dámaso May, and the rest of my companions
and myself escaped into the woods. They fired at us, but I don't know whether
anyone was wounded or killed. [I] [r]eceived no injury. I was five days in the
woods when I found a road homewards, and was returning when the Indians

---

1. The source of the following material is Archives of Belize (Belmopan), Record 74, 26 August
1861, 174–75.

2. I.e., 8 December 1860.

again met me and took me to Santa Cruz. I found they had taken Ambrosio Medina and Bonifacio Poot. What became of my companions, I do not know.

I was eight days with the Indians before we reached Santa Cruz, during which time they took three hundred and sixty prisoners. At a place eight leagues distant from Santa Cruz, called De Repente,[3] they killed all the male and female prisoners. The lives of fifty children only were spared.

I heard while at Santa Cruz that the Indians had crossed the Hondo into the English territory and forcibly carried away some cattle. I think I heard this in March. I did not see nor hear that anyone was punished for having done this. I must have known if any such punishment took place. I was servant to [Venancio] Puc, and whenever the Cross speaks, I, as well as every person in Santa Cruz, must be present. The Cross alone orders people to be punished, and no order was given by the Cross to punish any of the Indians who carried away the cattle from the English side. Without the orders of the Cross, Puc could not chastise anyone, although he is patron of the Cross. The Cross said with reference to what was done by the Indians at San Román in carrying off the cattle, that it was well done, and that if it had been a greater thing, it would have been all right.

I was in Santa Cruz on the 26th day of March last when a letter was received there by Puc from the superintendent of Belize. I read the letter. It was written in Spanish and was sent on by a soldier from Bacalar, who stated that it had been delivered to the commandant of that place by two English officers. The same night the letter was delivered, the Cross was consulted. It stated that it did not like the letter sent by the English, that it was insulting, and it gave orders that on their arrival in Santa Cruz, the two English officers and the two Spaniards should be taken out of town and killed.

On the thirtieth day of March, the officers with the two English soldiers and two Spanish interpreters arrived at Santa Cruz. They had a white flag with them. As soon as they were about one hundred yards from the church, the Indians ordered them to halt. The bugle was immediately sounded to assemble the troops and take them out to execution. Trejo, one of the interpreters who came with the officers, then began to speak and told Puc and the commandants that the letter did not convey the sentiments of the superintendent, that the English did not understand Spanish properly, and that no doubt some mistake had been made in translating it. They believed Trejo but placed him, the other interpreter, and the two officers and soldiers in custody.

At midnight the Indians took them down to the Cross; they were asked by the Cross, "What they came for? If they had not come as spies?" Trejo answered, "No, they came in peace and to promote commerce." The Cross asked, "How many *arrobas* of powder they were going to make a present to it." Trejo answered, "that with much pleasure they would give whatever the Cross

---

3. *De repente* means "suddenly."

asked." The Cross said that "it required as a present three hundred *arrobas* of powder and that they must bring one thousand *arrobas* to sell." The Cross then asked the officers if they would bring the powder. They replied they could do nothing without the superintendent's orders, but they would get the order and the Indians need not be afraid. The officers and their interpreters were released next morning, but the two soldiers remained prisoners. When Puc was drunk, I saw him compel one of the officers to take a mouthful of bruised peppers.[4]

I made my escape to Bacalar to sell hogs. I had for my companion a man named Romero. I don't know his Christian name, and we both ran away. I don't know where Romero is at present. I heard that he has gone to San Pedro, from whence he intends to proceed to Yucatán. He was a prisoner eighteen months with the Indians. The whole of the Indian male population does not exceed three thousand in number. The army does not consist of more than one thousand men. When these are called away into active service, all the servants in the plantations and boys of seven or eight years old, armed with carbines, are called in to guard the town.

---

4. I.e., crushed *habanero* chiles, a searing experience indeed.

17

"The Yucatecans Give Us a Very Bad Name"

John Carmichael's Visit to Chan Santa Cruz

John Carmichael was a merchant, militia captain, and son of a British entrepreneur with the same name. Both men were active in northern Belize in the 1860s and attempted to develop a gunpowder trade with Chan Santa Cruz during that decade. The younger Carmichael visited Chan Santa Cruz several times and at an extraordinarily successful moment in that community's history. In 1867 the rebels had recently foiled Mexican/Yucatecan attempts at reconquest and were preparing to gain control over the rival pacífico *communities of southern Campeche. Carmichael's descriptive letter, written on 15 November 1867, thus captures a critical moment in nineteenth-century Maya history.*

Carmichael's report boasts several unique features. It not only outlines the larger contours of rebel society but also contains intriguing details regarding the Chan Santa Cruz leaders, including their personalities, physical appearance, and leadership role in the community. Carmichael goes beyond this, however: he explores aspects of the daily lives of both leaders and followers, the geographical layout of rebel settlements, and the Mayas' attitudes toward the war and their principal antagonists, the Hispanic Yucatecans.[1]

Corozal, 15th November 1867

Having just returned from a visit to the Santa Cruz Indians in Yucatán and believing that some account of this hitherto unvisited tribe may be of interest, I take the liberty of addressing Your Excellency on that subject.

I started from Corozal on the 21st September last and arrived at Bacalar, the first outpost of the Santa Cruz Indians, on the 23rd, distant from Corozal 36 miles via the River Hondo and Chac Creek. Bacalar is now the remains of what must have been a very large town when occupied by the Yucatecans. The houses are nearly all built of stone, though at present mostly in ruins. The streets are laid out at right angles. The church situated in the center of the Plaza is a fine building still in good repair, although all images and decorations have

---

1. The source of the following material is Archives of Belize (Belmopan), Record 96, 15 November 1867.

been removed. The position of the town is well chosen, situated on the lake of Bacalar on a high bank about 60 feet above water level. The formation of the soil is limestone rock. The water of the lake has a slightly brackish taste consequent on the presence of marl, but excellent drinking water is obtained in the town by means of wells.

This town is the nearest outpost to British territory and is the principal trading post of the Indians. It has been held by them undisputed for the last ten or twelve years. The Indians always keep a garrison here of from two to five hundred men, and the command is entrusted only to a Chief of position and intelligence. They bring mules, horses, cattle, pigs, hammocks, hats, and other manufactures and productions in barter for British goods. Bacalar is surrounded by outlying pickets on each road entering the town. These *avanzadas*, as they are called, consist of a wall about six feet high made by piling stones one on the top of the other, with a rude hut for the men. They are much overgrown with underbrush and at a distance defy detection. The fort which faces the lake has been entirely demolished by the Indians; large trees now grow out of its ruins and almost hide it from view.

The Commandant of Bacalar, an intelligent looking Indian, received me on the wharf with a guard of honor of fifty men, with drums beating and bugles blowing, and conducted me to his quarters, one of the best houses at the corner of the plaza, where he entertained me most hospitabl[y] and furnished me with horses for myself, servants, and baggage, as well as six Indian soldiers as an escort.

Our road for the first thirty miles lay along the high banks of the lakes and was hard, dry, and open; here about one mile of swamp presented itself, but although it was the height of the rainy season, in no place did our horses sink below their knees. The road from here to the city of Santa Cruz resumes its former aspect, and is, what for the country would be called, a very good road, and with the removal of a few obstacles would be practicable for cart traffic for the whole distance. No villages or settlements are met with until near Santa Cruz; in fact, the first few days of the journey we had to make camp every night in the bush. Water is scarce after leaving the Bacalar lake and, with the exceptions of two small lagoons, is supplied by the wells belonging to the deserted ranchos and haciendas now in complete ruins. The water in these wells is nearly always bad.

I estimate the distance from Bacalar to Santa Cruz at 112 miles, and we required five days to accomplish it in.[2] The first village entered after leaving Bacalar is Xkanhá, containing about 800 inhabitants; we then passed through the villages of Chanchén, Tzul, Okom, Santa Clara, and others and met now frequently pickets of Indian soldiers stationed behind stone barricades, who

2. Carmichael was good with people but terrible with geography; the actual distance is fifty-six miles.

challenged, until arriving at the main guard outside the walls of the city of Santa Cruz. I was requested by the Chief in command to dismount and offered a hammock in the guard room, whilst he sent a messenger to apprise the Head Chief of my arrival. After waiting half an hour, José Crescencio Poot, the third principal chief, accompanied by a guard of honor of 200 men and a band of music of 30 performers, came to meet me, by whom I was conducted into the town through triumphal arches. At each cross street were soldiers who presented arms, while on arriving in the plaza or principal square, I found about 1,000 men under arms who saluted as I passed. I was taken to one of the best houses at the corner of the plaza built of stone with a raised veranda, which I found comfortably furnished as well as refreshments provided; and while a Chief of superior rank was told to be personally answerable for my safety, a guard of 12 men was placed over my quarters to keep out intruders.

Next morning I paid a visit to the Patrón, or Head Chief, Bonifacio Novelo. In front of his house is a guard room containing his body guard of 50 men. On entering the house, which is a large substantial one at the corner of the plaza, I was shown into the reception room, at one end of which was an altar with a cross profusely ornamented with gold and jewels. Presently the curtain dividing the room from an inner one was drawn aside, and the Patrón appeared. Without noticing me, he prostrated himself before the cross, and after five minutes devotion, rose and welcomed me. He is a man of about 60 years of age, immensely stout, and is of the lighter shade of color than the generality of the Indians. His expression of countenance is decidedly pleasing. He was dressed in a many-colored blouse made of cloth of Indian manufacture; white, loose cotton drawers trimmed from the knee downwards with rich lace; sandals of embroidered leather; and a scarf, also of Indian manufacture, round his waist, while round his neck was hung a massive gold chain with a cross attached.

He asked me if I was not afraid to have trusted myself in their hands, "[F]or," said he, "the Yucatecans give us a very bad name for treachery and cruelty, but," he added, "whatever our conduct may be toward them, I can assure you that our feelings are nothing but those of friendship towards the English, and the time may yet come when we will give you proofs of our sincerity." He went on to inform me that, owing to the war they were engaged in against the Mexicans, he regretted he could not allow the English to visit Santa Cruz, in case of spies taking advantage of this permission.

He vehemently denounced the cruelties and treacheries that have been perpetrated on the Indians by the Yucatecans, and frankly confessed to a retaliation on their part towards them, and stated that the war they were now carrying on was to recover their lands, which had always belonged to their ancestors. I asked him what he meant by their lands? He replied, the whole of Yucatán, recognizing the English boundary to the south and the District of Petén on the west (this includes the Indian tribes of Xloschá and Macanché, at present allied with the Santa Cruz Indians). That already two thirds of this vast territory had been successfully wrested from the Yucatecans, who had now entirely abandoned the offensive and were compelled to act solely on the defensive, while each year their circle was narrowed, till now the Indian patrols reached to within a few leagues of Mérida.

With respect to the Indians of Icaiché, who have recently been committing depredations on our frontier, he informed me that the actual number of Indians in the tribe was not more [than] 150 men; that the remainder were composed of Yucatecans, Central Americans, and Creoles, nearly all fugitives from justice; and that the whole gang was nothing but a band of robbers. That had they, the Santa Cruz Indians, been requested by the English, they would willingly have released the prisoners taken at Qualm Hill and exterminated the whole tribe; but, to use his own words, "[I]t was an English quarrel, and if we had interfered, you would have said England can fight her own battles without the help of Indians, and so what we had intended as friendship you would have viewed as an insult."

Bonifacio Novelo does not now take any active part in warfare. He is the head of the Church, and received all tithes and offerings for the same, and administers civil justice in Santa Cruz. He informed me that the Church was possessed of over $200,000—in specie, irrespective of jewels and gold ornament. This money is entrusted to three men who have charge of the Church, and who have buried the money in places only known to themselves. He asked many questions respecting Her Majesty the Queen, her relations with her subjects, [and] the English code of laws and mode of punishment with an intelligence which, considering his complete isolation, astonished me; whilst the firm yet impartial manner in which he administered justice, his kindness and benevolence to the lower class of Indians, and the many good traits his character displayed convince me that he is peculiarly adapted to govern these Indians and a very different character from what is represented by the Yucatecans.

I next visited Bernabé Cen, the second chief of Santa Cruz, who also had a guard of 50 men over his house. He observed the same ceremony of prostration before the cross as the Patrón before noticing me. He is a pure Indian, short, somewhat stout, with a frank, open countenance and an eye indicative of courage and resolution. He has the command of the whole army of Santa Cruz, which consists of 11,000 fighting men armed and equipped with rifles and accouterments taken from the Yucatecans in war. The Indians of Lochhá and Macanché, who form part of the Santa Cruz confederation, have to furnish 4,000 men of this number. Each Indian has to give 15 days military service in the month, during which time he has to provide himself with rations, which consist of a few hard, dry corn-cakes and red pepper. He receives no pay but on an expedition is allowed to appropriate what spoil he can lay his hands upon. They receive their rifles, accouterments, and ammunition from the Santa Cruz government.

When the tour of duty of a soldier arrives, he presents himself in Santa Cruz to his commandant, who assigns his station. If it should be Bacalar, he is allowed to take with him mules or horses or whatever produce he may possess to sell to the traders there. When the Indian soldier is not on guard or duty, he is not allowed to be idle in the barracks but is compelled to work at making hammocks, hats, ropes, or whatever his trade may be. When an Indian expedition returns to Santa Cruz from a foray on the Mexicans, each Indian soldier gives an account of his spoil to the government of Santa Cruz and is expected to make an offering of some portion to the Church. The military duty is performed most cheerfully by the Indians, and evasion of it is never attempted. Bernabé Cen spoke with the greatest contempt of the courage of the Yucatecan troops.

The city of Santa Cruz is the headquarters of the Santa Cruz Indians. It is built on high, dry, and rocky ground. The houses in the suburbs are made of pimento poles with thatched roofs and are at a little distance from the road, surrounded with orange and fruit trees, while the lot is always enclosed by a stone wall. In the neighborhood of the plaza, the buildings are all stone, many of them with some pretensions to architecture. The style is that usually adopted in Mexico, viz., flat roofs with arched piazzas in front. The windows are faced with iron bars, and the doors are loop-holed for musketry.

The most imposing building in the town is the church or temple, which occupies one side of the plaza. It is built of stone and is of immense height. It is in the form of a parallelogram with an arched roof and has two side wings with arched porticos. The walls are of great thickness, and the building reflects the greatest credit on the masonic skills of the Indians. It is here the celebrated cross is kept, which, when the government of Santa Cruz was in the hands of unscrupulous men, was made the instrument by means of ventriloquism of inciting the ever credulous Indians to commit deeds of unparalleled barbarity and ferocity. Now the Indians are not imposed on by these mockeries but taught to worship the Divine Being through the cross alone. With the exception of their belief in the efficacy of saints and the absence of priests, their religion is Roman Catholicism, but all prayers are addressed through the Santa Cruz.

Attached to the church is a school-house where children are taught the early rudiments in Spanish and Maya, the language of the Santa Cruz Indians. Facing the temple stands the palace of the Patrón, which is a magnificent building built of stone, with arched piazzas in front and at the back, and occupies an entire side of the plaza. The remaining two sides are occupied by the barracks, the prison, and the council-house. In the center of the plaza on a rock stands a sapodilla tree, under which their prisoners are executed, being cut to pieces by machetes or cutlasses. It is difficult to arrive at a correct idea of the population of the town of Santa Cruz, as the suburbs are very straggling, but I believe I am correct in supposing that it contains a population of some 7,000 inhabitants.

There is another Indian town about 60 miles from Santa Cruz and 20 from the south coast of Yucatán called San Luis, which contains an equal population. Near here on the coast are the remains in tolerable preservation of an Aztec city called Tulum, and which is said to exceed in size any of the ruins of Central America.

With the exception of maize, rice, and those vegetable productions necessary for their own consumption, there is but little cultivation, consequent on the present wars with Yucatán. The soil is most fertile and productive. The yield of maize per acre greatly exceeds that of British Honduras. Some of the finest quality of tobacco is grown, and while sugar cane and rice thrive admirably towards the coast, the interior is peculiarly adapted for cotton. The dense forests supply sapodilla, mahogany and cedar of large proportions, while in the neighborhood of the lakes is to be found logwood in abundance, as well as fustic and sarsaparilla.[3]

The climate of Santa Cruz is very similar to that of Corozal. The air is pure and dry and, owing to the low yet rocky formation of the land, a cool breeze from the eastward sweeps over the whole country, which contributes materially to its healthiness.

Before leaving the city of Santa Cruz, I attended a Council meeting of the three principal Chiefs. It was stated to me that some time ago, the government of Mexico had made propositions to them for peace on the following basis, viz.: that they, the Santa Cruz Indians, were to retain the land they had conquered from them for themselves (which, by the way, is about two thirds of the whole province of Yucatán); that a boundary line was to be drawn, which the Indians were on no occasion to pass, but were to draw their supplies from British Honduras; and that the land so given up was to be considered as no longer belonging to Mexico, but to be a distinct and separate government under the Santa Cruz Indians. This proposition was rejected by the Santa Cruz Indians, as they said they had no faith in the sincerity of this proposal, having been on every occasion duped and deceived by the Yucatecans. The question was put to me, in the event of a similar proposition being again made, would England be willing to take over this territory and make it part of British Honduras, they, the Santa Cruz Indians, laying down their arms, and becoming British subjects in every respect?

It is not for me to attempt to point out to Your Excellency the incalculable benefits that would accrue to our colony by this new accession to her territory. Fresh capital and that of no inconsiderable amount, an addition of some 15,000 laborers, a fresh impetus to trade, and above all, a state of security conducive to immigration, which would cause the colony to become one of the most flourishing and prosperous of Her Majesty's settlements in the West Indies.

I have the honor to be, Sir, Your Excellency's most obedient servant,

John Carmichael, Captain B, The Militia

---

3. Fustic (Spanish, *fustete*) is a tropical yellow wood used in the production of dyes. Sarsaparilla is a root used for the flavoring of such beverages as root beer.

18

"Active, Agile, Astute, and Generally Magnificent Marksmen"

An Anonymous Report on Rebel Military Capacity

The following anonymous account bears the title "Points and Infor-mation over the Current State of War of the Rebel Indians and the Possible Means of Opening a Decisive Campaign to Bring It to an End." Although the author is unknown, he clearly possessed de-tailed knowledge of the Mayas of Chan Santa Cruz, particularly in regard to their military practices. Details of the text date it between 1868 and 1875, the years of the respective deaths of rebel leaders Bonifacio Novelo and Bernabé Cen, even though the document itself bears the year 1878.

In addition to its thorough account of the rebels' state of military readiness, the anonymous narrative provides a review of the larger contours of the Caste War from its inception in 1847 to its decline in the late 1860s and early 1870s. Its author exhibits a clear under-standing of the obstacles that confronted the Yucatecan army in its efforts to end the Maya rebellion.[1]

After the disaster that the Indians suffered near Tihosuco in the year 1866, their main centers of population ceased to maintain their importance. Before that date, Chan Santa Cruz was well populated, and the most important chiefs lived there. Bonifacio Novelo, a relatively civilized mestizo, the head chief and more intelligent than any of the rebels, had his government relatively well organized, and the obedience and submission that they showed him was absolute. His influence reached, without exception, from one end to the other of the territory they occupied, passively and blindly obeying his orders. Their secondary villages also had more importance than now because they lived clus-tered more closely to one another, perfectly divided in military sections in order to spring into action at a given moment at the orders of their immediate superiors.

They then had their forces ordered so precisely and so easy to mobilize that it can be assured that in the years 1863 to 1866, there was not a month, with

---

1. The source of the following material is University of Texas, Austin, Nettie Lee Benson Library, García Collection, G559, Mérida, June 1878.

very few exceptions, that they did not invade our frontier, crossing the military line and mocking the vigilance of the soldiers of civilization; surprising our towns and frontier ranchos, destroying them with fire and claiming hundreds of victims; killing some and carrying off others as captives. It almost seems as though they came to show the inefficiency of the system of defense then adopted by the nation's troops. The lines formed an angle whose point of convergence was the garrison at Tihosuco, with Valladolid being the principal garrison of the eastern line, having in the middle the stations of Tixcacalcupul, Carolina (a *cenote*), and Majas; to the south, Peto was the principal garrison, with the intermediaries Dzonotchel, Ichmul, and Xcabil.

The Indians in their raiding parties numbering six or eight hundred crossed the woods in the space that lay between two stations, and they fell with a mathematical exactitude on the point that had been proposed. Because each of the intermediate stations is insufficient in itself (80 to 100 men), they were able to do nothing. When the force of the principal garrison was placed in movement and came to fill out its ranks with the stations in order to form a strong column and to strike with great success, the Indians had already had time to withdraw, carrying off prisoners and plunder, almost always with impunity. If some intrepid officer went to an encounter with insufficient forces because they had learned about their approach in advance, or if some small party on the march from one station or another entered into an unforeseen skirmish with them, then our troops were certain to be defeated, and many times the convoys of supplies fell into the hands of the enemy.

The inertia and the isolated life of the garrisons of the wilderness wore down the spirit of the soldiers, and boredom and desertion became inevitable. If some reverse was suffered, the mortification was complete. Even though in those years the troops were perfectly paid and supplied, the inefficiency of the adopted system made all efforts and sacrifices sterile.

The Indians, heartened by the good result of their excursions, by their constant victories, and by the discouragement of our forces, determined on a decisive campaign, a mass undertaking; and an army of more than four thousand savages laid siege to the advanced garrison at Tihosuco and closed off all roads, leaving the garrison completely incommunicado. The siege that they waged lasted for 54 days, day and night, without success until the enemy, weary of the indomitable resistance of the defenders of civilization, resolved on an assault on the early morning of 16 September 1866. It was for naught, then, that 500 men paid with their lives, their audacity, and all Yucatán suffered the inevitable consequences of such an immense tragedy. But when the first ray of dawn sparkled on that great day of the fatherland, everyone realized that they had the obligation to win a victory, and leaving their parapets, they struck up a bloody battle with the white arms, which forced the enemy to retire in defeat to the surrounding woods. On the 26th day of the same month, they definitively broke camp in order to return to their lairs, discouraged by the poor success of their bold enterprise. This was the most powerful effort of their feverish war activity, and from then on, their raids, although periodic, were always slower and less audacious.

Some time later Bonifacio Novelo died, and the lack of his authority and intelligence, abilities that everyone respected, was the reason that an intestine war erupted among them, this being the main reason why their disorganization began. From that moment began the fragmenting of their principal settlements; they formed small groups of houses isolated from one another, occupying the vast extension that stretches from the region of Cabo Catoche to the old fort of Bacalar. This same Chan Santa Cruz ceased to have the importance it once held; its inhabitants remained reduced to a small number of families and their more outstanding military *caudillos,* recognizing Crescencio Poot as the main chief.

From this epoch dates the rise in Tulum of a woman named María Uicab, who, it appears, assumed in herself all the attributes of sovereignty, dressed in sacred fashion, cleverly manipulating the Indians' superstitious nature, and who all blindly obey today. Through this means they have managed to maintain the principle of authority since the death of Bonifacio Novelo, although without the rigorous organization that they once had. The woman Uicab has a grand temple of palms in Tulum, in which there is an altar with three crosses that all the Indians venerate with exalted fanaticism and to which they attribute the powers of speech, and to the woman, the ability to understand or interpret their language. This is accomplished with great ceremony, after which she communicates their orders [to everyone, from] Crescencio Poot down to the last man, and she is obeyed without argument or comment. If one of the raids that she orders turns out badly or whatever order is not carried out exactly, the punishment of lashes is irremediably applied. They inform her of the result of the raids, as well as of whatever other news that might occur, and they faithfully hand over to her part of the booty. It is worth noting that this woman has been married three times and that none of her husbands has participated in the sacred power that they believe to be invested in her.

This point notwithstanding, there are reports that for some time now the Indians' ties of obedience have been loosening, as much from the weariness produced by their past activity as from living in a huge area spread out in isolated settlements, where the influence of authority makes itself felt with difficulty. Their current decadence is notorious, their excursions are less frequent, and they lack the importance that they had ten years ago; for the past year or so they have not crossed our lines, and when detected on various occasions, they have been soundly whipped. The number of the force that they bring when they invade us is currently four or five hundred men.

For the most part, they are farmers and cutters of wood, which they sell, along with the skin of animals they hunt, in the English colony of Belize or else trade these effects for gunpowder, lead, arms, and clothing, or other goods needed for their use. Austere by nature, their principal foods are those which they prepare as thick tortillas; *totoposte, pozole, atole,* and *pinole;* black beans and white beans, chile, and pumpkin seeds as food; for although they have some cattle and a great number of pigs, turkeys, and hens, they commonly do not use these meats other than in their religious festivals and private celebrations.

They are given to drunken sprees and use cane *aguardiente,* which they distill because they have various stills. In their days of drunkenness, there are always disorders, and sometimes one or the other is killed. The men dress in shirt and shorts of crude cotton; straw hat; and sandals, or *guaraches,* of tanned leather or a woven cutting of *majagua,* perfectly tailored and adapted to the foot.[2] The women dress in a *hipil,* or a tunic that reaches the knees; a petticoat, or *fustán*[3]; and a cloth for the head, also of crude cotton cloth. The product of their crops gives them the basis of their sustenance, and they pass the rest of their time in the woods occupied in the hunt, cutting some wood, or in lazy indolence.

They are fatalistic and await death with stoic indifference. Cruel and bloodthirsty, it is rare that they do not kill their prisoners with machete-blows, and although upon occasion they leave someone alive for a while, in the end they make him the victim of their ferocity. They are always armed with rifle, machete, and ax, and in their campaigns they carry cartridge belts and a large bag, or *habuco,* of henequen, where they carry clothing for rest and their supplies. They are tireless and travel in stages of up to 12 or 16 leagues. They endure the weather through all the seasons of the year. For war they are active, agile, astute, and generally magnificent marksmen. They almost never fire in vain, and each time that they discharge their rifle, it hits the mark. No woman accompanies them in their raids, nor do they take beasts of burden. To carry ammunition, provisions, and so forth, they have a section of troops, which they call *ligeros,*[4] who are only armed with a machete, and in their engagements their job is to recover the wounded and carry them away when they withdraw on stretchers, which they make from poles cut from the woods.

They are reserved, duplicitous, and maliciously cunning. They far prefer to suffer the worst torture than to provide information or to declare anything that might hurt their companions. Although they are valiant and tenacious, they almost never keep up an open battle, and they have a great ability for taking advantage of whatever opportunity to do as much harm as possible without serious risk to themselves. When they attack a town or try to assault a fortification in a defended area, it is always through surprise and in darkness. Very rarely do they try a direct frontal assault and in the light of day.

---

2. The *majagua* or *majahua* is known in English as the linden tree; the author refers to weaving its vines.

3. A *fustán* is the lace petticoat traditionally worn beneath the *hipil* that extends almost to the ankles.

4. This, like many other military terms and techniques of the Maya rebels, was borrowed from the Mexican army of the early national period. The original *ligeros* were units of lightly armed and highly mobile soldiers.

When they plan to carry out a raid, the main chief communicates his orders several days beforehand to the area whose warriors should form the section of operations. He informs them of the day and the place of meeting and how long the expedition should last. On the determined day they gather at the orders of their leaders, and these place themselves under the chief designated to assume command. Each one goes armed and well provisioned at his own expense, and they receive from the common fund only the ammunition that they consider necessary for each one, taking as well some boxes of reserve ammunition, which men of what they refer to as the *ligero* section carry.

Thus prepared and organized, they march out; and when they return with their prisoners and their booty, they invariably go to Chan Santa Cruz and there deposit their prisoners and spoils, which are distributed proportionally, leaving a part, which they sell in Belize, by which method they keep their war chest stocked. They withdraw to rest and a few days later get together once more to celebrate their victory with a religious festival, a bullfight, drunken sprees, and as a direct consequence, the slaughter by machete blows of some of the unfortunate lovers of civilization who had the bad luck of falling into their hands.

The vast and virgin forests of the peninsula are the Indian rebels' main element of defense. The war that they wage in their occupied territory is always by ambush, cutting the communication between combined forces and closing off, with many large tree trunks, all the communication lines of a settlement occupied by our troops. With tree trunks in the roads through which they think the army has to pass or around the village that those soldiers occupy, they put up their breastworks behind them or in the underbrush and wait for battle, which they sometimes provoke with small raids; and they allow others to pass through the fortified area without hostility in order to make them overconfident and to fall more easily into the ambush here or in some other place.

In these deadly engagements all disadvantages lie with the soldiers of civilization, and if through daring [these soldiers] manage to rout and to surmount all obstacles, it is at the cost of great losses. Then the enemy withdraws through the woods in confusion, regroups again, and the following day appears once more in the same or another location. If our soldiers are beaten back and withdraw in defeat, the enemy presses all its advantages. A mass of confused and disordered men, withdrawing through a narrow and winding trail that is nearly impassable because of the dead and wounded who block the march, is dismayed by the certain fire of the ambush; while another section [of the rebels], making a flanking movement, moves rapidly to block off the road of retreat and to threaten the troops until forcing them into a canton. All the wounded who remain on the field of combat are invariably killed; this fact has been the main cause of the state National Guard's demoralization. If the Indians approach a point occupied by the troops, the blockade is extended to leagues in circumference and through all the most important roads, for which reason the escapes are difficult and dangerous; and if a retreat becomes absolutely necessary, it is done in spite of terrific obstacles and at the cost of the most severe losses.

As examples of this point it is only necessary to cite two cases whose disastrous consequences form an epoch in the annals of this sad war. In the year 1860, Col. Don Pedro Acereto[5] led an expedition of more than 2,000 men . . . so ill-fated that it can be assured that more than a third of them fell victims, and the rest returned in complete defeat and in small bands, leaving in the enemy's hands their artillery, baggage, and ammunition. They had reached Chan Santa Cruz with no greater resistance than small exchanges of gunfire when they approached and entered the village; but the Indians were already prepared, and all the roads were closed with immense and impenetrable tree trunks, and when the troops took possession of the place, the enemy closed the circle, shutting off the only road that was still open, that which our troops had taken. In this situation the soldiers spent several days in the most inconvenient and inexplicable action, thus giving the Indians the opportunity to complete their woodcutting and to perfect their military position, conveniently situating their larger ambushes. When operations finally commenced—more for the need to find supplies, which in those days expeditions were not accustomed to carrying, always relying on spoils—in all the roads the columns encountered a resistance that [they] often could not overcome, and on other occasions [there were] numerous losses on our part.

After thirty days of unfruitful and deadly combat, demoralization set in; the supplies and ammunition gave out, and a withdrawal became imperative. As a preliminary operation they tried to carry out the wounded through the road to the Bahía de la Ascención. The strongest possible column set out to perform this delicate commission. Once on the road they were met with enemy ambushes and became embroiled in fierce combat; the column was destroyed, and few of the valiant soldiers that had taken part returned to the main camp. None of the wounded they had taken were saved from the terrible slaughter. No one had shown the prudence to secure this communication line, which later proved to be necessary and indispensable. After this lamentable disaster, there was no thought other than a de-occupation. They broke through the line at the point they thought the weakest; but during the evacuation, order broke down completely, and it can well be imagined how the enemy took advantage of the opportunities.

In the year 1865 a column of 500 men under the command of Col. Francisco

---

5. The Aceretos were an influential family of landowners, politicians, and military officers who dominated affairs in the Valladolid region from the 1830s to the early 1860s. The family patriarch, Agustín Acereto, twice "served" as state governor. An unscrupulous *caudillo* who built a fortune in selling captured Mayas as slaves in Cuba, he was eventually overthrown and killed in 1861 by forces loyal to Liberal statesman Liborio Irigoyen. His son, Pedro Acereto, controlled the military units that secured the family's power. Pedro escaped the disastrous defeat described here, but his misadventure in Chan Santa Cruz was a blow to the Aceretos' ambitions.

Cantón[6] advanced as far as Kampocolché. Apparently they learned that the Indians were on the move, and so [Cantón] ordered a retreat to Tsonot, five leagues from Tihosuco in the direction of Chan Santa Cruz. The Indians wasted no time in laying siege and at the same time took possession of all the roads in order to close them off from reinforcements. Don José María Gálvez, then chief of the brigade that covered the eastern line, set out from Tihosuco at the head of 500 men, half from the permanent force and half from the National Guard, along with three field mortars, to serve as reinforcement. Gunfire broke out one league from Tsonot, leading to a bloody battle in which the soldiers, throwing aside all the obstacles that they encountered in their path, managed to reach their destination. Five days later they decided on a withdrawal; initially it proceeded smoothly through a barely passable trail that the Indians had neglected to occupy. But as soon as they noticed the movement, they sprung into action and attacked the column, which, demoralized, was defeated and dispersed, leaving all their baggage, artillery, depots, and wounded. There could have been nothing more disheartening for the nation than this rough new blow of bad fortune. . . .

At the present moment, according to the most recent information, it has come to light that the Indian rebels, making a maximum effort, could assemble at the most 3,000 combatants. It is also known that there is discontent among them and that a certain portion would be disposed to surrender if circumstances favored that end.

It is also known that, because of their scarce capital, because of their lazy habits and poor system of agriculture, they have no grand deposits of basic grains. It is certain that whatever force that invaded there would put an end to their existence in six months and impede the harvest of their crops. . . .

There are some hamlets of middling importance around and a short distance from Chan Santa Cruz. The better part of their settlements lie to the south in the direction of Bacalar and to the north toward Tulum. There are few [villages] and of scant importance toward the Bahía de la Ascención. The latter is 12 leagues from Chan Santa Cruz; Bacalar lies 50 leagues, and Tulum 30.

---

6. Like both Pedro and Augustín Acereto, Francisco Cantón was a Valladolid-based *caudillo* active in both war and politics from the 1860s onward. A supporter of the French-imposed empire (in Yucatán, 1863–67), he managed to survive, supported the successful revolt of Porfirio Díaz in 1876, and served as state governor at the close of the century. His mansion is today the home of the state museum of archaeology.

19

"From the General on Down"

A Second Anonymous Report on Rebel Military Capacity

*Similar in content and perspective to the anonymous document in
the previous chapter, this anonymous report offers observations on
political, military, and economic affairs in southeastern Yucatán.
This account was presumably written in 1873 or later because it is
addressed to General Guillermo Palomino, who did not arrive in
Yucatán until that year. The information on the leadership of Chan
Santa Cruz suggests that it was written in the early 1870s, when
Crescencio Poot and Bernabé Cen were both still alive and vying for
power. The author was apparently a soldier who had been taken
captive but who managed to escape and flee to Belize.*

*Like the previous document, this narrative concentrates on mili-
tary matters, perhaps because these dominated life among the rebels
or perhaps because it was what most interested the Yucatecans
themselves. Although not as well developed as the preceding account, this report does provide useful supplemental information on
tactics and organizational structure, as well as exceptional details
on the internal workings of upper Maya leadership.*[1]

To Señor General Dn. Guillermo Palomino, in respectful proof of admiration: A report on the customs, situation, and elements of the rebel Indians of
Chan Santa Cruz and Lochhá, with the warning that I did not come to know the
settlement of Santa Cruz, although I was in Yoktsonot ten leagues from this
capital and in Bacalar, where I was able to save myself.

Customs or internal management . . . : In Santa Cruz there is a general who
wields all powers, and he is called or titled "Governor." At the moment the
man who holds this office is José Crescencio Poot, also titled "First General,"
who communicates directly with the "Cross," which, according to their beliefs,
is what gives orders on whether or not to leave on raiding expeditions. This
Governor is named by direct election, and all obey him blindly. His appointment has no limits, and he is only removed from office in cases of abuses. They

---

1. The source of the following material is Tulane University, New Orleans, La., Yucatecan Collection, 26, Box 2, Folder 14.

have other generals, and these are Bernardino Cen,[2] for which reasons he was removed from office; Ascención Cab, very reasonable, and today married to the woman who was "queen mother X-Bas"; J. Aké is also a general; [and] Pedro Tsul, who was as well, died of gunfire in an encounter with government troops in the year 1871, in which [the rebels] lost 84 men.

After each raiding expedition, each chief, officer, and soldier bears the obligation of presenting his booty, from which is deducted a portion to be used in the purchase of arms. Their weapons are generally poor, with the exception of those that they manage to seize in certain encounters or from unguarded settlements. The cannons are useless for anything more than ceremonial discharges during their celebrations, [but] they are the first things they protect when they have notice of an impending invasion. It never enters into their calculations to defend a settlement. Rather, their tactic is to allow the enemy to enter in order to immediately close off all roads so that at the moment of defeat, the troops, finding no way out, fall into their power. There [in Santa Cruz] all are soldiers from the age of ten years onward. It is also their custom not to take into the settlements more food or provisions than are necessary for each week. The rest is kept in the *milpas* so that, if there is an invasion, the troops will be deprived of all resources.

From the General on down to the corporals, all administer justice according to the exigencies of the case. Each subordinate officer immediately gives an account to the superior authorities, who approve or disapprove. In the latter case, the decision is respected, [but] he who gave it receives 12 to 50 blows.

Among these people the crime of theft is punished with 25 to 100 blows, according to the circumstances, and afterwards the culprit must pay for the thing stolen. The crime of adultery carries a punishment of blows for both men and women. The death penalty exists among them only for the so-called sorcerers or those who are caught fleeing to points considered hostile territory, and these are the villages of the State [of Yucatán] or the *pacíficos* of X-Mabén and Icaiché. Those caught heading for the English colony are only punished with blows because, they say, they recognize their queen as being their own.

Their lower officers are the commanders, captains, lieutenants, sergeants, and corporals. They have no sublieutenant nor sergeants of first or second class. Each captain leads 30 men, two lieutenants, two sergeants, and four corporals. And each commander leads three or four companies that he himself has formed, the command being hereditary, that is, as long as they are not removed for misconduct, in which case they remain soldiers. All officer appointments come from popular election, and there is no benefit of salary or special provisions because they abhor all form of taxes. There he who manages to get a peso

---

2. The anonymous author provides a gloss translating *cen* as "panther." I have been unable to find corroboration for this, and the gloss appears to be a mistake. The word *k'en* refers to something twisted or doubled over.

buries it, so that all seem poor. Their living quarters are generally small shacks, although well provided with supplies.

As a rule their settlements have neither streets nor supplies. A few are considerably removed, so that if some settlement is suddenly surprised, nothing more than a few families will be taken. The roads that they do have are of wide construction, whereas for their agricultural labors, they have footpaths.

They have distillation trains and some establishments for refining sugar and honey. Each pound of sugar is worth a *real,* and a bottle of *aguardiente* is worth four *reales.*

They have warning bombers stationed at every league for as far as five leagues around and [along] the road from Tihosuco to this point, ten leagues from Santa Cruz.

Lochhá has a general just like the one in Santa Cruz and named in the same fashion. The man who wields all powers is Julián Méndez, a *pardo* and ferocious in his campaigns, a man of very poor speaking abilities. He has a lieutenant-general who makes up for his shortcomings. Both take part in their incursions, whereas the settlements remain under the command of the most able sergeant or corporal, even when there may be chiefs and higher officers present.

The people of this area operate in concert with those of Santa Cruz; the number at this point [Santa Cruz] varies from 12,000 at the lowest to 15,000 maximum. In Lochhá the numbers do not exceed 2,000 because in their raiding parties, they never have more than 7–800, but in case of invasion, everyone becomes a soldier, even the sick. These people are generally poor. They exempt the muleteers and *carboneros* and their families from military service. Take, for example, the muleteers. Once the group has, through consent of the majority, resolved on a raid, the area [for the raid] is determined. The muleteers leave and head for the area with caution, with care, and when they enter the settlements, they mingle with the people, asking for horses or cattle of one sort or another; and in this manner, they survey everything and return to provide an account, and so it is determined where to go.

The *carboneros* are those who care for the gunpowder and war munitions, which they keep at a distance from the settlements. They must treat these supplies with extreme caution because the lives of the combatants hang in the balance. Some 500–1,000 barrels of gunpowder exist in Santa Cruz, always with the oldest used first. And this is purchased with the part deducted from their spoils.

The capital of the Lochhá [settlements] is Caunxaan, and the canton is the place that bears the name "Lochhá." It has a constant force of 150 men relieved every two weeks; it is not necessary to establish turns of relief because every captain knows when it is his responsibility. Each soldier and officer provides for himself, and only during shortages is corn distributed, for which contingency each captain and his company raise an annual patch of corn, which is called "of the troops." The canton is fortified, and for some two or three blocks all around, the streets are straight and wide. In this region or district, there are no springs or wells; rather, they have grand *aguadas,* where they supply them-selves.[3] In times of drought they suffer because they have to go three, four, and even six leagues from their settlements for water.

Bacalar is the commercial port with the colony [of British Honduras], and it is maintained by 180 men, of which 150 come from Santa Cruz, 30 from Lochhá. They are relieved each month with great punctuality. The roads lead-ing to this place are excellent in the dry season because all around is a forest of stout trees; during the rainy season the roads are terrible, so much so that the beasts are regularly stranded there.

Although Bacalar is destroyed, it still has some houses that serve as bar-racks. The church exists. The fort is destroyed.[4]

The merchants who come to that point are all Yucatecans. There no Eng-lishman is to be seen. These merchants are subject to a thousand outrages because when some commodity is scarce and for that reason the price rises, they snatch it away, paying the accustomed price; but in return for this abuse, the merchants buy everything very cheaply

On another occasion I will be more explicit.

---

3. An *aguada* is a pool or small lake found in southern Quintana Roo and Campeche.

4. The fortress of San Felipe de Bacalar, originally constructed in 1727, was part of the Spanish Bourbon effort to increase defense capacities in its American colonies.

III

THE DEEP SOUTH

Belize, Guatemala, and the *Pacíficos*

Although Chan Santa Cruz continued to be home to some 25,000 Mayas, others chose to flee the violence. They fled southward, forming refugee communities in places such as northern Belize, southern Campeche, and the Petén district of Guatemala. The settlements in Belize closely resembled those in prewar Yucatán, partly because a significant number of Hispanic Yucatecans fled with the Mayas, bringing their old lifestyle based on sugar haciendas. In Campeche and the Petén, however, the refugee communities were predominantly or completely Mayan. In southern Campeche, these groups (often former rebels) were known as the pacíficos del sur. *Although in theory the* pacíficos *were loyal to the Hispanic governments in Mérida and Campeche, they won a reputation as prickly isolationists. The following documents illustrate both the continuities and the changes among Mayas in the refugee regions of the deep south.*

20

The Story of a Troubled Wedding

Amado Belizario Barreiro's Travels among the War Refugees in Guatemala

From 1848 onward a significant number of Caste War refugees flooded into the Petén, the northern district of Guatemala. Attempts to integrate them into the religious or political life of either Guatemala or Mexico were sporadic and unsuccessful, owing to the dispersed nature of their settlements, the difficulty of the terrain, and the not-unfounded fears and suspicions of the refugees themselves.

Documentation on the Mayas of these remote hamlets is thin, but there are occasional glimpses. In 1858 Padre Amado Belizario Barreiro, a Yucatecan priest sent to administer the Petén, visited the refugee communities while traveling to Flores, the district capital. His main purpose was to discipline two less-than-obedient priests who had been working in the region without the proper licenses. While carrying out this mission, he had the opportunity to visit the refugee communities, allowing him to make some observations on their religious customs. He also recorded the case of an unorthodox marriage involving a cacique of one of the hamlets. Padre Barreiro wrote virtually without punctuation; his long, breathless sentences have been subdivided here to enhance readability.[1]

Since reaching the first village of the Petén, some 100 leagues away from the town of Flores, I began my conquest because I found myself among pure rebel Indians who have taken refuge in this wilderness. They have been forming villages, and all have their churches, even though most are quite small. But they meet in these every morning and every night to say their rosaries and sing songs of praise to the Lord. Unfortunately, the majority have no other adornments than a number of crosses made from firewood.

I began to preach to them. I called them to the confessional, and because they had a bit of confidence, they began to confess themselves. They asked to perform a marriage. . . . Daily and nightly I would rise to go to the confessional at one or two, more or less, after confessing all day and all night, until I would go to my hammock, half dead. Here I could not sleep, even with the help of the

1. The source of the following material is Archivo Histórico de la Arquidiócesis de Yucatán (Mérida), Decretos y Oficios Box 38, 15 September 1858, Flores.

exhaustion that gripped my body, because of the fleas, cockroaches, pigs, dogs, and mosquitos, because in these parts doors and windows are unknown, so that I wearied of scratching myself and turning in my hammock.

Thereafter I began to wonder about the two priests, both simoniacs[2] and abandoned by the hand of God. . . . Padre Milán married the *cacique* of these parts in the streets under a bower, saying, "Do you receive as your wife, etc., etc.," and the same thing to the woman without confessing the two. This *cacique* was marrying a woman whose daughter was about to give birth to [a child of] the same *cacique*. And when the two married, the daughter went crying, "Padre, how can you marry my mother to this man when he promised to marry me, and for which reason I am disgraced?" The *cacique* ordered that the girl go away, saying, "You never told me that the bride was your mother. How dare you come to interrupt?" Nevertheless, and in spite of all this, Milán married the *cacique* to the girl's mother.

---

2. Simony is the sin of using the clerical office for personal profit; a simoniac is someone guilty of this sin.

21

The Methodist and the Mayas

Richard Fletcher's Ethnography

The Methodist missionary Richard Fletcher is an important but previously unexamined source on life in the refugee communities of northern Belize during the Caste War. He began his missionary work in Sierra Leone. In 1857 he was transferred to Corozal, British Honduras, where he served for some twenty-five years with his wife and five daughters. The Methodists had been developing a presence in British Honduras since the 1830s, but Fletcher was the first and virtually the only missionary to attempt to reach out to Yucatecan refugees, both Mayan and Hispanic.

Between 1854 and 1880, Fletcher wrote more than 140 letters describing conditions among the people of his area. The following document, the most important of his communications with the Wesleyan home office in London, is his description of the Maya peoples among whom he worked. Fletcher also promised to write a comprehensive account of Maya beliefs, but, much to the regret of the modern historian and ethnographer, this report was either lost or never completed. Nevertheless, the following letter, written on 30 December 1867, is a valuable depiction of Maya life in the wake of twenty years of warfare.

Several points recommend the inclusion of Fletcher's previously unexamined ethnography in this book. It constitutes one of the most far-reaching nineteenth-century attempts to capture Maya culture through writing. Fletcher identifies many of the key features of Maya life, including its dual orientation to the home and the milpa, *its basic material culture, aspects of its religious life, and a few broad brush strokes of recent Maya history. He also incorporates some of the vibrant hues of Maya folklore. At the same time, Fletcher's own predispositions shine through. These include his censorious disapproval of Catholicism, which he considered the universal root of evil; and his interest in phrenology, or the science of reading personality by studying the shapes of skulls. The Corozal manuscript is thus both an ethnography of the Mayas and an account of the nineteenth-century, English-Protestant-missionary mentality.[1]*

---

1. The source of the following material is Wesleyan Methodist Missionary Society Archives (London), microfiche, 30 December 1867, R. Fletcher, Corozal.

Corozal, December 30, 1867

Reverend & Dear Sirs,

At your request I will endeavor to give you some particulars respecting the Maya Indians. Corozal before the year 1847 was only a mahogany work. The Indians of Yucatán, rising against the government, spreading destruction on every hand, and destroying great numbers in a most barbarous manner, especially Spaniards, caused many to flee from the country and seek a place of safety and a home elsewhere. Many found their way to this part; they cleared away the bush and formed a town, to which additions were made for several years after by newcomers from Yucatán. In February 1858 the Indians routed a second time the inhabitants of Bacalar, who were loyal to the government of Mérida, consisting of Spaniards, Indians, & Africans; many were killed in the attack, many taken prisoners and afterwards killed, but those who managed to escape made their way to Corozal. The house we now occupy, on our first arrival we found filled with fugitives who had just arrived.

Corozal and neighborhood have a population of about four thousand Yucatecans, but in the colony, according to the census of 1861, there are about 13,000 of the Spanish and Indian races, who, with few exceptions, speak the Maya language and some of the Spanish as well. Many since their coming have advanced in the world, and more would have done so but for the gambling and other evil habits. Some Indians are employed on the sugar estates, and they are always thought of as very good laborers, giving very little problem to their employers when they once know their duty; but the greater portion of them are farmers on a small scale.

The early origins and history of the Indians are still mysterious, as no writing nor tradition exists among them; there can be no doubt but great numbers of Indians were formerly living in what is now British Honduras & especially in the northern part of it. The mounds, the heaps of loose stones overgrown by trees, the idols, & other Indian curiosities found serve to convince one that once a large population existed here. The mounds could only have been made by a people numbering tens of thousands, for some of them are about 70 feet high, with a base of as many feet and the top about 30 ft. On these mounds there seems to have stood some buildings reached by steps, & joining to it there seems to have been a large yard enclosed by walls and buildings; & within these walls the Indians met, no doubt, to worship their idols, & to witness the offering up of their sacrifices, & to take part in their national games and customs.

As the city with its temples existed at Petén less than 200 years ago . . . , it is almost certain that the buildings now in ruins here were about that time in a state of perfection; but the Indian *caciques,* priests, altars, & people have since disappeared from this soil, and till within 20 years back not an Indian was found living on this part of the land of his forefathers. The treatment the Indians received at the ruthless hands of the pale faced bearded man who took possession of his land & home, and deprived of his treasure & life, was such as makes the mind sad to contemplate. The heart grieves while the mind brings to view the past, the teeming population of other days, the wonderful buildings, & the skill of the aboriginal tribes, and contrasts it with the present condition of Yucatán, with its diminished, degraded, and miserable inhabitants.

Do we ask what has produced the desolation? Do we ask what the religion of the Spanish invaders, which they forced upon the Indians by the drawn dagger, has done for Yucatán? It has done everything but spread happiness. It is plain that papacy is not Christ's religion, is not the religion to advance and bless any people, or why has it not advanced Yucatán during the last 300 years? It has made Yucatán a shattered wreck. The ruined cities, the decreased population, the loss of civilization, and the prevailing ignorance and misery prove this. The religion that has blessed Fiji, and all people who are really happy on the face of the earth, is the religion that Yucatán needs, the religion of Christ as found in his word.

This is the appearance of the houses of the Indians present. The size of most is about 6 yards by 4 yards. Some are larger and some smaller. Eight hardwood posts are planted 3 ft. from the ground & stand about 6 ft. above the ground. When the house is large, more posts are required. The poles which may be regarded as the wall-plate are dropped into the open[ing] made at the end of each post. Both ends of the house are rounded. When the house is ready for putting on the leaf, it presents this appearance. The square in the roof of a well made house is about 12 in. and received, when well thatched, 7 & sometimes 8 leaves, and from inside looks like this. The bay leaf from a kind of palm tree is used for thatching. The thatching is commenced from the bottom of the rafters, which are thin poles, and each course of leave laps over the others. A part of the leaf is made to go over the cross stick fastened on the rafters and needs no tying. It is separated in this way at each side of the stem of the leaf. All the braces and principal rafters are got with prongs like this so as to be able to span the wall plate pole.

The houses of the Indians are erected without the use of a nail. Only wicks (*aak'*) are used to secure the poles together. They are very strong and durable and display much skill. The house we live in is not less than 16 years old, & the leaf is not yet worn out, & it has stood many a strong blowing. Indian houses are generally enclosed by poles stuck up side by side, & bay leaf put outside of them as on the roof. Some few plaster inside the poles, but Spaniards of means enclose with stone work. In an Indian house, there is no window but a door [on] each side of the house. What is used as a door are sticks fasted together with wicks and called *makab aak'*. Indians help each other in making their houses. The inside forms one room, there being no partition. They make no bed but sleep in hammocks (*k'áan*) made of string, which they hang across the house. Few houses have less than 3 and some have many more.

The cooking is done in the house; 3 stones form the hearth, which they call *k'óoben*. Each family has an iron pan or two and earthen pots (*kuum*) in which the corn is boiled, soup, &. They boil the corn before rubbing it, and in the water white lime is put. The stones are of this shape. A bench with long legs is used for putting them on. The woman stands at the end of the bench & takes hold of the round stone with both hands, & as the corn is rubbed between the two stones, it falls on the bench. After rubbing two or three times over, it is formed into a fine paste (*k'u'um*) & is ready to make corn cakes of. The iron on which the cakes are baked is about 10 inches in diameter & 5 inches thick. This is called *xamach*. Hammocks serve for chairs, but they have also little blocks of light wood to sit upon, which they make into different shapes (*k'áanche'*) about 9 inches high & 15 inches long. On one of these the woman sits while she makes the corn into round cakes & bakes them. The dining table agrees with the low seat; it is about 16 inches high, with a round top of 15 inches diameter & three legs stuck in it.

Small gourds serve for plates and cups, as they both eat & drink out of them. Large gourds holding 2 gallons are used instead of large basins; they have also pails. When traveling they carry their water in a gourd of this shape (*chúuj*). Gourds are cut through, serving as little boxes in which they keep things. When on a journey they put their hammock, clothes, &, in a thing of this shape, which they carry on their back; it is very light and keeps the water out. One of the youngest children sits on it and is tied to the back. It is platted of a kind of palm leaf, and one half laps over the other. They have a thing made of wicks hung from a beam on which they put their cornbread, called *peten aak'*. They have a few wooden bowls in which they wash clothes. The only thing remaining to be mentioned as regards the content of their houses is a kind of table, made sometimes of sticks, on which two or three crosses are placed.

The food in common use among the Indians is very soon told. They chiefly subsist on cornbread, which they dip into a kind of soup made of ground pumpkin seeds & chile or bean soup and chile. When they kill game, some of it is prepared with the soup. They seldom buy meat or kill a chicken or even make use of eggs, so that their food is not very nutritive. Plantains, yams, rice, & other vegetables they make very little use of themselves; they cultivate them on a small scale to sell. As a substitute for coffee, they roast corn, rub it on the stone, and pour boiling water on it, to which salt or sugar is added. This drink is called *k'eyem*. They make another drink of boiled rubbed corn, called *k'áaj*, and another of dry rubbed corn, called *sa'*. The same kind of diet was spoken of by the Spanish invaders, as now in use. The corn bread or cake is made of different thicknesses from $1/16$ to an inch thick, some hard & some soft. When hard and thin, it is called *sak pet waaj;* when soft and thin, *pok jaachbil waaj;* when $1/2$ inch to 1 inch thick, *pimpim waaj;* and when corn is cooked under the ground with fowl in it, [it] is *pibil xkaax;* when with pork, *pibil k'éek'en*. *Cháamcham* is a pastry they make of corn & meat or corn & beans. They have two meals a day, early in the morning & late in the afternoon, and by eating fruit or taking a little corn drink, they keep off hunger during the day.

Comparing the description of the dress of the Indians given by the invaders of their soil with what they now wear, there can have been but little change. The men wear a short white shirt outside their white cotton trousers or drawers (*eex*) & a straw hat and sandals, which completes their dress. The sandal is a piece of leather cut the size of the foot and, by cords from it fastened round the ankle, is secured to the foot.

The women wear a cotton chemise and a cotton shirt. A border of needle work consisting of a large flower or some other striking pattern is worked on the bottom of each of them, when for special use, and round the open cut in the chemise (*hipil*). The bottom of the skirt reaches nearly to the feet, but the chemise [stops] about 9 inches from the feet on the top of the skirt (or *piik*), and in this way 2 borders are formed. I enclose a specimen of one of the borders, which I got one of their school boys to paint. A small shawl is thrown over the head, which I suppose they have adopted from the Spanish; this they call *bóoch'*. The slippers, which only some of them wear occasionally, are made of cloth, silk, or satin; they are such as are worn by Spanish females. Some have earrings and other ornaments about the neck.

Neither men nor women have many changes of arrayment. The hair of women is tied in a ball behind the head. In hot weather the men sometimes sit in their houses without their shirts. I have heard Europeans say, who look only at the very white clothes on their backs, how very clean they are. A mistake, for under the bleached cotton, the skin is often anything but clean. They have no custom of oiling the skin, nor have they the custom of frequently washing it.

Bugs, fleas, chiggers (small fleas which bury themselves under the skin & make ulcers if allowed to remain there) abound in their houses. Having so few articles in them, it would be an easy matter to keep them clean and tidy, but all is disorder. The floor ground is seldom swept, and pigs, dogs, & fowls are allowed to go out at pleasure. Firewood, old bottles, stones, gourds, corn bags, corn sticks: all in confusion. The houses of Spaniards are not much better. If cleanliness & godliness go together, there is very little of the latter among them.

Indians, in their way, cultivate the soil to a considerable extent. Their farm, which is sometimes near the house & sometimes several miles distant, is called *kool*. If possible, they get fresh land every year for their corn and rice, which are the chief articles they cultivate. After the land has laid idle for several years & become covered with a thick bush, they clear and plant again. The corn is planted in the early part of June when the rains set in. About three months before this, they commence clearing the ground of its underbush, which becomes perfectly dry. At the end of May or beginning of June, fire is set to this mass of dry wood, which in a few hours is consumed, excepting a few large trunks.

During a heavy fall of rain, they commence putting in the corn. A hole is made in the ground by the pierce of a pointed stick, in which four grains of corn are thrown; they are made about a yard apart. In a few days the blades of green corn make their appearance, & when it has grown 2 or 3 feet high, the grass and underbush are weeded out. Nothing more is needed. In November the corn is ready to be harvested. Before the corn is ripe, while it is green & tender, the Indians begin to eat it, roasting or boiling it, but especially by making a kind of porridge of it, called *sa'*, of which they are very fond, and another kind with meat in it, called *k'óol*.

The rice, when gathered in, is hung from the roof of their houses in bundles. The corn is packed close together in a little house (*ch'il*) made for the purpose. The leaves then enfold the corn not being removed &, when kept dry, it does not spoil for a year or two. The Indians have a custom before eating or drinking any new corn themselves of taking some of the *sa'* to the farm for the lord of the land, whom they call *Balam*, or *yumil k'áax*. For a good crop & for success in shooting game and the like, they look to him. *Balam*, it is said, sometimes robs boys when following their father through the bush to the farm & that they, in their turns, become *Balams;* moreover, it is said that the *Balams* often make music at night in the bush.

The Indians do not generally build their houses together & form villages, but make them in the bush alone or two or three houses together. In Yucatán as many live in towns as on the small farms. And near to their houses they raise small quantities of beans, bananas, oranges, limes, arrowroot, pumpkins, squash, cassava, yams, & other vegetables. Families living near each other show their friendliness by often sending each other cooked food. The work of women is to rub corn,[2] cook, wash, & sew. Sometimes they go with their husbands to help them in the farm, in which the men employ themselves. A cutlass and an ax comprise their farming implements. With the cutlass they make holes in the ground & use no hoe, and also use it as a billhook. An Indian has generally his cutlass at his side when he stirs out of his house, & it is always at hand when in it. By their farming & raising poultry & great frugality, many of them have saved money, which they often bury in some secret place. If they die & leave it there, they have a notion that they will come back again to enjoy it.

Many are living together unmarried, & the married frequently leave their own wives & take those of other men. There are not many cases of polygamy, & fewer of infanticide. Indian families are not large. It is a rare thing to find 6 or 7 children belonging to the same family, more frequently 3 or 4. Children when young wear a shirt or chemise. When boys are about 7 years old, they wear cotton trousers; [at] 7 they begin to go with their father to the farm. Sometimes Indian parents beat their children very severely; at other times they frighten them to obey by threatening to take them into the bush [so] that some animal may eat them, at the same time tying their hands. When penitent, they are ordered to kneel before the crosses with their arms folded. Children are weaned when about 12 months old. With few exceptions, they grow up with large hard

---

2. I.e., to grind it.

bowels, the consequence of the indigestible food they eat, and many of them are killed by worms. Living away in the bush, they grow up almost without amusement and in entire ignorance, as there is no one to teach them, but those living in Corozal are more highly favored. Indians being professed Roman Catholics, their children have been baptized by the priests of that church, who make a charge of 4 pesos. The following are a specimen of their names: Juan Tsib (John Write), José Ek (Joseph Star), Manuel Pech (Emanuel Tick), Pedro Miis (Peter Cat), Isidore Che (Isidor Tree), Tomás Na (Thomas House), Bernabé May (Barnaby Hoof).

The sick are treated after their own stoical character. They acknowledge that sickness comes from God, & they wait for him to cure them, sometimes suffering for days & weeks without applying any remedy. Their remedies are generally herbs. Of drugs they have a dread, and they trust themselves more readily in the hands of an Indian herbist than the most skillful doctor. The attention a sick Indian receives is small even during the day, but the whole night long he is left very much to himself, even when in a dying state. If he cannot eat the corn bread, corn gruel is made for him, from which he seldom gets a change. They are reluctant to kill a chicken to make soup of, though they have plenty running about the house. I saw a sick Indian lately who was rich, but who seemed to value his money more than his life, and did not wish to spend any of it with a view to restore his health. Neither in sickness nor health do they put any pillow or cloth under their heads to preserve them from resting on the string of which their hammocks are made.

When it is seen that a father is at the point of dying, his children are brought to the side of his hammock that he may put his hand on their heads & give them his dying blessing. Two or three crosses are then laid on his breast, and a lighted candle held in his hand. After he is dead, leaves are put under him on the floor on which he is laid, & his arms are folded. If he has a change of clean clothes, they are put on. The bereaved friends then purchase a quantity of rum to give away to neighbors, who soon assemble. A wake is kept, & the whole night is spent in drinking & gambling. Such a mockery of death is most awful, of which Spaniards are alike guilty. Even in Corozal Spaniards have put the dead in a sitting posture near the table, as if engaged in card playing. A more Satanic occasion cannot be imagined than an Indian or Spaniard funeral wake.

Indians dying in their farms are buried without a coffin & without a priest officiating. When a priest buries anyone, it is service that must be paid for, and I am told that the lowest charge made in Corozal for burying an adult is 28 pence. With extras, for those who can pay for them, the charges soon run up to more than 4 pounds.

Maya Indians are not a race of large stature. An Indian 6 feet high is not often seen. Out of 12 men measured, the tallest was 5 feet 6$^1/_2$ inches, the average height being 5 feet 1$^3/_4$ inches. I have not been able to weigh them, but I am sure that but few of them weight 160 lbs. Corpulent Indians are nearly as rare as tall ones. Most are spare and sinewy and capable of great endurance. The neck is short, the shoulders square, the chest tolerably broad, & the bowels rather large. The feet are small, & the toes turn in. The head, which is round, is often covered by a mop-like mass of strong hair, very black, which is allowed to hang over the forehead, but those who live in town follow the custom of cutting the hair short. Many have no whiskers, & others a very little. The eyes are rather small & wide apart, black, and observant. The cheek bones being high, the chin and forehead small, the outline of the face is oval. The greater part have bold roman noses, but the profile is not vertical, as both the forehead and the chin slope back. (I mean the chin slopes off from the mouth to the neck.) The enclosed profiles will give you some idea. They are taken by casting the shadow of the face on the wall. I regret that I am not able to give you photographs, but at some future time, I hope to be able to send you some.

The aspect is somber and reserved, his melancholy features seem immovable, & whatever of passion he feels is concealed & not exhibited. According to phrenology, they possess much firmness and veneration; benevolence and the intellectual faculties are not very largely developed, but destructiveness & secrecy are. They are very stubborn and hard to move when once they fix their mind to a certain course of action. Still, they have good abilities, as is displayed in the case of those who have had opportunities of learning trades. Indian scholars, I find, possess quick memories; they apply themselves diligently to their lessons & make good progress on learning. Their complexion is copper colored, but I have observed some of a darker shade than others. This was noted by the early Spaniards.

They are not long lived. The average life must be very short. Old people are rare among them. From 40 to 50 years of age, they begin to look old. From their disregard to health, hard drinking, night exposure at wakes, & other causes, their constitution is early broken up, & they pass away before they have lived out half their days. I have been pained to witness how few and evil their days are. Very few, indeed, are to be found who are 70 years old. Since writing the above, I have noticed the census of 1861 with regard to the age of the different races in this Colony, & I find that in every thousand Yucatecans (Indians & Spaniards), there are 4 persons of 70 years & upwards, but in every thousand of the colored people, there are more than 40 of 70 & more years.

The Indians living on British territory are very quiet and well behaved, and if it were not for their feasts & wakes, when drink is freely given away, we should seldom, if ever, hear of any act of violence committed by them; but on such occasions when nearly everyone gets drunk, quarrels arise, cutlasses are sometimes used, & evil is done.

They profess the Roman Catholic religion, & most of them have crosses in their houses, but their knowledge of divine truth is very limited, and their mind is wrapped in darkness. This is not to be wondered at. It would be strange if it were otherwise. They have grown up without instruction, crosses have been put before them instead of good books in their own language, and when they attend the services in the romish church, they understand nothing of the prayers, being in Latin, nor of the sermon, being in Spanish, except by here and there one who has learned a little Spanish. They stand like horses & know no more than a horse would, as one of them once expressed himself to me. As a result of their false religion, truth is trifled with, lying is common, & to break their word is nothing thought of. Other sins prevail among them, but this noble race, under the influence of a preached gospel in their own tongue, are capable of better things.

They seemed to have no idea how their forefathers worshiped their idols, but in some other letter, I will endeavor to give you such information as can be collected about their present superstitions & charms, their notions of witch-craft, their mode of divination, and also something about their herb medicines. I have been fortunate in obtaining two clay idol[s]; one is quite perfect. The arms and legs of the larger one are broken, also the nose, a part of the crown, and the collar round the neck (the back part of it). It seems as if stained with blood, particularly the face. I enclose drawings of them.

Though a few families are all that generally live together in many different parts of the bush, yet many live in villages with Spaniards & Ladinos[3] (Spanish Indians), forming villages with Yucatecans. The following is about a visit to one of their villages containing 300. In the afternoon of Nov. 24, I rode to a place nine miles distant, accompanied by Mr. Núñez. We found one of the priests there, who in the morning had been scolding them for having attended Protestant preaching since his last visit. We at once went among the people, borrowed the house in which I have generally preached, and invited them to attend. A bell was sent round by the priest to announce that there would be a procession. The priest seated himself at the door of the next house in which I was to preach that he might see who attended &, if possible, prevent them. Those who had generally attended showed that they appreciated the preaching & were not to be hindered from doing so, neither by the priest's presence, scolding, nor curse.

We had just finished our service as the procession passed along the street, which was made up [of] a few women, 3 or 4 men & some children. They stopped at the crossing of a street near[by], when the priest addressed the people in Spanish & wished those who had attended the preaching also to hear, shouting in a loud voice "that the Yucatecans were shameless, or they would not attend Protestant preaching." Fewer than usual attended our preaching, but we had more men than were with the procession & out of the most influential

---

3. *Ladino* was a Central American term originally designating a person of indigenous ancestry who had ceased to live the indigenous, community-based lifestyle. Over time it came to refer to anyone identified as non-Indian. Common in Guatemala, the term was rarely used in the Yucatán Peninsula.

in the village, most of whom accompanied me down the street in the opposite direction & waited till we got our horses ready & started. The priest has publically declared that there is now no morality in the village because they now know better than [to] pay for mass or go to confession.

Three weeks since in another part, among Indians only, I held a very interesting service. About 40 men, women, and children came from their scattered homes, & I could see that they were pleased with the service & drank in the words of truth. After the arrival of Mr. Giolma, we shall be able to visit these places more frequently, & I am sure we shall be made a blessing to them. I may make a remark here to show why more has not been done. It is true we regard this as an Indian & Spanish mission, yet, being the only missionary living in this part of the colony, I have had to employ a large portion of my time in preaching to the English-speaking people and in daily teaching the children of these nations.

The Indians living in Yucatán have manners and customs which those living under British rule do not practice, such as [those that] relate to war, plunder, treatment of enemies, & the infliction of punishment on offenders. There is a large body of Indians at Santa Cruz, about 60 leagues from here & nearly the same distance from Mérida, the capital of Yucatán. They do not number less than ten thousand & live principally by plunder. All the men & boys act as soldiers, & it seems from what I hear, they are always glad to go on expeditions of plunder, as they share in the spoil. Yes, boys of 10 & 12 years of age are sent "to play at killing," as an Indian said the other day who was talking to me about them. The cruelties they practice, especially on Spaniards, are as diabolical as man can be guilty of. And yet, it is a just retribution of providence on Spaniards for the cruel treatment the Indians suffered at their hands. Just before the Indian insurrection 20 years ago, as I have heard the Spaniards admit, the poor Indians were robbed of their labor, flogged, enslaved, & ground to the earth to support lazy & profligate Spanish masters. Now the Indian is getting the upper hand, & he is likely to maintain it. One of the Commandants of the Indians of Santa Cruz, who called to see [me] some four months ago, said that for 20 years they had held their independence, & clenching his fists, he declared that they would still hold it.

They worship the cross, but they have no priest among them. It is said they have a cross that speaks, and the Indian who interprets is called *tatich,* and whatever the cross commands is done. Though they have such intense hatred to[ward] the Spaniard, it is remarkable that their president is one: Bonifacio Novelo, who was elected by the Indians after they had killed Puc, who was their chief. But the two generals who govern with him are Indians, Bernabé Cen & Crescencio Poot. I am told that they are all very cruel and tyrannical men. A small crime of disobedience to authority is punished with death, which is inflicted by chopping up with a cutlass. It is a great risk to any stranger to venture among them, but I hope the day is not distant when we shall be able to go

to Santa Cruz to do them good. I have told some of their captains who have visited Corozal that I would visit them if they would not force me to drink & kiss
their crosses, which I hear all have to do. I have enclosed two articles from the
paper published in this colony, which throw some light on these Santa Cruz
Indians and how they are regarded here by the merchants & others, for and
against.

(January 3/68) Yesterday I fortunately met with a book called "Memorias del
Secretario General del Gobierno del Estado de Yucatán, 1862,"[4] from which I
give the following facts respecting the population of that state.

Total Population	248,156
Of the white race (Spanish & Spanish Indians)	88,020
(Of these, 39,437 are males; the females are	
9,146 more than the males.)	
Of the Indian race	160,136
(There are 7,252 Indian females more than males.)	
Total number of females in Yucatán more than males	16,398
Nearly 6½ per cent more.	
It is considered that 7 to 8,000 of the white race, out of	
the total males [of] 39,437, are fit to take arms.	
White race living in the towns, cities, forts	68,102
Indians " " "	80,335
White race living in rural places	19,918
Indians " " "	79,801

Out of the total population of 248,156, only 8,142 can read and write (I have
seen specimens of their best writing, and they are certainly very poor writers),
being 3.28 per cent. If the reading & writing [percentage is] restricted to the
white race, [then it is] 9 ¼ per cent. Of the 99,719 who live in rural places on
the small farms (white race, 19,918; Indian race, 79,801), not one percent can
read (0.92). Here we have a view of what popery, dark ignorance loving popery,
has done for the instruction of Yucatán.

The following excerpt will interest you. "From the census of the State taken
in the current year, of which I give you the particulars in the present 'Memorias,' it is ascertained that of the total population, only 3.28 per cent know how
to read and write. It is clearly seen from this fact the neglect and abandonment
which there has been of elementary instruction during our fifty years of independence. This in part is palliated by the bad customs in which the colonial

---

4. The document to which Fletcher refers is *Memoria del Secretario General del Estado de
Yucatán* (Mérida: José Dolores Espinosa, 1862). A copy of this document is included in Crescencio Carrillo y Ancona, ed., *Documentos interesantes del Estado de Yucatán, 1851-1902* (unpublished collection), which is archived in the Centro de Apoyo a la Investigación Histórica de
Yucatán.

government left our education and by the malignant supervision, more or less to the present time, of a clergy greedy and covetous of riches, acquired from the ignorance of the people, shielded by the holy books and ceremonies of a religious worship which is only turned to their own benefit, concerning themselves but little about the true worship of God & the real good of their flock." A little further on is the following, which is also a credit to the writer: "We ought to consider the want of this education a greater evil than the war of castes."

The State in 1862 consisted of 4 cities, 8 towns, 171 villages, 1,049 estates, 856 small farms. These, compared with the census of 1846, are less by 24 villages, 216 estates, & 817 small farms. In some of the existing towns & villages, there is but a fraction of their former population. The decrease in the population during the 16 years is given as 184,386. It is the opinion of the most intelligent Spaniard here, who was formerly secretary of the State & who still knows much of its affairs, that the population now is not more than 200,000.

Things in Yucatán are growing worse year by year, & unless God in his providence interpose[s] on their behalf, Spaniards & Indians within the next 50 years will nearly all have passed away. May God's people at home pray for them & for the other doomed States of Central America. On our border we hear of Indians fighting with Indians, & within the last fortnight, Indians belonging to those of Santa Cruz have taken from British territory, within 20 miles of Corozal, about 50 peaceable Indians—men, women, & children & their property. The day after Christmas day a party of 30 armed Indians came within a quarter of a mile of Corozal & were taking away 5 Indian men as prisoners. The magistrate, hearing of this, informed the captain in command of the soldiers, who followed them & captured 13 & also brought back the prisoners. The soldiers just the week before came from Belize out of the way of the cholera, which I am sorry to say is raging there, or things would have been worse. More soldiers came this morning with large guns. A communication has been sent from the Governor to Santa Cruz. How things will turn is hard to say, but forbearance cannot be exercised toward them much longer. This I know, that Indians living 4 & 6 miles away from Corozal at night leave their houses & sleep in the bush for fear of the plundering Indians taking them by surprise.

I wish to live for the good of these Indians, & I intend to labor to bring many of them into the fold of Christ. I remain

Your obedient servant,
Richard Fletcher

22

"Sweet Idleness"

Alfredo Giolma on the Corozal Community

Alfredo Giolma was another Methodist missionary who worked with Caste War refugees in northern Belize. Years of residence on the island of Gibraltar had given him a fluent command of Spanish, and he seemed a likely choice to assist Richard Fletcher in Corozal. After several months (1869–70) in this community, however, the two men fell into a bitter quarrel. Giolma abandoned Methodism, became an Anglican priest, and, much to Fletcher's chagrin, returned to Corozal to minister to the Spanish-speaking populations.

On 29 October 1868, before his defection, Giolma wrote the following letter to the Wesleyan Methodist Missionary Society's home office in London. Although he lacks Fletcher's extensive experience and flair for ethnographic reporting, Giolma reveals engaging details about life among the Yucatecan refugees. One gets the impression that Giolma was not terribly enamored of the people he proposed to save.[1]

After the writing of the enclosed report,[2] I have thought it well to add to it, as it were, a few things about the life and morals of the people among whom we are laboring. As to the whole life of the people here, it bears in a great measure the impress of the Italian saying *il dolce far niente*.[3] They never hasten busily through the roads as it is done, for example, in London or Paris. Their time is never to be taken up with anything at all, but in gambling, drinking, and in laying in their hammocks as much as they possibly can. The females lead the most hothouse life that European[s] could imagine.

Between twelve and one o'clock, a kind of dinner is eaten, which chiefly consists of *tortillas* and *frijoles*. The first are a kind of pastry made of ground corn in the shape of a thin disk as large as a plate, white and quite tasteless. *Frijoles* are little black beans, which they mix up with every kind of stew they make and which, when nicely cooked, make a very nice and tasty food. Besides,

---

1. The source of the following material is Wesleyan Methodist Missionary Society Archives (London), microfiche, 29 October 1868, A. Giolma, Corozal.

2. The report to which Giolma refers concerns internal matters related to missionary operations and has been omitted here.

3. "Sweet idleness." I extend special thanks to Corinne Pernet for clarifying this point.

we have also the *tamales,* which consist of a ragout of fowl prepared with *chile* (a kind of pepper)[4] and tomatoes, or as they are called here, apples of paradise, which once in the mouth, it burns almost forever.

As to the religion of this people, it consists in having in their homes a little altar and many pictures of saints, crosses, and crucifixes. There are many of the Indians, especially those that come from "Chan Santa Cruz," who believe that the cross, a wooden cross, speaks. I think the words of the Apostle to the Athenians are most applicable to this people here. The moral state of the whole place is very low, and it must be so until the influence of [the] Gospel is felt by them.

The climate here is not so hot as it is in Belize [City]. Here is always a nice breeze from the sea—the trade winds—which cools both the place and the people. It is only about mid-day when it is excessively hot. . . . As to the Maya language, I find it quite difficult, especially in the pronunciation of the following letters: ɔ, k, pp—, th—, tz.[5] These letters are very difficult to pronounce, and some time is required before a foreigner is able to master them.

---

4. Giolma refers to the *habanero* chile.

5. The letters shown by Giolma represent orthographic conventions devised by the Franciscan missionaries to capture spoken Maya in written form. The style was continued with the introduction of printing presses in Central America in the nineteenth century. I have left the letters in the original orthography. These sounds are as follows:

Original Orthography	Modern Orthography	Pronunciation
ɔ	ts'	glottal ts
k	k'	glottal k
pp	p'	glottal p
th	t'	glottal t
tz	ts	nonglottal t

23

"This Flower of All Things Beautiful"

A Speech to the Emperor

In the years 1862–67, a French army occupied Mexico, imposing as its figurehead emperor the unfortunate Maximilian, younger brother of the Austro-Hungarian ruler Franz Joseph. In southeastern Mexico, the states of Campeche and Yucatán surrendered to French forces in 1863, and in the following year they were consolidated under the administration of a single imperial commissar, or regional governor. Maximilian's rule enjoyed few successes, but it did make some tentative efforts to win the loyalty of Mexican peasantry.

On 28 January 1865, a group of Maya pacíficos were brought from southern Campeche to Chapultepec Castle in Mexico City to have an audience with Maximilian. During their brief time with him, they delivered the following speech. It was subsequently reprinted in the Mérida newspaper El periódico oficial, along with an inexact Spanish translation. I have retranslated their speech in a manner more faithful to the original text. The version shown below captures some of the elaborate ceremonial language that the nineteenth-century Mayas used in more formal speech and correspondence.[1]

Sir and great king: The glory of your name has reached even to the dense forests where we live and to all the land of the reign of your great esteemed honor. We assure you, great king, that if we chose to live in the forest, never knowing submission to a single government of Mérida, it is because we have never seen even one ruler who dignifies us with love like your great esteemed honor.

What is done, sir, is that we have come to submit to your great beloved honor, and [for that reason] it does not frighten us that we pass over so much land and cross so much ocean,[2] we who have never once chosen to leave the place where we were born.

Receive this flower of all things beautiful,[3] because thus we know and thus we commend you to our lord of the heavens and the earth, beloved of God.

---

1. The source of the following material is Hemeroteca Pino Suárez (Mérida), *El periódico oficial,* 15 February 1865, 3.

2. Before the mid-twentieth century, there was no road connecting Yucatán with central Mexico. The Maya representatives would have had to travel to the port of Sisal, take a boat to Veracruz, and travel overland to Mexico City.

3. *El periódico oficial* renders this phrase as *tuláakal uf,* clearly a mistake because the letter *f* does not exist in Maya. The correct rendering is almost certainly *uts,* meaning "good," "beautiful," etc.

24

"No People Is Like Them"

Maya Rebels Visit the Corozal Community

The relationship between the Mayas of Chan Santa Cruz and the settlers in northern Belize remained problematic. These two accounts, each by missionary Richard Fletcher but written four years apart, capture different aspects of interethnic relationships on the Mexico-Belize frontier.

Both letters describe visits that Chan Santa Cruz leaders made to Corozal. The first visit occurred in late 1869, when the southeast was once again in a state of armed conflict. Mérida and Campeche had recently liberated themselves from the Empire, a French-imposed puppet state that drew heavily upon Mexican conservatives as a base of support. The imperialists had invested a great deal of their political capital in the proposed reconquest of the rebel Mayas, and their eventual fall in the first six months of 1867 had much to do with their failure to complete that project.

The Empire's collapse, however, left much turbulence in its wake. In Chan Santa Cruz, veteran leader Bonifacio Novelo had recently died (May 1868), and his two surviving associates, Crescencio Poot and Bernabé Cen, were vying for supremacy between themselves while also struggling to gain the upper hand with the pacífico *communities of southern Campeche. At this time, the danger of imminent warfare was in everyone's mind, and the visit of Bernabé Cen, regarded as the most warlike of the generals, sparked panic. Among other details, the 1869 letter illustrates Fletcher's attempt to broaden the Maya leaders' horizons and reveals the ceremonial pecking order within the Chan Santa Cruz military ranks (specifically, who ate first).*

The second and briefer letter, written in 1873, depicts a much more relaxed scene. Although power struggles continued both in Yucatán and among the Mayas, the larger regional conflicts had begun to subside, and average people were able to concentrate once more on subsistence and trade.

A STRESSFUL VISIT FROM BERNABÉ CEN, 1869[1]

We are again in the midst of excitement and alarm produced by the notorious Indians of Santa Cruz. On the night of the 19th, a number of these armed Indians went to Consejo[2] & took a man and his wife and such of their things as they thought worth taking and carried them to Bacalar, where generally about 200 Indian soldiers are stationed 30 miles distant from this. A trader from Consejo, being there at the time they arrived, succeeded in purchasing the liberty of the woman, but the man was carried on to Santa Cruz, where it is expected he has been killed after their fashion. A little while since, in the presence of the Santa Cruz Indians, this man called them a set of robbers, etc.

Things are now quite upset; and as we have no soldiers here and no prospect of getting any, . . . no one here feels safe, and especially since the Indians have said that they intend to come to Corozal for about 20 Spaniards, whom they say have offended them. Many Spaniards and Indians have gone out of the [area], and many more are going.

About 2 months since, a number of Indians paid a visit to Corozal, consisting of officers, about 50 soldiers, & their head chief Bernabé Cen, whose name is associated with indescribable horrors. They went about the streets armed, contrary to the wishes of the magistrate, who had no power to enforce order. They bought a large quantity of gunpowder and other articles. I went to see them several times and spoke to their chief about the good that would result to his people if he would allow a missionary to go work among them. I told him that I should like to go and preach to them and teach their children. He did not give me much encouragement, but he called to see [me], accompanied by many others.

The son-in-law of Cen, a young captain, I was glad to find could read fluently both in Spanish and Maya. He read some of our translations to the chief, who approved of what he heard & wished to take some of the books with him. In addition to Maya books, I gave him Bibles and other books in Spanish. Knowing that they have an idea that no people is like them, I gave them a volume of the *British Workman* & a volume of the *Illustrated London News,* which happened to contain many views of soldiers on the battlefield.

Cen had his heavy cutlass by his side, which a day or two before I had in my hands, as it was attached to a green cotton scarf made at Santa Cruz, which he handed [to] me to see. He and his officers were breakfasting together at the time on thin corn cakes, a little meat, which looked like deer, and a preparation of corn to drink. They had . . . only a calabash, which contained their substitute for coffee. What they left was handed to others of lower rank.

---

1. The source of the following material is Wesleyan Methodist Missionary Society Archives (London), microfiche, 30 November 1869, R. Fletcher, Corozal.

2. I.e., Punta Consejo.

MELLOWER TIMES, 1873[3]

The Indians from Santa Cruz in Yucatán, nearly 200 miles from here and where some 30 thousand of them are living, frequently come to Corozal to trade, in numbers from 20 to 60.[4] I have had an opportunity of preaching to some of them, and as there is a very good feeling existing between the English and them, we may often have the privilege of doing them some good. A person living here who acts as a kind of consul for them has been sick for two months, & he has received my visits gladly. He has generally a number of Indians staying with him, which on my visits I am thrown amongst; in this way, I am becoming acquainted with them, & they with me.

---

3. The source of the following material is Wesleyan Methodist Missionary Society Archives (London), microfiche, 7 November 1873, R. Fletcher, Corozal.

4. Like John Carmichael, Fletcher tends to exaggerate distances; ninety miles is closer to the mark.

25

"Waiting for the State to Remember Them"

Salvador Valenzuela Visits the Petén Mayas

The Petén remained the home of Yucatec Maya refugee communities for decades after Amado Belizario Barreiro's visit in 1858. The world around them, however, began to change. In 1871 Justo Rufino Barrios overthrew the old Conservative government of Guatemala and set up a new Liberal system that emphasized commercial export agriculture (principally coffee) and the reduction of communal Indian rights. As part of his national development program, Barrios sent Salvador Valenzuela to the Petén in 1879 as Inspector of Agriculture. His travels took him to the Maya communities that had formed along the roads leading to Yucatán in the northern part of the district.

Ultimately the Petén failed to share in the emerging coffee economy. Valenzuela's report, however, remains an important testimony to the nature of life in this region during the late nineteenth century. His distance from the early years of the Caste War led him to make some mistakes of history, but his observations on the lifestyle, economy, and attitudes of this heavily Maya region still merit attention.[1]

Toward the north, along the road to Yucatán and throughout an area of some 80 to 100 leagues, one finds the villages of Chuntuquí, San Felipe, Concepción, Yaxché, Santa Cruz, San Antonio, Tankach-Ahal, Dolores Xtanché, Santa Clara, Conhaus, Silvituc, Bolon Petén, Tubucil, and Nohbecán. These fourteen villages are known only to merchants who travel the road to Yucatán. Their inhabitants come from that state and are Indians who have fled because of the wars from 1853 onward.[2] They have formed without the protection of the [Guatemalan] authorities. These Indians are hardened and restless and are accustomed to living in total independence; and the authorities of the Petén have also become accustomed to fearing them. For this reason none of the

---

1. The source of the following material is Salvador Valenzuela, "Informe sombre el departamento del Petén, dirigido al Ministerio de Fomento," reprinted in *Anales de la Sociedad de Geografía e Historia* 24, no. 4 (1951): 397–410.

2. A mistake on Valenzuela's part; the wars began in 1847.

corregidores of the past government, the *jefes políticos* of the current era, have dared to visit them, their hostile character being much exaggerated.[3]

However, I have managed to pick up certain facts about their situation and have been informed that every year they come to the head town to report on the election of *alcaldes*[4] and on the pitiful tax revenues they collect; they even bring insignificant sums, which they charge *ad libitum*[5] on *aguardiente,* gunpowder, and other products which come from Belize. In addition, some travelers inform me that in these villages one can find every sort of assistance in accommodations, supplies sold at extremely low prices, young men working as porters, and so forth. They cultivate corn, beans, yams, some vegetables, and tobacco that is both well-cleaned and well-cured, and they sell these things in Yucatán or to those passing through the villages. They are very much given to raising hogs and domestic fowl, which items they possess in abundance; among them one also finds cattle, relatively rare in those parts.[6] They also trade with Belize, where they obtain clothes, arms, gunpowder, and *aguardiente.*

All this makes me realize that the authorities here exaggerate the risks to be run if they try to extend political control over the refugees. Undoubtedly an annual visit from the *jefes políticos,* without use of force, treating those Indians kindly and skillfully, will result in their eventual, if not rapid, organization. Those Indians are undoubtedly waiting for the state to remember them. When the *jefe político* issued a circular announcing the visit that I was planning to make, they prepared to receive me and proceeded to clear the roads; this indicates that there is not such a hostility on their part against the established authorities.

---

3. The *jefe político,* or "political chief," was an administrative official immediately below the governor (or, in the case of Guatemala, the president), who was charged with overseeing the political activities of a *jefatura política,* or district, each of which comprised several municipalities. This political structure became universal in Mexico from 1835 onward. The *jefe político* was often a vehicle for imposing authoritarian rule from above and was finally abolished in the wake of the 1910 revolution.

In Guatemala, however, the term *corregidor* was used during the colonial period and under the rule of Rafael Carrera (1838–65), the Conservative dictator to whom Valenzuela refers in the phrase "the past government." Borrowing from the Mexican model, *jefe político* became the new term for the same position under the Liberal governments from 1871 onward. At any rate, Valenzuela erred because numerous officials had visited the Maya refugee communities during the 1850s and 1860s.

4. The *alcalde* was a town mayor. The head town to which Valenzuela refers was Flores, the capital of the Petén district.

5. "At will."

6. Cattle raising was the principal industry of *peteneros* before the rise of chicle cutting in the late nineteenth century. The brands used by the Maya refugees are listed in the massive register of 1873, found in the Archivo General de Centroamérica in Guatemala City.

26

"Strange to the Century in Which We Live"

Three Accounts of Life among the *Pacíficos*

One legacy of the French intervention in southeastern Mexico was a prolonged initiative to bring the autonomous communities of pacified Mayas once again under the control of church and state. The first missionaries dedicated to this cause arrived in 1865, and they remained in the region at least until 1869, when renewed warfare made their presence untenable. The three missionary letters reproduced here explore various aspects of the pacíficos lives, including their religion, population, political authority, and water usage. Written during the height of the French Empire's control over southeastern Mexico, the letters also make occasional references to the new order.

The first two letters deal primarily with the missionaries' plans and activities, not the lives or culture of their intended subjects. Buried within them, however, are several intriguing observations, particularly regarding problems of water and political authority, all of which are found in the excerpts reproduced below. The third letter, by missionary Juan Bautista Aguilar, unquestionably provides the richest ethnography and is therefore reproduced in full. The missionary correspondence highlights the mixed sentiments of the pacíficos: to dissociate themselves from the Caste War by claiming (at least titular) allegiance to the Mexican church and state, but also to conserve their autonomy as much as possible.

LETTER OF JUAN DE LA CRUZ CAMAL[1]

Parish of Maxcanú, 26 January 1866, Juan de la Cruz Camal

I had been appointed to provide spiritual care to the pacified Indians of the South, and to that end I departed from [Mérida] at the end of last April, bound for Mesapich with my companion, Padre Juan Bautista Aguilar. We arrived on 4 May. On the way we reached Noh-ayín, the first of their cantons, at 7:00 P.M. on the third day, when I found its inhabitants united in a procession dedicated to the Immaculate Conception. We took advantage of the opportunity and

---

1. The source of the following material is Archivo Histórico de la Arquidiócesis de Yucatán (Mérida), Asuntos Terminados 15, 26 January 1866.

immediately explained to them why we had arrived and what was our mission there: namely, to teach them the obligation that all men have to God, to themselves, and to their fellow men; and to guide them to the path of virtue.

LETTER OF PEDRO JOSÉ SÁNCHEZ LÓPEZ[2]

Ecclesiastical Commission to the Indian Tribes of the South,
Noh-ayín, 21 February 1866, Pedro José Sánchez López

Since September 20 of the past year, when by your order I arrived to assume responsibility for the spiritual administration of these tribes, I came to see that the work of the commission could not limit itself to the purely formal activities of our ministry. For although it is true that the divine Religion to which we are unworthy ministers exerts its salutary influence upon civil society, . . . the same cannot be said of the South, where everything is anomalous and irregular. Their government (if such a term can apply to the barbarous regime that they follow), their lives, customs, inclinations, habits, nature, and character, all are exceptional and strange to the century in which we live. For this reason, I have found it indispensable to extend our efforts into new areas. . . .

With respect to the numerous tribes or families that live dispersed throughout the woods: so that they may associate, join together, and form large populations in order to enjoy in this manner the advantages of society, the commission has labored a great deal. But on one hand, they are accustomed to this sort of life and fear the incursions of the eastern Indians. On the other hand, the lack of water obliges them to search for water holes and to cluster around them. To my mind, the place that promises the greatest hopes for settlement is the canton of Xmabén, where cisterns abound (known under the Maya name of *chultunes*[3]), in which rainwater collects as it comes down from the surrounding hills. In this regard, and taking advantage of circumstances, namely, a horrific event that came to the attention of the commission, we wrote to General Don José Antonio Uc, commander of that canton, posing to him some serious reflections over an affair that might have been avoided if he had kept his followers in sight.

One person of this *partido* (Xmabén), who, like many others, had his home in the deep woods, in a fit of madness or for who knows what reason, killed his wife and children with a machete. Then, after burning down the house with the bodies inside, he hid in the woods to escape the consequences; and he could only be brought to justice by hunting him down, like some wild beast. For this reason, and (thanks be to God) heeding my advice, the town's chief has given orders that all the families living dispersed in the woods be resettled

---

2. The source of the following material is Archivo Histórico de la Arquidiócesis de Yucatán, Asuntos Terminados 15, 21 February 1866.

3. From the Maya *ch'uul tuun,* or "wet stone." A number of these devices for storing rainwater can be seen at archaeological sites, such as Uxmal and Chichén Itzá.

around the plaza of Xmabén. And, in fact, they *are* being resettled by soldiers who have the responsibility of carrying out these orders.

Because of their large *aguadas,* Noh-ayín and Can-akal offer the same hope, all the more if circumstances allow the paternal government of his excellency the Commissar to carry out his plans in a constructive manner.[4] I have said that the Commission ordinarily operates out of Mesapich because it is the center of the other cantons. But it is almost certain that this summer its residents will relocate to Noh-ayín or Xmabén because during this season Mesapich suffers from a severe shortage of water. To my mind, Xmabén would be the most appropriate as the head of the parish.[5]

LETTER OF JUAN BAUTISTA AGUILAR[6]

Izamal, 20 August 1866, Juan Bautista Aguilar

[The South] is the name of that part of the peninsula inhabited by the *indios pacíficos.* It covers 15 square leagues, excluding two cantons removed by a considerable distance: the first fifteen leagues away and the second 70, both being situated to the southwest of Mesapich, the southern center.

This land is fertile and well suited to sugar cane, rice, and tobacco, somewhat less so to corn and cotton. It suffers from a complete lack of springs, and the inhabitants are limited to the rainwater that collects in artificial repositories, which the prehistoric inhabitants of the peninsula bequeathed to posterity. The region is filled with the ruins of colossal monuments, which testify to the genius of these ancient peoples.

The new settlers are the enemies of all society because they live dispersed throughout the forests, so much so that there is almost a different settlement for every family. In the entire south there are only two cantons where one finds a number of families gathered together, and these are Noh-ayín and Xmabén. Each probably has sixty loosely organized households, more or less.

According to my calculation, all the inhabitants, including women and children, add up to about 25,000, while the number of men suitable for military service is at most 4,000. But not all of these have arms, nor can they form battalions or substantial columns, owing to the lack of discipline and the insubordination they show to their leaders. They are naturally cowards and not much inclined to war, the proof of this being that they never retaliate for the

---

4. The Imperial Commissar of the peninsula was José Salazar Ilarregui. Up to the time this letter was written, imperial policy had been based on a military campaign against Chan Santa Cruz, coupled with the gradual insinuation of Mexican political authority among the *pacíficos.* Neither aspect of the plan came to fruition, and, in fact, by the time of this letter, Ilarregui found himself fending off almost constant rebellions.

5. Parishes (*parroquias*) were divided into head towns (*cabeceras*) and outlying communities (*sujetos* or *auxiliares*).

6. The source of the following material is Archivo Histórico de la Arquidiócesis de Yucatán (Mérida), Asuntos Terminados 15, 20 August 1866.

invasions that they have suffered at the hands of the eastern Indians, whose victims they have been.

Their government is democratic, and they practice the principles of liberty and equality. They elect their leaders, but these scarcely have any authority to punish individual misdeeds because in civil and political matters, the voice of the people is the only sovereignty. The leaders remain in power and govern according to the whims of their subjects, while those who have tried to rule by themselves have been removed and in some cases assassinated. These people are very keen on their independence from the white race, to the extreme of preferring the woods of the Petén rather than subjecting themselves to the Empire. They pay no form of tax or levy, nor do any of the functionaries, even the governor, enjoy any sort of salary.[7]

The southern cantons that have communications with our own towns are Lochhá, 27 leagues south of Peto; Macanché, 20 leagues southeast of Tekax; Noh-ayín, nine leagues east of Iturbide; and Xmabén, 20 leagues east of Dzibalchén. These are the areas through which the government should send its forces when it wants to reconquer the Indians, without forgetting their road of retreat, which leads from Icaiché all the way to San Antonio in the Petén. Such a project would require a thousand men and should be carried out in a single stroke.

This campaign is indispensable for the prosperity and civilization of the country. The reason is that the area serves as a lair for the deserters, thieves, escaped servants, and every sort of criminal, who by emigration have increased ever more the size of the South, while at the same time depleting our own population and consequently weakening the power of the government.

They carry on an unfettered commerce with Belize, Tekax, and Campeche. From the first of these places, they commonly import cloth and gunpowder, but they export nothing of their own. They travel overland until reaching a place known as Corozal, from which they sail for Belize, although they can travel by land as far as the Hondo River, then sail to the same place. Their commerce with Tekax and Campeche is in reality barter. The hard currency found here is brought by whites, who come to buy hogs, lard, and tobacco, which they take away in considerable quantities; and it is worth noting that the whites even supply themselves with gunpowder here because it is sold more cheaply than elsewhere. The *pacíficos* profess the Catholic religion and respect its ministers, but among them one can find certain vestiges of idolatry and beliefs contrary to the dogmas of the church. Their medicine men heal by means of a crystal, which they call *saastun*, a talisman through which they pretend to see and cure the diseases. These men are little more than imposters who have invented such

---

7. It is not entirely clear to whom Aguilar refers when he mentions *el gobernador*. The term apparently denotes an individual whom the Yucatecan authorities recognized as head of all the *pacíficos*, but judging from his previous comments, such an individual had only limited influence over his people.

a lie to exploit their companions, since they do not cure using herbs, of which I believe them to be ignorant.

The Indians of the South harbor a deep aversion toward the whites, since on many occasions I have met them on the road, and they have treated me with profound arrogance and disdain. Despite this fact, there are at least a thousand able-bodied white people living among them with their families, the majority of them deserters, since as I have said, this is the lair of all sorts of criminals.

27

"The Beautiful and Sacred Principles
That Religion Teaches"

A Letter from the *Pacíficos del Sur*

Connections between the pacíficos and the states of Yucatán and Campeche continued throughout the century. In this 1875 letter, a collection of southern chiefs write to Bishop Leandro Rodríguez de Gala to request that a priest be stationed permanently among them. The letter was part of a long dance of diplomacy, in which the southern communities cultivated social and economic ties while keeping the outside world at arm's length. Its style and phrasing, however, are suspiciously elegant for a band of isolated Mayas.

What survives of this document is merely a recopied version of the original. It may represent a translation from the original Maya, or the signatories may have had assistance in its preparation. The letter, however, captures the pacíficos' attitudes. These include their propensity toward flowery rhetoric, their appeal to patron-client relations, their dislike of outside authorities (here, the priest of Hopelchén), their willingness to manipulate fears of Indian uprisings, the persistence of folk Catholicism, and the popular opposition to fixed taxes.[1]

Illustrious Sir,

We, the undersigned, chiefs and officials of the cantons of the *pacíficos del sur,* before your Most Holy Illustriousness with the appropriate respect, have the honor to state that we profoundly regret the insuperable obstacles that have been weighed in the decision or ruling that was made regarding the request that we previously made to you.

Your Honor, we cannot understand how one of the Church's greatest and most illustrious heads would deny a humble petition that has neither evil intentions nor personal ambitions. The principal motive of those who wrote to you before, and who write now, has been nothing more than to revive in the hearts of the people who make up this territory (who number some 13,000 or more) the Christian religion, which is on the point of disappearing among them.

---

1. The source of the following material is Archivo Histórico de la Arquidiócesis de Yucatán (Mérida), Decretos y Oficios Box 44, 8 May 1875, Xcanhá.

We believe strongly that men who lack the beautiful and sacred principles that religion teaches will stray from the path of virtue; and this apostasy will, God forbid, unleash great upheavals and bloody episodes, whose terrible and barbarous consequences we, perhaps, will be the first to suffer.

Above we state that insuperable obstacles have come before us because Your Illustriousness will certainly concede that we live in a savage wilderness. We lack even some of the most indispensable necessities of life; and for this reason, and because we are the appointed guardians of civilization in these cantons that form the front line, which protects those who make up the important *partido* of the Chenes[2] against the raids and ambushes of the barbarous Indians, we should by law enjoy certain special rights, such as those that we receive from the civil government. In this regard and in matters that touch Your Illustriousness, we believe it right and proper that we be exempted from paying the monthly twenty pesos of support demanded as the necessary condition for sending us the priest that we request, and whose presence is so sorely lacking in these parts.

We believe, Your Illustriousness, that the *cura* who might be appointed to help us would need no salary whatsoever. In part, this is because his expenses in these villages would be extremely small because everything is so cheap. In equal measure, [this is] because in our humble view, his monthly income would probably not fall below forty pesos, more or less.[3] To this we should add that if Your Illustriousness stations a priest here in these parts, which form part of the parishioners of the diocese that is his responsibility, he will be fulfilling one of the dearest and most sacred of philanthropic duties, and for this reason, will receive the applause and gratitude of all the inhabitants of the wilderness of the southern *pacíficos*.

We also see as an obstacle, and one of enormous consequences, Your Illustriousness's idea of leaving this part of the south under the authority of Hopelchén. We say this because under such an arrangement the priest who comes to work here will have to be under the command of interim *cura* Don Cenobio Aguilar. We cannot fail to point out to Your Illustriousness that said *cura* of that parish is utterly unacceptable for all the sons of these villages because of the excessive strictness with which he treats them. And, if his title of *cura* includes these parts as well, he will come to visit us some day with his sermons that consist of little more than curses, condemnations, and outrages. These stir up anger among certain uncouth and unprincipled men, never lacking even among the most refined people, all of which diminishes and profanes his character as a priest. This is precisely what we wish to avoid, and at all

---

2. Essentially the lower third of Campeche state; "Chenes" refers to natural wells, or *ch'e'eno'ob*, found in certain parts of the district.

3. The income to which the chiefs refer is presumably based on fees for incidental religious services, such as baptism and marriage, although their estimate of $40 was highly exaggerated.

costs, so that our subordinates may conserve the singular respect that they profess toward ministers of the church.

For all the reasons we have expressed, we ask with fervor and tenderness that Your Illustrious Sir see it worthy to grant our request. First, that a parish be founded in this territory befitting its size and needs. Second, that the parish receive the appropriate decorations, something that reason and justice demand because we find ourselves in the most frightful poverty, as previously stated. Third, that we be exempted from paying the twenty-peso monthly salary for the priest we are requesting. And fourth, that we receive an independent parish with a priest, who (we most profoundly wish, although with no desire to wound anyone's sensibilities) will be a clergyman of highest virtue so that in his mission to this wilderness, he may grace the people with his sterling example. . . .

Xcanhá, 8 May 1875

General Eugenio Arana

Colonel Francisco Mian	Commander Perfecto Escamilla
Commander Jacobo Ku	Commander Manuel J. Ku
Commander José A. Cab	Commander José María Cab
Commander Justo Pech	Commander Ceferino Couoh
Captain José Pantí	Captain Miguel Caach
Captain José María Fuentes	Captain Juan José Yupit
Captain José Camal	Captain José Keb
Captain Dámaso Poot	Captain Juan Balam
Lieutenant Guadalupe Chan	Captain Mag
Daleno Canul	Lieutenant José Xeceb

"Comparing the description of the dress of the Indians given by the invaders of their soil with what they now wear, there can have been but little change" (Richard Fletcher, missionary). This drawing, which accompanied B. A. Norman's *Rambles in Yucatan* (New York: J. & H. G. Langley, 1843), in fact, reveals the considerable European influence on clothing.

"The Indian woman is beautiful in form, beautiful for her dark eyes so deep and alluring, and finally for the warm reflection of her coppery skin, which accentuates the white *huipil,* the *huipil* of Mexico" (Ludovic Chambon, traveler). This highly stylized drawing comes from Frederick Ober, *Travels in Mexico and Life among the Mexicans* (Boston: Estes & Lauriat, 1887).

"Because the greater part of the Indians and the women of the villages go barefoot on good roads, carrying their sandals (*alpargatas*) to reserve for use in the cities, it happens that here they acquire an extraordinary dexterity in the use of their feet" (Federico de Waldeck, traveler). In this scene from B. A. Norman's *Rambles in Yucatán,* barefoot Mayas carry a foreign visitor to his destination.

"The houses of the Indians are erected without the use of a nail.... They are very strong and durable and display much skill" (Richard Fletcher, missionary). Frederick Starr's *In Indian Mexico: A Narrative of Travel and Labor* (Chicago: Forbes & Company, 1908) includes this scene of rural Yucatecan architecture, complete with plastered siding.

"They have also little blocks of light wood to sit upon, which they make into different shapes (*k'áanche'*) about 9 inches high & 15 inches long. On one of these the woman sits while she makes the corn into round cakes & bakes them" (Richard Fletcher, missionary). This illustration from Frederick Ober's *Travels in Mexico* captures this quintessential scene of daily life.

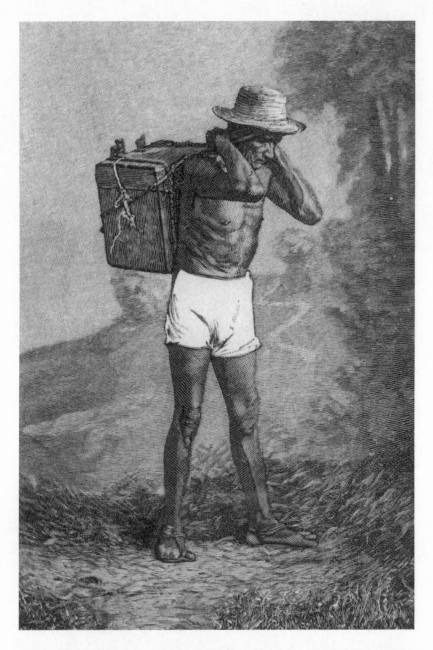

"The Indian . . . performs the menial labor of the country, and there is an appearance of apathy in his looks and actions, which seems to carry with it the signs of a broken or at least a subdued spirit" (B. A. Norman, traveler). Frederick Ober's illustration of a Maya porter, printed in *Travels in Mexico,* captures a mixture of strength, determination, and stoicism.

"We must work ever harder to win the Indians away from certain practices, inspiring in them the love of work and obligating them to acquire certain needs that will awaken a desire to improve their lot. We must also show them that their interests are those of the estate owners" (José Demetrio Molina, Indian defense attorney). Frederick Ober's scene of daily labor in *Travels in Mexico* reveals the real disparity between hacienda opulence and Maya misery.

"I left and went to the *castillo,* that is, where the corn market is located, and here I sat down" (Marcelo Uc, escaped hacienda worker). The public market where Marcelo Uc spent his lost weekend continues to be a meeting place for people from across the peninsula. Photograph by Terry Rugeley (2000).

"They have an idea that no people is like them" (Richard Fletcher, missionary). This early-twentieth-century photograph of the Mayas of Chan Santa Cruz is from Thomas W. F. Gann, *The Maya Indians of Southern Yucatan and Northern British Honduras,* Smithsonian Institution, Bureau of Indian Ethnology Bulletin, no. 64 (Washington, D.C.: U.S. Government Printing Office, 1918).

"For years a favorite pastime [was attending] the *vaquería* dances, which began at night with a high-spirited opening *jarana* that summoned the people" (Santiago Pacheco Cruz, schoolteacher). This photograph, from Frederick Starr's *In Indian Mexico*, captures the spirit of popular celebrations on the haciendas.

"Both children and adults play many games, most of which have probably been introduced since the conquest" (Thomas Gann, archaeologist). In Yaxcabá, the town that inspired one of Yucatán's most famous ethnographies, modern-day residents excel at playing soccer, seen here against the backdrop of the colonial church. Photograph by Terry Rugeley (2000).

IV

LIFE IN PACIFIED YUCATÁN

The Caste War was primarily a rebellion of Maya peasants, but it is important to remember that most peasants did not join the rebel cause. Most peasants fled, served as auxiliaries or even combatants in the army of the Yucatecan state, or relied on the influence of prominent hacendados to keep them out of military service.

By the mid-1850s, much of the Mayas' world had returned to normal. The following documents offer a panorama of the problems and persuasions of these unrebellious peasants. These narratives paint vivid portraits of hacienda labor conditions, migration, military service, land tenure, religious beliefs, and the ceaseless struggle to make a living and keep families together.

28

"Finding Ourselves Near to Death"

The Will of a Condemned *Batab* and Two Associates

In August 1847, shortly after the outbreak of the Caste War, Creoles living in Mérida fell into a paranoid fear that Maya leaders (batabs or caciques) were plotting against them in all quarters. This panic quickly subsided, but not before the caciques *closest at hand became the victims of a witch hunt, which resulted in their arrest and, in some cases, their execution.*

The following document is the will of the cacique *of Motul, Bacelio May, drawn up shortly before his death in August 1847. It illustrates the modest possessions and the close family ties of the more successful Mayas. The circumstances and wording lend a ring of pathos to the document. This will and those of other condemned* caciques *are preserved in the notary archives in Mérida, Yucatán.*[1]

In the name of God Our Father, amen, may it be known by this public document that we, Bacelio May, *cacique* of the town of Motul, José Miguel Pech, and Nicolas Kuk, residents of the same town and currently [here in Mérida], being healthy in body and mind and with the natural judgment that Our Lord God has seen fit to give us, but finding ourselves near to death in this chapel, condemned to capital punishment for the crime of conspiracy against the Whites, . . . make the following declaration:

I, the first [Bacelio May], declare that, although I have been married, nonetheless I have four natural children through María Eusebia May, their names being María Isidra, José Gerónimo, María Catalina, and María Luciana May y May.

I declare as my possessions one-half of my house lot, located in the village of my residence, which I jointly purchased with my brother José María May, including the palm trees found there.

I also declare the 40 *mecates* of *milpa rosa* that I have near the lands of Padre D. N. Rivas and 30 *mecates* of *caña*, with the provision that from the yields on the *milpa rosa*, which are two *cargas* of corn, it is my wish that it be given to satisfy María Eusebia May after the harvest. Her brother Rafael May will show her where said *milpa* is located.

---

1. The source of the following material is Archivo Notarial del Estado de Yucatán (Mérida), 27 August 1847, 220–21.

I also declare my wish that the possessions to which I have referred remain in the power of María Eusebia May and that they be divided among her and my children. I recommend to her their care. She can sell my estate in order to raise and educate them. She can also liquidate all the harvest of this current year, according to an agreement that I formed with my brother, and after the harvest, they can make the appropriate division, each receiving what belongs to them. . . .

I, the second [José Miguel Pech], declare that I have been married . . . to María Domingo Pech, in which matrimony we have produced as our legitimate daughter María Anselma Pech y Pech, noting that at the time of our union, my wife owned six head of cattle, of which five have died and only one remains with her two calves.

I also declare that I have no possessions other than 22 *mecates* of *milpa caña* a short distance from my house and 12 *mecates* of *milpa rosa* on the property of my father-in-law, Faustino Pech. It is my wish to leave both to my said wife in order that she maintain herself in reward for her faithful service to me. I have also given to her the expenses necessary for the marriage of my daughter, and for that reason, [I] cannot further indemnify her for such costs. I appoint my wife the executor of my few belongings; and I declare in similar fashion that at my house I have a mare with her foal, which I also leave to my wife, requesting that if the mare should produce another foal, it be given to my daughter. . . .

I, the third [Nicolas Kuk], declare myself to be a bachelor and to have no possessions other than 20 *mecates* of *milpa* among the lands of Don Tomás Mendiburu. Regarding these, I declare as my legitimate heir my mother, Juana María Cé.

29

A *Lunero's* Journey

The Testimony of Marcelo Uc

*By 1856 peace had returned to a large part of the Yucatán Penin-
sula. Life, however, remained difficult for many, particularly the
urban poor and rural laborers, two groups that were predominantly
Mayan. The following story illustrates this hardship. Taken from
court testimony for 5 January 1856, it concerns the lost weekend of
Marcelo Uc, a hacienda worker who left the estate to look for his
master in Mérida. Arrested on suspicion of being a spy from Chan
Santa Cruz, he told the story reproduced below.*

*Narrated with ingenuous charm, Marcelo Uc's account captures
many features of the times: hacienda labor conflicts, heavy drinking,
the lure of the city market, the rootlessness of rural people newly
arrived in Mérida, and the client-patron relationships that prevailed
between poor Mayas and their social superiors. Although a hacienda
peon, Uc seems to have been relatively adept at finding assistance.
His testimony also highlights the comradery that prevailed among
rural Mayas who came to the big city.*[1]

My name is Marcelo Uc, native and resident of the hacienda San Juan
Actún of Maxcanú *partido*. I am married to María Felipa Euán, who still lives
on that hacienda, where I am a *lunero*.[2] Although I don't know my age, I would
say that I am about 40 years old. I do not know who arrested me or where
because I was drunk, and I think that they did so because I had been drinking.

I abandoned the hacienda on Friday the 28th of last December in the early
morning, without telling the *mayordomo*, and I arrived at the capital on the
morning of Saturday the 29th of the same month. I came for the purpose of
informing my master, Don Juan Manuel Castellanos, that the *mayordomo* had
unjustly beaten me because I had been wasting time with my companions
when we were shucking corn, putting the husks in the grain baskets. I warned
him that I would complain to the master, and he replied that he was going to
beat me.

---

1. The source of the following material is Archivo General del Estado de Yucatán (Mérida),
Fondo Justicio, Penal, Box 1855–56, 5 January 1856.

2. A *lunero* was a hacienda peon who, in exchange for access to hacienda land, worked on Monday, or *lunes*.

After I arrived, I sat at the doorstep of my master; when he saw me he asked why I had come, and I told him the reason for my visit. He answered me that, because his son had gone to the hacienda to determine what had happened, I too should return to the hacienda, and he gave me a *medio-real* to buy something to eat. After I left and began to make my way back, I came across two residents of Maxcanú, Juan de Dios Rodríguez and José Canul, at the corner of Don Manuel Silvestre Herrera's home. This was about three in the afternoon because I had spent all of the day at the house of my master, where I had eaten. Rodríguez and Canul invited me to drink *aguardiente,* and we drank all that they had in a gourd. I remember that after drinking, the three of us wandered into the vegetable market, and they gave me something to eat. Somehow I reached the portico, where they sell corn. It was now about seven at night, and finding myself here with no place to stay, I spent the night asleep there without knowing where my companions had gone.

At dawn on Sunday the 30th, I headed to the house of Regina Reyes, who lives on the corner of the plaza of Santa Ana, looking for her brother Francisco Reyes, who is the *mayordomo* of the hacienda Cholul in Hunucmá *partido.* Cholul's owner is Don Manuel Pinelo. I wanted to ask Reyes for something to eat and drink because I was hungry and thirsty. I explained what I needed to his sister Regina, who gave me a cup of chocolate and who scolded me for drinking liquor. Afterwards she offered me a *medio-real* to clear the weeds away from the door, which I did. I finished this work around one in the afternoon; I ate there and spent the rest of the afternoon and that night at her house.

At dawn on Monday the 31st, I left Regina Reyes's house and walked as far as the church of Santa Lucía.[3] In a store on the corner, I bought a *cuartilla* of *anís,* which I drank without having eaten breakfast beforehand.[4] I left the store and went to the vegetable market, where I bought another *cuartilla;* it was now about eight in the morning. From there I left and went to the *castillo,* that is, where the corn market is located, and here I sat down because, as you know, a person who is drunk, no matter where he is, wants to sit down. Sometime around eleven in the morning, I got up and went to wander around the portico of the corn market, and I remember that some gentleman gave me a *medio-real,* which I used to keep drinking. I stayed under the portico until I saw that the moon had come up, and that in the main plaza there were lights and tables where things were being sold, and that there were people there singing and playing music. After a while I went to sleep again, and I woke up under the portico on Tuesday the first of this month.

Without food and without the money to buy it, I began to go from door to door looking for work; at a small store a block away from the main plaza, the woman hired me to carry water and gave me some money, which I used to buy

---

3. The distance to which he refers is about two blocks.

4. A *cuartilla* was approximately .188 liters; old-timers inform me that it was sold in hip flasks. *Anís* is anise-flavored *aguardiente* and is still commonly available in southeastern Mexico.

aguardiente. I half remember that when I left there I went back to the barrio [of San Cristóbal], where I earned a *real* for clearing weeds from a house whose location I can't remember; it was on an unfamiliar street. I finished at three in the afternoon, and from there I went to the vegetable plaza, where I bought some food and tortillas, and in a store on the corner of the same plaza, I bought a *medio* and a *cuartilla* of *anís,* which I drank alone. After that I returned to the corn porticos and went to sleep. I remember that I was still there at four in the morning when some people from Maxcanú arrived to sell pottery, people I had never met before.

Soon afterward I saw Francisco Moo and José Ek; Moo asked me what I was doing there. I told them that I had been working in a hacienda, and that some time before I had run away. They asked me why I didn't leave Mérida. I told them that I probably would leave because I had nothing to eat; they told me to wait until they had finished selling and then we would leave. At nine in the morning they finished their work, and together we went to the vegetable plaza to buy food, which I ate with them. Before coming to the plaza, Moo bought a *medio* of *anís* and Ek bought a *cuartilla,* which we shared equally. After eating, we three went to the corn portico to buy salt; Moo bought half an *almud*[5] of salt, and then we returned to the corner of the vegetable plaza, where Moo and Ek bought another *medio* of *anís,* and we drank together. Immediately thereafter, I asked Moo to loan me a *real;* I used half of it to buy liquor and kept the other half. After that I don't remember where I went, what I did, or how they brought me here because, as the mayor knows, I was drunk, and when I sobered up I found myself here, a prisoner.

---

5. A dry measure of volume common in colonial times and still used up until the early twentieth century. An *almud* equals 3.5 kilograms.

30

"Like the Ancient Gypsies"

Juan Pablo Ancona on Maya Religious Practices

Padre Juan Pablo Ancona, author of this brief description of Maya beliefs, was born in 1822 and served for many years as a priest in various villages in central Yucatán, including his hometown of Tixkokob. He had the bad luck to be stationed in Valladolid when the town was besieged by Mayas in 1847–48 and made various trips into the surrounding countryside to negotiate with rebel leaders. When he wrote the following account in 1865, Ancona was collaborating with the French-sponsored empire of Maximilian and, in fact, hosted the empress Carlota during her visit to Yucatán. He was briefly imprisoned for his political activities after the empire was overthrown in 1867; once released, he served quietly as cura of Tixkokob[1] until his death in the 1890s.

Even in 1865, Ancona had considerable firsthand experience with rural life. The following memoir is brief but contains useful information about the rebels of Chan Santa Cruz, the pacífico settlements of the deep south, and the more generalized ceremonial practices of the Yucatec Mayas.[2]

El registro yucateco,[3] volume 2, pages 165 and 291, contains a report concerning the Indians of Yucatán that gives [a] very close idea of their general character and of their superstitious practices. If this has decreased somewhat, it would only be among those who live in the capital and the principal towns of the state. They have a false idea of our religion. For them the Cross is God himself; it is the true object of their cult, and if at any time they stray from their devotion to this object, it is to focus on the image of San Antonio or some other saint.

The rebels, whether by erroneous persuasion or by some wretched scheme of theirs, make the Cross speak and appear to consult it on serious and solemn

---

1. Tixkokob is a town twenty-four kilometers east of Mérida, located on the road to Izamal.

2. The source of the following material is Centro de Apoyo a la Investigación Histórica de Yucatán (Mérida), Manuscritos, XLVIII, 002, 1865.

3. *El registro yucateco* was a four-volume literary journal that appeared in 1844–45. Edited by man of letters Justo Sierra O'Reilly, its highly readable articles still open windows to nineteenth-century Yucatecan life and culture. The *Registro* provided the first published version of the ethnography of José Bartolomé del Granado Baeza, which was reprinted in chapter 1 of this book.

occasions, principally when they want to sacrifice some victim, always doing it to comply with divine will as known through the Cross, which they are accustomed to make speak in a way that is clumsily false. A certain José Na, who was a sort of ventriloquist who served in these instances, was assassinated in 1863 in Chan Santa Cruz; but the cult of the Cross continues among the barbarous rebels, among the *pacíficos,* and among those who live in the main towns, albeit with some modifications.

The *tich'* is very strange. This superstitious ceremony consists of a banquet to which friends gather to eat a huge bread of corn mixed with beans and a turkey cooked in special seasoning. During the meal they drink a lot of *balche'* (*pitarrilla*). The object is to propitiate the spirit of the bush so that he will protect the crops and make them prosper.

Stranger still are cases of idolatry, but there is not lack of them. In these cases they hide themselves in the most remote parts of the bush, and gathered with their close friends and fellow believers, one of whom plays the role of priest, they use clay censers (*pom*) to burn a substance known as *copal,* which serves them as incense. The same Indians refer to these ceremonies as *tóok pom* (burnings of incense), and it is a forbidden term, even among them. For this reason, the superstitious practice is condemned.

The healers and herb doctors also use *pom* before confessing for their baths as a propitiatory ceremony. They invoke the winds and in this mode conjure them. The practice is altogether common because the Indians prefer these herb doctors to the most famous doctor, and beyond that, they consider herb doctors as the wisest of counselors. They use a piece of ordinary glass, which they call *saastun* (clear stone), and through this instrument pretend to see and observe the most hidden things. They are a type of talisman for good luck, like the ancient gypsies, and they do not fail to have their points of similarity with the mesmerists,[4] although they labor through mere superstition, without any idea of the reasons on which those latter base the effects of double sight.

The *koj kaan*[5] is a common operation to cure illnesses among the Indians. It is a type of purging that they carry out by means of a hollow fish bone, which they use to make a crude perforation in the skin of the affected area. For them, bloodletting is the trusted remedy for all sickness.

They are accustomed to eating the rattlesnake meat as a remedy for syphilis. A snake that in its old age has become long and thick is called *ajua kaan* (king of the serpents). Idolaters take them as the objects of their worship.

---

4. Ancona uses the term *magnetizadores,* or "magnetizers."

5. "Serpent's tooth." The operation was at times performed with the hollow fang of a serpent.

31

"The Question of Village Lands"

The *Abogado Defensor de Indios* States His Case

In the years 1863–67, Yucatán, like other parts of Mexico, fell under the power of a French-imposed "monarchy" known as the Empire. Among other initiatives, the imperialists set out to win the support of the rural peasantry by providing guarantees of land and legal access. In the southeast, the work of overseeing Maya-related problems fell to the newly created Indian Defense Attorney (abogado defensor de indios), whose job it was to hear complaints, file petitions, and represent the Maya peasantry in the law courts. The position fell to a highly competent lawyer named José Demetrio Molina. Molina, however, soon found himself caught between the Mayas' heightened expectations and the resentment and resistance of prominent landowners.

The following passage was excerpted from a larger report that Molina wrote in 1865, following a month-long tour of eastern villages. It offers an unusually thorough review of the intricacies of peninsular land tenure. Molina realized the difficulties of dealing with mostly illiterate rural peasants, and his frustration with their complaints and demands comes through quite clearly. Despite its limitations, the account of the Indian Defense Attorney merits inclusion as a textbook study of attempted reform and the corresponding methods of evading and manipulating that reform. It is worth noting that the revolutionaries who won national power in 1920 used the same basic strategy—land reform and governmental protection—on a grander scale and with far greater success.[1]

One of the matters that most occupies the Defender's time is the question of village lands. At this moment the Indians are in a state of ferment because they have been led to believe that the coming of the Empire means the reestablishment of the village *ejidos* and at the dimensions that those *ejidos* enjoyed at the time of the conquest. The Indians do not hesitate in insisting that the Defender use judicial means to give them lands that are now private property. For this

---

1. The source of the following material is Centro de Apoyo a la Investigación Histórica de Yucatán (Mérida), Manuscritos, XLVIII, 005, "Relación de los trabajos hechos por el abogado defensor de indios de la visita a los pueblos del oriente en el mes de enero de 1865."

purpose they usually provide no more proof than scraps of paper showing crude sketches of property boundaries, and no other documentary evidence whatsoever. But because there is a law of the Republic, a law which in my opinion is still valid, which establishes the limits of the *ejidos* according to the number of inhabitants, it does not seem prudent to me to promote this type of lawsuit, which the villages so desire. And indeed, it might well put the entire peninsula in an uproar because, according to the Indians' way of thinking, there would be no landowner whom I would not bring to court. . . .

The lands called *ejidos* were granted to the villages by the kings of Spain in order to sustain their peoples, to provide firewood, and so that the Indians and poor *vecinos*[2] could carry out their plantings. A law (whose date I have momentarily forgotten) established that each Indian could have 60 *mecates* of the lands surrounding his village for annual cultivation. Against this law the village magistrates, taking advantage of the ignorance of the Indians, have converted the *ejidos* and communal holdings into their own private property, using them on a grand scale and leaving only the worst parts for Indian cultivation. So it happens that currently the magistrates of some villages have plantings of more than 400 *mecates* on public lands, while their privileged position also allows them to rent out private lands for additional plantings, leaving only the remaining common lands for the use of the poorest.

This same situation led to still another abuse. Once the lands of some villages had been taken over, the magistrates and other *vecinos* incited the Indians to dispute various points about their land, providing them with cash loans to cover the fees of an attorney, who represented them purely for private interest and not for the good of the community. Indeed, the goal [of the *vecinos*] has always been to have free lands in order to carry out large-scale plantings. Fortunately, the institution of the Indian Attorney has partially eliminated this abuse. But not totally. Since the magistrates now can no longer find an attorney to do their bidding, they instead manipulate the Indians into seeking out the services of the Defender. And when he turns them down, they denounce him for being unresponsive to their needs.

It also requires a tremendous effort to convince the servants of rural estates that, by Imperial law, they are not free to abandon their service whenever they want, without reference to the agrarian law of 1847, a piece of legislation that regulates rural labor. They act as if contracts could be voided merely by the wish of one of the involved parties. This is a serious abuse which, in my opinion, could be gradually remedied by making them understand that the 1847 law is still in effect. I have tried to do exactly that with the Indians who have come to me in such cases. And for the most part, I have managed to persuade all the *caciques* of the villages that if Your Excellency, out of sympathy for their difficult situations, has appointed me to see that their rights are not trampled,

---

2. A *vecino* is a non-Maya resident of a rural community.

so too I am not obligated to cover for their abuses. As I have remarked, the principal defect of the Indians is the profound indolence that stems from a lack of civilization and from the excessive use of *aguardiente*. At the same time, I have made the *caciques* understand that their subordinates must remain industrious; that they must work *milpas* that are not only sufficient for their own needs, but that also yield a surplus with which to advance themselves; and that above all, they must moderate their use of *aguardiente,* which is the main cause of all their quarrels and missed obligations.

I firmly believe, Your Excellency, that we must work ever harder to win the Indians away from certain practices, inspiring in them the love of work and obligating them to acquire certain needs that will awaken a desire to improve their lot. We must also show them that their interests are those of the estate owners. Whatever the difficulties, I am confident that because this is a labor of peace, in the end it must prevail.

32

"My Sad and Wretched State"

Two Personal Accounts of War

For most rural people, the Caste War was probably neither the dawn of a Maya millennium nor the defense of a cherished fatherland; it was simply a time of prolonged violence, when ordinary people found themselves trapped between rebel raids and state demands for donations and military service. From the late 1850s to the mid-1870s, the suffering was compounded by the continual wars that Hispanic elites waged amongst themselves.

The following accounts, both dated 1866, were selected from a thick packet of petitions, in which both Mayas and Hispanics asked for exemptions from taxes and labor drafts, usually because of the sacrifices they had made via military service during the Caste War. These documents provide interesting human details about a period known mainly for its macropolitical contours. Both petitions were granted.

PETITION OF LAUREANO AKÉ[1]

I, Laureano Aké, resident of the village of Dzemul,[2] appear before Your Honor with the most profound respect to say that at a tender age I fell into a well, breaking my backbone and leaving me an invalid and unable to work. In spite of this and with no consideration for my condition, the magistrate of my town sentenced me to service in the troops commanded by General Navarrete.[3] But when he was defeated by Col. Cepeda,[4] we were forced to retreat while carrying boxes of ammunition. . . . The result was a hernia on my left side, which left me completely incapacitated and which grows worse each day. I cannot work to support my abandoned family or my elderly mother, who accompanies me in my sad and wretched state.

---

1. The source of the following material is Archivo General del Estado de Yucatán (Mérida), Poder Ejecutivo Box 164, Gobernación, "Excenciones a la contribución personal y de tequios vecinales," 23 July 1866.

2. Dzemul is a town twelve kilometers north of Motul.

3. Gen. Felipe Navarrete (dates unknown), whose Conservative revolution of June 1863 set the stage for the Second Empire in Yucatán.

4. Col. Manuel Cepeda Peraza (1828–69), the man who led the military victory over imperial forces on the Yucatán Peninsula.

I beg that Your Honor, in consideration of the documents that I am including, . . . decree that I be freed from the taxes that I ordinarily pay, as well as from the labor obligations. I ask this favor because of Your Honor's well-known humanity, and I swear that I am not acting out of bad intentions.

PETITION OF SANTIAGO CAHUM[5]

I, Santiago Cahum, resident of the village of Huhí, appear before Your Honor with the appropriate respect to say that, knowing for certain that I have been placed on the list of those who are to make up the *república de indígenas* in my village for the coming year of 1867, before I am called to occupy the position for which I have been named, I have come to this Capital to express before Your Honor that my right hand has been left useless by a bullet wound that I received while serving as a *hidalgo* in the campaign against the rebel Indians. I cannot carry out the services to which I have been called because I can barely earn a living for my family. I present myself in person before Your Honor so that, seeing me with your own eyes, you will understand that I am disabled.

---

5. The source of the following material is Archivo General del Estado de Yucatán (Mérida), Poder Ejecutivo Box 164, Gobernación, "Excenciones a la contribución personal y de tequios vecinales," 13 December 1866.

33

"I Commend My Body to the Earth"

A Poor Maya's Will

The Caste War created enormous hardships and dislocations for the Mayas living in the pacified areas of Yucatán and Campeche, and its effects continued for years after the original conflict had subsided. On the evening of 29 August 1877 in the town of Tekax, witnesses were called to hear the last wishes of Atanasia Ku, an illiterate Maya woman living as a domestic servant with one of the town's families. This is her declaration.

Although Ku's will is written in the phrasings of one of the town's lawyers, it captures important features of her life, including the uncertainties generated by the Caste War (she was a war orphan) and a poor person's dependence on her more affluent patrons. The document also alludes to a sexual relationship with one of the town's Creoles. The designation of a tutor for Ku's underaged son, Herculano, reflects what had become a common practice by the 1870s.[1]

In the name of Almighty God, amen. Be it known by those present that I am Atanasia Ku, 35 years more or less, single, employed in the labors of my sex in this home. I do not know who my parents were because as an small child I was taken from the territory of the rebel Indians, an orphan.[2] Physically ill but sound in soul, memory, understanding, and intention, . . . I make this, my declaration, which I ask to be taken as my last, final, and deliberate will.

First, I commend my soul to Our Lord God, who rescued it from the abyss and redeemed it from sin at the infinite price of his precious blood, asking that he have mercy on it at this, my final moment.[3] And I commend my body to the earth, from which it was formed. And having no one to grieve for me, I ask of the charitable souls that it be granted a Christian burial.

---

1. The source of the following material is Archivo Notarial del Estado de Yucatán (Mérida), Protocols of Tekax, Book 3, 29 August 1877, no page numbers.

2. If the age thirty-five is correct, Ku would have been four or five years old at the outbreak of the Caste War.

3. These religious invocations, found in both Maya and Hispanic wills, were largely formulaic, although they attest to the pervasiveness of Catholic belief even after the Liberal reforms of 1855 onward. They invariably precede the testator's inventory of his or her material goods and the designation of both executors and heirs.

I declare that I have never been married, but that I have had a son named Herculano, who is now 16 years old or more. His last name is Peraza because my *compadre,* Don Lorenzo Perazato, has deigned to grace him with his own name.

I declare as my final wish that my son, Herculano Peraza, have as his tutor Don Manuel Tenreyro Ramírez of this neighborhood, asking my son that he obey him submissively and carry out for him all the obligations of a son; just as I ask the aforementioned Tenreyro that he attend him and educate him in a Christian manner and with all the benevolence of a father.

I declare that I possess few and insignificant belongings, which are known to my son and which he will collect when I am deceased, in order that he do with them as he sees fit.

I declare that I have no properties, nor any debts active or passive, for which reason there is no need to appoint an executor because my aforementioned son is my heir.

34

"They Did Acquire Certain Properties"

A Prosperous Maya's Will

In many ways Juan Bacilio Tzuc was the opposite of Atanasia Ku. A landowner and entrepreneur in the town of Ticul, Tzuc was undoubtedly among the most prosperous Mayas of the mid-nineteenth century. Tzuc, who was illiterate, married twice and produced a large family. Some measure of the man's success can be seen in the fact that his son Juan Asunción Tzuc became one of the few Maya priests of the century.

Juan Bacilio's will, dictated before a local magistrate, highlights the complicated family relations and business dealings. Tzuc's hatred for his second wife is also noteworthy and is reflected throughout the document. Family problems notwithstanding, Tzuc's will illustrates a key point: in virtually every part of Yucatán, a small class of successful Maya entrepreneurs persisted, despite the dislocations from prolonged warfare and the continued expansion of the hacienda system.[1]

In the city of Ticul, on the 15th day of the month of July 1870, . . . there appeared Juan Bacilio Tzuc of this town, of whom I testify as follows: that being of advanced age and finding himself sound in mind, . . . he declares his last wishes in the following manner:

First, he entrusts his soul to Our Lord God, who raised it from nothingness and who redeemed it at the infinite price of his most holy blood; and he entrusts his body to the earth, from which it was formed.

He declares as his last wish that the mandatory donation be made, and only once, as is the custom.

He declares that he has been married first to María Leona Couoh, now deceased, to which marriage they brought nothing, and that during their bonds they did acquire certain properties. As legitimate children they produced Juana María, Rosalía, Fermín, and Juan Asunción Tzuc y Couoh. The first of these is married to Nazario Chi, and the two of them live in San Esteban, a village of the English flag. The second is a widow and lives in the town of Peto. The third

---

1. The source of the following material is Archivo Notarial del Estado de Yucatán (Mérida), Protocols of Tekax, Book 1, 15 July 1870, no page numbers.

died, leaving as his legitimate heirs Juan Santos and Manuel Jesús Tzuc y Bacab, legal adults. The last of their children died while serving as a priest, leaving a few possessions of little value to Tzuc in an execution of a will filed in the state of Campeche. [Tzuc] declares that after the debts of his late son have been paid, along with the costs of the *testamentaría*,[2] this estate reaches 80 to 100 pesos.

He declares that he married a second time to Manuela Dzul of this town, to which matrimony he brought the possessions itemized below. As legitimate offspring they produced Silveria, María Loreto, Enrique, and Damián Tzuc y Dzul; and although six years ago he divorced this woman for valid reasons, which he omits to mention as they are documented elsewhere, nevertheless he has continued to support said wife and children to the present. Moreover, it is notorious that from their wedding to their separation, Manuela Dzul, far from making herself useful, has instead squandered part of the wealth that he brought to their marriage.

He declares it his last wish that Buenaventura Tzuc of this town be named executor to carry out the articles of his will, and he relieves him of whatever need for bonding.[3] He also names him as guardian of his children Silveria, María Loreto, Enrique, and Damián Tzuc y Dzul, all minors; and of his grandson Juan Santos Tzuc y Bacab, . . . with the condition that his wife Manuela Dzul is in no way to take part in managing the possessions of these children.

He declares as his property a small undeveloped plot[4] located in the confines of this city, along the road leading east to the village of Dzan. It is called San Benedicto and includes a small adjacent plot of 100 *mecates*. It is his wish that after his death it be given to his married daughter, Juana María Tzuc y Couoh, now living in San Esteban. In the event of her death, it should go to her heirs.

He declares as his property an urban lot of three square *mecates*, located two and a half blocks to the southeast of the church of that city. He purchased this from Gregorio Marín, and of it he leaves half to his daughter Juana María Tzuc y Couoh. He states that after his death, his executor is also to see that she receives 32 beehives, with the condition expressed in the preceding article.

He declares as his property a spot of land named Xkuil, two leagues to the south of this city. It consists of some 2,000 *mecates*, and it is his wish that after his death it be given to his daughter María Rosalía Tzuc y Couoh, along with the other half of the urban lot mentioned in the previous article, . . . noting that while living he gave her 32 beehives, which she in turn sold to the late Don Luis Francisco Medina when she left Ticul to live in the villa of Peto.

---

2. A *testamentaría* was the legal process of executing a will.

3. The *fianza*, or bonding of executors by a third party, was a common though not universal practice in writing wills during the nineteenth century. As with the bonding of would-be political officeholders, it was a way to help guarantee good conduct.

4. The word used here is *sitio*, which normally applies to a small and relatively undeveloped parcel of land used for cattle, beekeeping, or agriculture.

He declares as his property another plot of land named Xkocoh, measuring some 2,000 *mecates,* more or less, located two leagues to the south of this city and bordering on the aforementioned property. It is his wish that after his death the executor divide it equally among Tzuc's grandchildren, Juan Santos and Manuel Jesús Tzuc y Bacab, sons of his late son Fermín Tzuc y Couoh. To these same grandchildren he also leaves an urban lot measuring three square *mecates,* located two and a half blocks to the southeast of the same church. This lot was formerly owned by Nicolás Uk and contains 32 active beehives.

He declares as his property a small spot of land named Zoh-Akil, approximately 1,000 *mecates,* bordering on the aforementioned Xkocoh, and it is his wish that after his death it go to his daughter Silveria Tzuc y Dzul, to whom he also leaves half of the urban lot in which his wife, Manuela Dzul, currently lives, two blocks to the southeast of the church, with the other half going to his daughter María Loreto. In similar fashion, he leaves to the said Silveria 15 beehives.

He declares as his property another spot of land measuring some 1,000 *mecates,* located one league south of this city, and it is his wish that after his death it be given to his daughter María Loreto Tzuc y Dzul, along with 15 active beehives and the half lot mentioned in the previous article (the same in which his wife now lives).

He declares as his property another spot of land measuring some 1,000 *mecates* called Cehkal, located two leagues to the south of this city and bordering on the aforementioned Xkocoh, and it is his wish that after his death it remain with his son Enrique Tzuc y Dzul, to whom shall also be given half an urban lot with a well, located slightly more than two blocks to the southeast of the same church. He purchased this property from the late Juan Miz, and it contains more than 15 active beehives.

He declares as his property a *milpa* of 90–100 *mecates* of recently planted corn. He also declares the small debt owed by three servants, which is recorded in his books and which is known to his grandson Juan Santos Tzuc. It is his wish that after his death Juan Santos assume charge of the *milpa* and servants, using the profits to pay for his burial and other costs associated with his funeral.

He declares that the testament of Padre Juan Asunción Tzuc y Couoh, to whom he refers in the third article of this document, is currently in the hands of Don Adrián María Medina of this city, to whom he has given power of attorney. However, as of today he has not received from said Medina any of the inventoried goods and valuables that appear in the proceedings of the will's execution. And it is his wish that after his death his executor collect what is owed to him by the aforementioned Don Adrián María Medina.

He declares as his final wish that whatever remains from the said testament of his son Juan Asunción Tzuc, to whom he refers in the previous article, be invested in equal parts to pay for masses for the good of his soul, for the soul of his late wife María Leona Couoh, and for the soul of his deceased son Juan Asunción Tzuc.

He declares that he does not owe a single cent to any living soul.

And to carry out his final wishes, he names as executor the aforementioned Buenaventura Tzuc. To serve as guardian of his underaged children named in the fourth article, he names his grandson Juan Santos Tzuc y Bacab. He relieves both the executor and guardian of bonding, as he is aware of their Christian behavior. And he names as his legitimate and universal heirs his aforementioned children Juana María and Rosalía Tzuc y Couoh, as well as Silveria, María Loreto, Enrique, and Damián Tzuc y Dzul, and Juan Santos and Manuel Jesús Tzuc y Bacab.

V

THE CLOSE OF THE CENTURY

The divisions among rebels, refugees, villagers, and labor-ers persisted to the century's end. Each group found itself worn down by different pressures. The deep south gradu-ally welcomed to rubber tappers, merchants, and even archaeologists. Between 1898 and 1901, the Mexican fed-eral government firmly established itself in what is now Quintana Roo, forcing the descendents of the original Maya rebels into smaller and more isolated communities.

Refugee communities, such as Corozal and Orange Walk, gradually became less Yucatecan and more Belizean. Pacífico settlements offered reservoirs of labor for the rub-ber tappers. In Yucatán proper and in northern Campeche state, the economy and culture of the henequen hacienda displaced much of what had once been autonomous vil-lage life. Continuity accompanied change, however. The documents of this final section illustrate the persistence of many cultural traits throughout the Maya region.

35

"Courageous, Efficient Soldiers"

Karl Sapper on Late-Nineteenth-Century Maya Settlements

*Prior to 1880 the area of Belize, northern Guatemala, and the south-
ern Yucatán Peninsula remained a relatively unknown part of the
globe. The Mexican federal government entertained dozens of plans
for reclaiming its lost territory, but these never got beyond the
prospectus stage. The final two decades of the century, however, witnessed a gradual entry of scientific explorers from the more developed nations: geologists came as part of a larger process of mapping
and analyzing the natural world, whereas archaeologists sought out
the remains of classic Maya civilization. At the same time, the
increasing demand for chicle as an ingredient for chewing gum
brought traders and chicle tappers. All of these individuals made
contact with the Maya rebels and refugees who had come to inhabit
the area as a result of the Caste War.*

*Among those who roamed the tropical forest was German geogra-
pher Karl Sapper. Primarily involved in scientific exploration, Sapper
also developed a keen interest in the history, culture, and political
geography of the area. He traveled to most of the important Maya settlements. This report, originally published in German in 1895, offers
an overview of regional history as well as important observations on
the lives and polities of various independent Maya groups. Although
writing as a man of science, Sapper manages to insert his own biases
in places. For example, he seems captivated by the military organization of life among the rebels, an attitude that contrasts visibly with
his censorious disdain for the black Creoles of Belize. Nevertheless,
the Sapper report remains a critical and often cited source on the
region's late-nineteenth-century political geography.[1]*

It is a well-known fact that the conquest of Yucatán offered the Spaniards
great difficulties and that the *adelantado* Don Francisco de Montejo,[2] although

---

1. The source of the following material is Karl Sapper, "Independent Indian States of Yucatan,"
trans. Charles P. Bowditch, in *Mexican and Central American Antiquities, Calendar Systems, and
History,* Smithsonian Institution, Bureau of American Ethnology Bulletin, no. 28 (Washington,
D.C.: U.S. Government Printing Office, 1904), 625–34. The article originally appeared in *Globus,*
vol. 67, no. 13 (1895).

2. The term *adelantado* means "trailblazer" or someone who arrives in advance. It was commonly
applied to the early conquistadors.

he fully understood the art of craftily turning the dissensions among the different Indian states to his own advantage, at length found himself forced to call on Ferdinand Cortés for aid. After the conquest of the peninsula was finally accomplished, the Indians rose here and there to regain their freedom. The Spaniards suppressed the insurrections with brutal force but could never dispel the hatred toward their white oppressors, which, even to this day, smolders in the hearts of the Mayas and manifests itself from time to time in a renewal of bloody insurrections, like those which took place in the middle of the last and of the present century (1761 and 1847). The latter rebellion has had a lasting influence on the political development of the peculiar conditions which exist today. For this reason, I will enter into a somewhat detailed discussion of them.

The [Caste War] began among the eastern tribes, who were soon joined by those of the south; a large number of villages were destroyed, and in the year 1848 Bacalar, the last important place of the Mexicans in southern Yucatán, at that time a city of more than 5,000 inhabitants, also fell into the hands of the eastern Indians under Venancio Pec, Juan Pablo Cocom, Teodoro Villanueva, and others. In the following year (May 3, 1849) the Yucatecos, under Colonel Cetina, succeeded indeed in regaining possession of the city, but in June of the same year the eastern Indians, under Jacinto Pat, reinforced by the southern Mayas of Chichanhá, under José María Tzuc, made another vigorous attack on Bacalar and were repulsed only with difficulty. The siege lasted for years and was only interrupted when the Mexican garrison received large reinforcements.

It was not until Gen. Don Rómulo Díaz de la Vega assumed command in Yucatán that the war was carried on with greater energy by the Mexicans. This general marched by way of Chan Santa Cruz, the "sacred city" of the eastern Indians, to Bacalar, where he arrived on March 1, 1852. The southern Indians, whom the Mexicans had defeated, now offered to negotiate for peace with the Yucatecos, which enraged the eastern Mayas, who turned against them, unexpectedly attacked their principal town, Chichanhá, and almost entirely destroyed it. But soon afterward (July 1852) Díaz de la Vega surprised the principal town of the eastern Indians, Chan Santa Cruz, which had been fortified in the meantime, and in this engagement the dreaded chief, Venancio Pec, and his adjutant, Juan Bautista Yam, fell. The Mexicans, however, were not able to achieve a permanent victory over the eastern Mayas, to whom, in the year 1858, they finally lost Bacalar, which has now become an important base of operations and rallying point for these Indians.

In 1871 the Mexicans made another armed incursion into the territory of the eastern tribes, again captured their principal city, Chan Santa Cruz, and again withdrew without the slightest permanent success. After the withdrawal of the Mexican troops, the Indians quietly returned to their former habitations and occupy today the same territory that they formerly occupied. From time to time, they make predatory expeditions into the Mexican territory of Yucatán or into the territory of the southern tribes; but their military operations no longer aim at great enterprises and seem to be directed only to the occasional acquisition of booty.

Thus, while the eastern tribes have stood uninterruptedly on a war footing with the Mexican Government since the year 1847, the chiefs of the southern tribes, José Maria Taz, Andrés Tzima, and Juan José Cal, concluded a treaty of peace as early as 1853 with the Mexican agents, Doctor Cantón, Colonel López, and P. Peralta, through the instrumentality of the English superintendent at Belize, Ph. Ed. Woodhouse, the conditions of which were recorded in both the Spanish and Maya languages. Unfortunately, I have not been able to examine the terms of this treaty; but the conditions actually existing indicate that full independence in the conduct of their internal affairs (civil and judicial administration, etc.) was guaranteed to the Indians, while the latter formally recognized the suzerainty of Mexico, and their *caciques* have to be confirmed by the Mexican Government, that is, the *gobernador*[3] of the state of Campeche.

The southern tribes are divided into two distinct states, whose chief towns at present are Xcanhá in central Yucatán and Icaiché in southern Yucatán. Both states, in the main, have faithfully kept their treaty with Mexico, but in 1869 Mexican troops were obliged to enter the district of Xcanhá to suppress an insurrection of the Indians under General Arana, the brother of Gen. Eugenio Arana, now in office. On the other hand, both states have had to repel occasional incursions of the eastern Mayas, who have been hostile since the conclusion of peace in 1853, and thus the southern Indians have served as a bulwark and outpost, as it were, for that portion of the state of Campeche which is under Mexican authority.

Among the Icaiché Indians, who retreated farther southward after the destruction of Chichanhá, the warlike spirit once roused would not be quieted and manifested itself in numerous raids into the territory of British Honduras, where at one time the Indians advanced as far as the neighborhood of the city of Belize. In 1868 the Icaiché Indians, under their leaders Marcos Canul and Rafael Chan, occupied the city of Corozal but withdrew through fear of the Santa Cruz Indians; and in 1872 the warlike Gen. Marcos Canul attacked the city of Orange Walk but was fatally wounded during the siege by a Swiss named Oswald, whereupon the Indians withdrew.

The British Government complained to the Mexican Government of the repeated Indian invasions, and when the Mexicans explained that the Icaiché Indians were not under Mexican authority but were an independent tribe, the English pointed out that the leaders of the Indians were Mexican generals. The protest, however, was not followed up, since the Icaiché Indians made no more raids into British territory after Canul's death, neither under Rafael Chan, Canul's successor, nor under the excellent Santiago Pech, nor under the present *cacique,* Gen. Gabriel Tamay.

---

3. I.e., the governor.

At present, indeed, great warlike enterprises on the part of the Icaiché Indians are quite inconceivable, for their number has been continually reduced by war, rum, and pestilence; and in the year 1892 virulent smallpox and whooping-cough epidemics swept away about half their number, so that now the entire population of the once feared Indian state can be estimated at only about 500 souls. Nevertheless, in Icaiché, a few Indians are always stationed as sentinels in a special hut called the *cuartel* (barracks); and in the house in which I lived during my residence there, five loaded repeating rifles hung on the crossbeams of the roof, a sign that the Icaiché Indians are always on their guard against the Santa Cruz Indians, who, in fact, a short time before (during the rule of General Tamay) had made an unsuccessful attack upon the village.

In Xcanhá there are a larger number of soldiers on guard day and night in the barracks, under the command of a captain, and although they do not wear a uniform any more than do the Indians of Icaiché, they are a somewhat nearer approach to disciplined military, inasmuch as they use drum and trumpet calls, etc. In the district of Xcanhá the population has also diminished, compared with its former number, especially through smallpox epidemics and owing to an utter lack of good medical aid, and a few years ago Gen. Eugenio Arana ceded the important village of Chunchintok to the state of Campeche. Nevertheless, the population of the independent territory of Xcanhá is probably about 8,000.

At the beginning of the rebellion, the population of the Santa Cruz territory was stated to be about 40,000; but since then the number has also greatly diminished and is estimated by those familiar with the country at 8,000 or 10,000 souls. Indeed, it seems as if the depopulation of the forest regions of the peninsula (eastern and southern Yucatán) [was] constantly progressing, although it is probable that even before the conquest, these regions were more scantily populated than the drier and more salubrious districts in western and northern Yucatán.

The population of Chan Santa Cruz is chiefly confined to the strip of territory between lake Bacalar and Ascención bay, for the fierce and long wars have resulted in an ever-increasing concentration of population on the part of the eastern Indians and also on that of their enemies; in consequence of which uninhabited tracts of land lie between the two factions, in which the former roads have been rapidly overgrown and rendered impassable by the luxuriant forest vegetation. Even though Indians can use these overgrown roads in case of need in single file, the Santa Cruz Indians will always be obliged to open new roads for incursions on a larger scale, which will serve to warn the inhabitants of the threatened district well in advance.

The state of civilization of the independent Mayas is low. There is no educational system at all, and although for Xcanhá, which is probably more directly dependent on Campeche than Icaiché owing to its proximity to it, the position of schoolmaster is provided for in the state budget of Campeche; nothing is gained by it since no candidate ever applies for the position. Maya is exclusively the language of common intercourse, and in each of the three independent districts, the clerk who is appointed by the general as secretary and interpreter is the only man in the state who speaks Spanish well and can also read and write a little. In ecclesiastic matters, the Mayas of Santa Cruz are dependent upon Corozal, those of Icaiché upon Orange Walk, and those of Xcanhá upon the neighboring villages of Campeche. In Xcanhá, it is true, I saw in the church a smoothly shaven Indian, not otherwise distinguished from his fellows, who, morning and evening, conducted religious services, consisting largely of song, in the Maya tongue; but he was evidently not a genuine priest.

The public and private buildings of the independent Mayas, without exception, are thatched, wooden huts, such as are customary elsewhere among the Indian inhabitants of the peninsula. The houses of sun-dried brick or stone have fallen to ruins, and in Santa Clara Icaiché,[4] for example, the numerous foundation walls and cellars still recall their former existence.

In dress the independent Indians scarcely differ from the rest of the Mayas. The women wear a white cotton skirt and a white *huipil* of the same material reaching to the knees, which is often ornamented with red embroidery around the hem and the neck of the bodice. The hair is gathered in a knot at the back of the head. Their ornaments are large gold earrings, while necklaces, so popular among the Indian women elsewhere, are seldom worn here. The men wear white cotton trousers and shirts, straw hats, and sandals, which are fastened to the feet with cords.

The Indians cultivate the more important plants for food, luxury, and textile fibers; raise cattle, swine, and poultry; spin and weave their clothing; and braid their straw hats and hammock, etc., so that they are obliged to import comparatively few articles: only arms, ammunition, salt, ornaments, and the like. The products of the chase are of great importance to the household of the Indians of Icaiché and Santa Cruz, who live in the forest regions. The chase is of less importance to the Mayas of Xcanhá, who live in the region of the dry brush-covered plains and border only on the south and east on the region of unbroken primeval forests.

A few English have settled in the district of Chan Santa Cruz and a few English and Yucatecos in the district of Icaiché for the purpose of cutting mahogany and logwood. For every ton of wood that they export, they pay a certain sum to the general of the district, and out of this income he meets the public expenses, such as the cost of arms and ammunition and the salary of the clerk. Any surplus remaining seems to belong to the general himself. There are no taxes or duties. As the Xcanhá district is nowhere contiguous either to the sea or to navigable rivers nor is intersected by highways, the logwood, which is

---

4. Mexican towns often have two names: an older, pre-Hispanic name to which was added the name of a Christian patron saint. The two names—in this case, "Icaiché" and "Santa Clara Icaiché"—could be used interchangeably.

present in considerable quantities, can not be made marketable. On the other hand, the people collect a good deal of chicle, a kind of gum obtained from the milky juice of the *chicozapote*. I do not know from what source the public revenues of Xcanhá are derived.

The Indians of Santa Cruz trade chiefly with Corozal, the Mayas of Icaiché with Orange Walk, while the trade of the people of Xcanhá is chiefly with Campeche. A short time ago, it is true, General Arana had a direct bridle path cut from Xcanhá, by way of Cluchanhá,[5] to Santa Cruz on the Río Hondo and to Orange Walk for the purpose of reviving the direct trade with the British colony and the once active carrying trade from there to Campeche; but as this route passes near the territory of the Santa Cruz Indians and the trading caravans are therefore in danger of highway robbery, and as most of the imported wares are at present not appreciably cheaper in British Honduras than they are in Campeche, very active traffic on this road can not be expected.

Commercial relations have a decided influence upon the monetary system of the independent Maya states. Since in British Honduras the small coins of Guatemala, as well as Chilean and Peruvian silver dollars, are mostly in circulation, these coins are also most in use in the districts of Santa Cruz and Icaiché. In the Xcanhá district, on the other hand, Mexican money is the only currency; but when some years ago the old fractional currency was discarded in the Republic of Mexico and a new one based on the decimal system was adopted, the Xcanhá Indians did not conform to the innovation but continued to use the Mexican and old Spanish *medios* and *reals,* which long ago had been withdrawn from circulation in Mexican territory.

The office of *cacique* is not hereditary in any particular family, but at the death of the general, the next below him in military rank, the *comandante,* advances to the position, while at the same time the senior captain is promoted to the rank of *comandante,* etc. During the absence of the general, the commandant acts as his representative. The general has supreme command in war, and he fills the office of judge, for which reason the *caciques* of Xcanhá and Icaiché, when they are confirmed in office by the *gobernador* of Campeche, are as a matter of form officially appointed to the position of *jefe político* and *comandante de armas* as well as to that of judge. Both generals use a stamp which bears, besides the Mexican eagle, the inscription *Pacíficos del Sur,* in accordance with the customary division of the independent Mayas of Yucatán into the *Indios sublevados pacíficos* (peaceful insurgents) of Xcanhá and Icaiché and the *Indios sublevados bravos* (fighting insurgents) of Chan Santa Cruz.

The general seems to be in some measure answerable to the popular assembly for his actions, in so far as these do not directly relate to military matters or to his judicial office, as I think I may infer from some remarks made by the

---

5. This name is possibly a misspelling of *Chichanhá.*

clerk of Icaiché. Even after General Tamay had given me permission to travel in his district, I had to leave behind me in Icaiché a copy of the circular addressed to the authorities of the Republic, which I had obtained from the ministry of the interior, so that the general could have in this document a justification of his actions before his fellow citizens, who had been called to meet in a popular assembly on the day after my departure, March 1, 1894. If I had not come to Icaiché as an official of the Mexican government, I should in all probability have been refused permission to pass through this territory.

The general of the Santa Cruz Indians has, as I gather from my inquiries, the same authority as the chiefs of the Xcanhá and Icaiché Indians. On the whole, the conditions in the three independent Maya states are almost identical.

Among the independent Mayas, military service is compulsory; every man capable of bearing arms is obliged to perform military duty and is drafted for sentinel duty. The firearms in use are quite miscellaneous; modern repeating rifles are seen side by side with heavy, old-fashioned, muzzle-loading muskets. In general, the independent Mayas are considered good shots and courageous, efficient soldiers skilled in the stratagems of war. The Mayas who accompanied me as guides through the interior of Yucatán always carried their shotguns on their shoulders, loaded and cocked, with percussion cap on, and usually with great promptness brought down the game which crossed our path.

The administration of justice is prompt and summary, but it is, I believe, very conscientious, in favorable contrast to the dragging, uncertain methods of Mexican courts. The accused is either set free or flogged; or in serious cases, among which, as I was assured, rape is reckoned, he is shot. There are no prisons and no punishment by imprisonment.

The existing laws are strictly enforced. I myself experienced a slight proof of this, manifested in a logical though somewhat petty decision of the authorities. I had obtained in Icaiché three Mayas as guides and interpreters and had made a legal contract with them before the clerk of Icaiché, according to which they were to accompany me to Xcanhá, receiving in advance half of the pay agreed upon, the rest to be paid at Xcanhá. When we reached Xcanhá, the three Icaiché men voluntarily proposed that for a certain sum they should accompany me still farther to the railroad station, and that I should there pay them the whole amount. To this arrangement I agreed.

The Indians of Icaiché and Xcanhá are compelled to have passports, and therefore my Icaiché men could not journey farther without the express permission of the Xcanhá authorities. As General Arana was absent, my guides had to transact their business with the commandant, the contract I have mentioned serving to prove their identity. After a while I was also summoned, and the commandant informed me through his interpreter that I had not fulfilled the contract, since the Icaiché Indians had not yet been paid. Although they did not in the least wish it, I nevertheless hastened to pay them, while the commandant looked on attentively. He then informed me that a new contract might now be made. He conferred with the Icaiché Indians, communicated their conditions to me through his interpreter, and when I declared myself satisfied with them, the clerk was instructed to draw up the contract and to sign it "in the name of General Arana," upon which the Icaiché Indians, after the proceedings had lasted about an hour, received permission to accompany me farther.

Although the whole affair was of no importance whatsoever, I was glad to observe how much trouble the commandant took to protect against possible fraud the Indians who, on their part, did not in the least distrust me, and how quietly and straight to the point the whole transaction was conducted. The mistrust of foreigners is very easily explained when one knows how frequently the Indians are defrauded and cheated of their stipulated pay by the half-breed element of the population.

As to the character of the independent Mayas, I can make an almost wholly favorable report from my own experience. Having come from Honduras, where the indolent Negro and half-breed population, spoiled by the too liberal laws, can often be kept only with difficulty to the fulfillment of engagements with which they have entered, I was particularly impressed by the reliableness of these Mayas, by the punctuality with which they fulfilled a promise once given, and by the fidelity which they showed to me on my journey. My Maya guides freely shared their hunting booty with me and the bearers who accompanied me from Guatemala. Everywhere, even in the most isolated hut, we found hospitable entertainment.

Family life was peaceful and quiet wherever I had an opportunity to observe it, and although the Mayas are somewhat reserved and more silent than the tribes of Guatemala and Chiapas, they are by no means of a sullen disposition, but, on the contrary, [are] very quick to appreciate a harmless jest. It is often said of the Mayas that they are honest in important matters but that they readily steal trifles; but I have never had the least thing stolen from me during my travels in Maya territory. On the other hand, drunkenness is a prevailing vice; and I can believe the accusations of cruelty against the Mayas, the more readily as from my own observation I judge that a certain trait of cruelty is peculiar even to the mildest of the Central American Indians. The blood-thirsty cruelty and warlike readiness which the Santa Cruz Indians in particular evince in their expeditions have made their name exceedingly feared and have caused the generally accepted report of their great numbers and invincible armies.

This reputation and the slight commercial relations of the independent Mayas are probably the principal reasons why scientific travelers so seldom visit these regions and why their topography and peculiar political conditions are so little known. Engineer Miller, the account of whose travels in the *Proceedings of the Royal Geographical Society*, 1899, is unfortunately not accessible to me, was the first European since the rebellion of 1847 to visit Chan Santa Cruz,[6] the

---

6. On this point Sapper was mistaken because British merchants and officials, as well as Hispanic priests, had visited Chan Santa Cruz from the 1850s onward.

chief city of the eastern Mayas; and toward the end of 1893 two Englishmen, Mr. Strange and Mr. Bradley, passed through the same village, at that time almost depopulated, on their way to see the chief of this tribe at his place of abode, the neighboring Chanquec. I could ascertain even less concerning the Santa Cruz territory when, at the beginning of the year 1894, I intended to advance through that region to the civilized northern portion of the peninsula. Orange Walk was the first place where I could obtain fairly accurate information regarding the route to be followed.[7]

---

7. Here I have omitted Sapper's discussion of available maps of these areas.

36

"The Thin Veneer of Civilization and Restraint"

Thomas Gann's Description of the Maya Indians of Quintana Roo and Belize

Thomas Gann was a British archaeologist who worked in the region of Belize, the Petén, and what is today southern Quintana Roo during the late nineteenth and early twentieth centuries. Among other accomplishments, he discovered the now-destroyed site of Santa Rita, a late Postclassic site in northern Belize. At the time of his expeditions, the Mexican federal government was involved in a prolonged process of establishing non-Maya settlements and national political authority in what would eventually become the state of Quintana Roo. During those years, however, Maya culture persisted in rural areas. Gann's explorations consequently brought him into extensive contact with Maya villages that had formed in the wake of the Caste War and acquainted him with the people, their language, and their customs.

The following selection consists of excerpts from Gann's most extensive ethnographic account, The Maya Indians of Southern Yucatan and Northern British Honduras *(1918). One of the most comprehensive ethnographic pieces ever written on the Yucatec Mayas,* The Maya Indians *merits inclusion for its treatment of a wide range of cultural matters not covered in other pre–Carnegie Project writings. Gann discusses such diverse topics as gender differences, material culture, illness and medicine, games, political succession, religious beliefs, and even methods of capital punishment. In these passages, the author strikes an ambivalent tone, a mixture of disdain, astonishment, and admiration; perhaps it is this interpretive tension, together with an eye for anecdote and detail, that continues to infuse Gann's writings with a sense of immediacy. Given the archaeologist's own highly logical organization of material, I have chosen to omit his subtitles.[1]*

---

1. The source of the following material is Thomas W. F. Gann, *The Maya Indians of Southern Yucatan and Northern British Honduras,* Smithsonian Institution, Bureau of Indian Ethnology Bulletin, no. 64 (Washington, D.C.: U.S. Government Printing Office, 1918).

The women are, on the whole, both physically and mentally superior to the men, and when dressed in gala costume for a *baile*[2] with spotlessly clean, beautifully endowed garments, all the gold ornaments they possess or can borrow, and often a coronet of fire beetles, looking like small electric lamps in their hair, they present a very attractive picture. They are polite and hospitable, though rather shy with strangers; indeed, in the remoter villages, they often rush into the bush and hide themselves at the approach of anyone not known to them, especially if the men are away working in the *milpas*. They are very fond of gossip and readily appreciate a joke, especially one of a practical nature, though till one gets to know them fairly well, they appear dull and phlegmatic.

When quarreling among themselves, both women and girls use the most disgusting and obscene language, improvising as they go along with remarkable quick-wittedness, not binding themselves down to any conventional oaths or forms of invective, but pouring out a stream of vituperation and obscenity to meet each case, which strikes with unerring fidelity the weak points in the habits, morals, ancestry, and personal appearance of their opponents. The young girls are as bad as, if not worse than, the older women, for whom they seem to have no respect. They are extremely clean in their persons and wash frequently, though with regard to their homes they are not nearly so particular, as hens, dogs, pigs, and children roll about together promiscuously on the floor, and fleas, lice, and jiggers abound only too frequently. . . .

The women are very industrious, rising usually at 3 or 4 o'clock in the morning to prepare the day's supply of tortillas or corn cake. During the day they prepare cigarettes; gather cotton (*taman*), which they spin (*k'uuch*), weave (*sakal*), and embroider for garments; weave mats of palm leaf and baskets (*xúux*) of a variety of liana (*aak'*); make pottery (*u'ul*), and cotton and henequen cord, of which they construct hammocks (*k'áan*). In addition to these tasks, they do the family cooking and washing, look after the children, and help their husbands to attend to the animals.

Till late at night the women may be seen spinning, embroidering, and hammock-making by the light of a native candle or a small earthenware cahoon-oil lamp,[3] meanwhile laughing and chatting gayly over the latest village scandal, the older ones smoking cigarettes; while the men squat about on their low wooden stools outside the house, gravely discussing the weather, the *milpas,* the hunting, or the iniquities of the Alcalde. Among the Indian women of British Honduras, the old customs are rapidly dying out; spinning and weaving are no longer practiced, pottery making has been rendered unnecessary by the introduction of cheap iron cooking pots, and even the *metate* is rapidly superseded by small American hand mills for grinding the corn.

---

2. I.e., a dance.

3. The cahoon is a type of palm common in southern Quintana Roo and northern Belize.

The men's time is divided between agriculture, hunting, fishing, and boat and house building, though at times they undertake tasks usually left to the women, as mat and basket making, and even spinning and weaving. The Indians of British Honduras who live near settlements do light work for the rancheros and woodcutters; they have the reputation of being improvident and lazy, and of leaving their work as soon as they have acquired sufficient money for their immediate needs, and this is to some extent true, as the Indian always wants to invest his cash in something which will give an immediate return in pleasure or amusement.

The men are silent, though not sullen, very intelligent in all matters which concern their own daily life, but singularly incurious as to anything going on outside of this. They are civil, obliging, and good-tempered and make excellent servants, when they can be got to work, but appear to be for the most part utterly lacking in ambition or any desire to accumulate wealth with which to acquire comforts and luxuries not enjoyed by their neighbors.

It happens occasionally that an individual does perforce acquire wealth, as in the case of the head chief of the Icaiché Indians, who was paid a salary by the Mexican Government to keep his people quiet and royalties on chicle cut on his lands by various contractors. He accumulated a considerable sum, all in gold coin, which he has stored in a large demijohn and hid in the bush. At his death, as no one knew the place where the demijohn was buried, the money was permanently lost.

They are remarkably skillful at finding their way in the bush by the shortest route from point to point, possessing a faculty in this respect which amounts almost to an instinct; they are skillful also at following the tracks of men and animals in the bush by means of very slight indications, as broken twigs and disturbed leaves, imperceptible to an ordinary individual. The men are very stoical in bearing pain. I have removed both arms at the shoulder joints, with no other surgical instrument than a long butcher's knife and no anesthetic except several drinks of rum, for an Indian crushed between the rollers of a native sugar mill, without his uttering a single complaint.

The Indians are undoubtedly cruel, but not wantonly so, as the shocking acts of cruelty reported as being perpetrated by them from time to time are usually by way of reprisal for similar or worse acts on the part of the Mexicans. Before the rising of the Indians in 1848,[4] they were, throughout this part of Yucatán, practically in a state of slavery and were often treated by their Spanish masters with the utmost barbarity. As an instance of this, it is recorded of a well-known merchant of Bacalar that he was in the habit of burying his Indian servants in the ground to the neck, with their heads shaved, exposed to the hot sun; their heads were then smeared with molasses and the victims left to the ants; and this punishment was inflicted for no very serious offense. It is hardly

---

4. Gann errs: the war actually began in 1847.

to be wondered at that such treatment left in the Indians' hearts an undying hatred for their masters which, when in their turn they gained the ascendency, found vent in acts of the most horrible cruelty—flogging, burning, mutilation, and even crucifixion.

The men wear hats of platted palm leaf, which they make themselves; those woven from coarse split palm leaf are known as *xani p'óok,* those of very fine leaf, like Panama hats, bearing the name *bomi p'óok.* They wear cotton trousers (*eex*), or in some sections, short cotton drawers (*xkuleex*), with a short, loose, shirt-like jacket of cotton hanging outside the trousers. On the feet they use sandals of danta hide[5] (*xanab k'éewel*), held in place by a leather or henequen thong passing between the great and second toes and around the back of the heel to the front of the instep, where it is fastened. Formerly the cotton was grown, spun, and woven at home, but nowadays it is giving place to cheap imported English and American goods, while the sandals are being superseded by moccasins and even by imported shoes. The moccasins the Indians make themselves, tanning the hides (usually of deer or antelope) in lime and red mangrove bark and stitching the parts together with thin strips of leather. These moccasins, which are made on crude wooden lasts, are very comfortable and wear well.

The women wear two garments of cotton: the *huipil* (*yupte*), a loose, short-sleeved blouse, cut square at the neck and reaching nearly to the knees; and a short skirt reaching to between the knee and ankle, known as a *piik.* The neck, the lower border, and the armholes of the blouse, and the edge of the skirt were formerly beautifully embroidered in varicolored floral and geometrical devices; now, however, cotton manufactured in England or the United States and stamped in colors to imitate the original embroidery is rapidly coming into use. The women formerly went barefooted or wore loose slippers; now they frequently wear imported shoes, often with high heels, a feature which renders their walk and carriage awkward and stilted. They often go bareheaded but sometimes wear a sort of shawl (*bóoch'*) around the head and shoulders. Many of them wear large round or oval plaques of gold (*tuup*) in the ears, survivals probably of the enormous round ear disks worn by the ancient Maya.

Some of the women wear long gold chains with religious medallions attached, while the smaller children wear a variety of curious objects, [such] as small coins, shells, beads, dried seeds, and berries, with figurines in wood, stone, pottery, and metal strung round their necks. Many of these are worn as charms or amulets to protect the wearer against diseases, accidents, or evil spirits or to bring good luck. A charm worn by nearly all children consists of a small cross of *tankasche'* bark, which is regarded as a sovereign remedy for flatulence, a complaint from which, owing to the nature of their diet, nearly all suffer. . . .

---

5. *Danta hide* refers to either deerskin or the hide of the tapir, both common in the region in those times.

The villages vary in size from two or three houses to two hundred or more, with inhabitants numbering from 10 to 12 to more than 1,000. In the smaller villages, the houses are very irregularly disposed; in the larger, they are arranged more or less regularly so as to form streets around a large central space, or plaza, where the dance house and church are usually situated. Each house is surrounded by its own patio, or yard, generally inclosed in a fence of *tasitas*,[6] in which the bush is allowed to grow to a considerable height in order to provide a convenient latrine for the women and children. Dogs, pigs, and vultures serve as scavengers.

Many of the Indians, especially the Santa Cruz, are at great pains to conceal the whereabouts of their villages. Along the main roads only a few scattered groups of huts will be seen, while the larger villages are approached by tracks so inconspicuous that they may easily be missed. The villages themselves are surrounded by a maze of narrow, tortuous paths, in which a stranger may wander about for some time before finding his way in. The Santa Cruz are said sometimes to cut the tongues from their cocks in order to prevent them crowing and so betraying the situation of the village.

The Indians are very jealous of outside interference in their affairs and do not permit foreigners to reside in their villages. An exception was made in the case of a number of Chinese coolies imported into British Honduras many years ago, most of whom ran away to the Santa Cruz country, where they were well received and married Indian wives. Among their offspring, it is interesting to note, are found a very unusual proportion of defectives. On one occasion the Mexican Government commenced to cut a road through from Peto to Santa Cruz, the Indian capital. Five of the Santa Cruz Indians went to see the work going on and were well received and given useful presents. On returning to their own country, however, they were executed by the head chief as traitors for encouraging the entry of outsiders into their territory.

The Indian girls married formerly at about 14 or 15, the boys at about 17 or 18 years. After the conquest of Bacalar, however, and the expulsion of Yucatecans from Indian territory, a law was passed making marriage compulsory for all girls of 12 years of age and upward. This was probably done with the idea of increasing the population, which had been considerably depleted by the long-continued war. Formerly, the first question of a girl's father to her suitor was *Jaay tsak a kool, jaay tsak taman?* (How many *mecates* of corn and cotton have you?); but at the present day, there are not enough men to "go round."

The Indians of British Honduras are usually married by the Catholic priest, though the actual ceremony is often performed months or even years after the young couple have set up housekeeping together, since owing to the remoteness of many of the Indian settlements, the priest can visit them only at long

---

6. The term *tasita* is probably a Hispanic variation of the Maya term *tas che'*, or the stick latticework commonly used to isolate the latrine areas that Gann describes.

intervals. Among the Santa Cruz, marriages are not considered legal unless performed by an official known as the *yumxcrib* (probably derived from the Maya *Yum,* "lord," and Spanish *escribano*), who holds a position somewhat analogous to that of colonial secretary in a British colony.

The babies and smaller children in general are pretty, merry little things. The mothers almost invariably nurse them well into the second year, as the mammary glands are remarkably well developed, and the secretion is abundant and long continued. Children are much desired by both parents and are well treated and loved, though not spoiled. If the father and mother separate, the very young children remain with the mother; of the older children, the boys go with the father, the girls with the mother. If small children are left destitute by the death of both parents, the nearest relative takes them, and in the absence of relatives, they are distributed by the subchief among families of his choosing in their own village.

When a man dies, his widow takes the home, furniture, domestic animals, corn, and plantations; other possessions, if such exist, are divided equally between the widow and the older children, each taking such articles as will be most useful to him or her. When a woman dies, her jewelry, ornaments, and clothes are divided between her daughters. The marriage tie is a somewhat loose one, and the more the Indians come in contact with civilization, the looser it seems to become. In British Honduras, where the Indians are closely associated with Spaniards, Mestizos, Negroes, and other races, the women change their partners with the utmost facility.

The Negroes are called *kisin boox,* "black devils," by the Indians, a term which, however it originated, is now employed without any particular opprobrious significance, as many of the Maya women show no repugnance to a Negro husband. A good deal of the immorality is brought about by the cheapness of rum and the facility with which it is obtainable by the Indians. The husband takes to drink, neglects his wife and family, and probably gets entangled with some other woman; the wife, in order to obtain food, clothing, and a shelter for herself and children, is driven to an alliance with some other man who is a better provider. The consequence is that in British Honduras, all degrees of racial mixture are to be found between Indian women and European, East Indian, Chinese, and Negro men, who, again intermarrying, produce a bewildering racial kaleidoscope.

The Indians are a short-lived race, a fact due partly to their indigestible and badly cooked food and partly to the prevalence among them of malarial fever (*chokwil*), with accompanying anemia (*xkan muk'uy*) and splenic enlargement (*kanchikin*), but chiefly to overindulgence in alcohol whenever an opportunity offers. Notable exceptions to this rule are, however, not uncommon, and once an individual passes the four-score mark, he or she is quite likely to live to well over 100 years; dried up, wrinkled, and feeble, but clinging to life with an almost incredible tenacity.

Landa[7] frequently mentions the fact that in his day drunkenness (*kaltal*) was the curse of the Indians and the cause of many crimes among them, including murder, rape, and arson. At the present time, these remarks apply equally well; indeed, drunkenness is probably more prevalent than formerly, as the rum is made locally and is far more intoxicating than the *balche'*, which Landa describes as a drink made from fermented honey, water, and roots. Moreover, the people drink rum at all times and seasons, whereas both the preparation and consumption of *balche'* were to some extent ceremonial, as was the resulting intoxication.

Drunkenness is not considered in any way a disgrace but is looked on rather as an amiable weakness. The women, especially the older ones, drink a good deal, but they usually do so in the privacy of their own houses. I have seen, however, a little girl of 14 or 15 purchase a pint of rum in a village liquor store and go out on the plaza, where she drank it in a few gulps; then, lying down in the fierce heat of the afternoon sun, she lapsed into alcoholic coma.

Alcohol effects an extraordinarily rapid change for the worse in the Indian's temperament; from a quiet, polite, rather deferential individual, he is converted almost in a moment into a maudlin idiot, staggering about, singing foolish snatches of native songs, and endeavoring to embrace everyone he comes in contact with. When thwarted while in this condition, his temper is likely to flare up at the slightest provocation, whereupon the thin veneer of civilization and restraint is sloughed in a moment, and he becomes savage, impudent, overbearing, and contemptuous toward the stranger, and ready to draw his machete and fight to kill, with friend or foe alike.

On the death of the head chief (*noj kalam* or *nojoch yum taat*) among the Santa Cruz and Icaiché, the oldest of the subchiefs (*chan yum tupilo'ob*) is supposed to succeed him; as a matter of fact, there are always rival claimants for the chieftanship, and the subchief with the strongest personality or greatest popularity among the soldiers usually succeeds in grasping the office. There are nearly always rival factions endeavoring to oust the chief in power, and the latter rarely dies a natural death. The village subchiefs are elected by the people. The power of the head chief is practically absolute over the whole tribe.

Some years ago, when Roman Pec was head chief, one of the subchiefs came to Corozal, the nearest town in British Honduras, to purchase powder, shot, and other supplies. He remained some time, as he had many friends in the place, and obtained, among other things, a bottle of laudanum to relieve toothache. On returning to his village, he was met by three soldiers, who informed him that he was to go with them at once to the head chief, as the latter was angry with him on account of his long absence from the country. Aware that this was the equivalent to a sentence of death, he asked permission to

---

7. Diego de Landa was a Franciscan missionary and the main force behind the spiritual conquest of Yucatán. His *Relación de las cosas de Yucatán* (Madrid: Hermanos García Noblejas, 1985) remains an important source on Maya culture at the time of contact.

retire to his house for a few minutes to get ready for the journey, and taking the opportunity, he swallowed the whole contents of the bottle of laudanum. This began to take effect very shortly, and long before reaching the capital, he was dead.

The method of executing those sentenced to death is curious. The accused does not undergo a formal trial, but the evidence against him is placed before the head chief; if he is convicted, he has an opportunity of defending himself and of producing witnesses in his behalf. Three or four soldiers are chosen by the chief to carry out the sentence; this they do by chopping the victim to death with their machetes when they catch him asleep or off guard. Several men always perform this act, all chopping the victim at the same time, so that no single individual may be directly responsible for his death.

Imprisonment as a punishment for crime is unknown, fine, flogging, and death being the only three methods employed for dealing with criminals. Fines and flogging may be administered by the subchiefs, but sentence of death can be passed only by the head chief. The severity of the flogging is regulated by the nature of the offense, and after it is over, the recipient is compelled publicly to express sorrow for his crime and go around humbly kissing the hands of all the spectators, after which he is given a large calabash of anise to drink. The heaviest punishment is inflicted for witchcraft or sorcery, as the *pul ya'aj,* or sorceress, is greatly dreaded by the Indians. She is literally chopped limb from limb; but, whereas the bodies of other victims executed in this way are always buried, that of the *pul ya'aj* is left for the dogs and vultures to dispose of.

Military service is compulsory for all adult males among the Santa Cruz, though many avoid such service by payment to the chief of a certain sum of money or its equivalent. Small garrisons were kept up at Santa Cruz, Chan Santa Cruz, Bacalar, and other Indian towns where soldiers were permanently stationed. No uniform was provided, though many of the men were armed with Winchester rifles. They were provided also with a ration of corn and beans and often took their wives along with them as cooks.

Indian men and women of all ages and classes, when attacked by any serious malady, are found to be lacking in vitality and stamina; they relinquish hope and relax their grip on life very easily, seeming to hold it lightly and as not worth a fight to retain. An elderly man or woman will sometimes take to the hammock without apparent physical symptoms of disease beyond the anemia and splenitis from which nearly all suffer, and merely announce *Je' in kimli,* "I am going to die." They refuse to eat, drink, or talk, wrap themselves in a sheet from head to foot, and finally do succumb in a very short time, apparently from sheer lack of vitality and absence of desire to continue living.

Malaria is without doubt the chief scourge of the Indian's existence. Many of the villages are built in low-lying situations, with mosquito-breeding swamps all around them, while the scrubby bush and rank vegetation are allowed to grow in the yards right up to the houses, furnishing good cover and an excellent lurking place for the insects; moreover, the Indians seldom use mosquito curtains, as they seem to have acquired a sort of immunity to the irritation caused at night by the noise and biting of the pests.

Practically all Indians suffer from malaria, which is the main cause of the splenic enlargement and anemia so prevalent among them. In some cases the spleen reaches an enormous size, nearly filling the abdominal cavity, and deaths from a slight blow or fall, causing rupture of this organ, are by no means uncommon.

Malaria is usually treated by means of profuse sweating (*k'íilkabankil*), the patient lying wrapped in a cotton sheet in the hammock, with a fire burning beneath and drinking sudorific bush medicine. This in itself is an excellent remedy, but in the midst of the sweat, patients frequently plunge into cold water, thus becoming thoroughly chilled, a procedure very apt to bring on pneumonia, to which they are peculiarly subject.

The splenic enlargement is treated by applying a number of small circular blisters (*xakal*) containing *chichem* juice to the skin over the affected organ, which seems to be remarkably efficacious in reducing the swelling.

In the winter, when the nights are cold, the Indians often lie out all night in the wet, a practice which frequently results in pneumonia and death. Hookworms and many other varieties of intestinal parasites are prevalent, owing to the earth-eating habits of the children, the earth being taken usually from the immediate vicinity of the house, where pigs and other domestic animals have their quarters. This disgusting habit no doubt accounts in part for the swollen bellies and earthy color of many of the children.

Smallpox (*k'áak'*) invading an Indian village is a terrible scourge, far worse than in a more civilized community of the same size, where partial immunity has been acquired. Sometimes the whole unaffected population depart en masse, leaving the dead unburied and the stricken lying in their hammocks, with a supply of food and water, to do the best they can for themselves. The Indians employ the same mode of treatment for this disease as for malarial fever—sweating followed by immersions in cold water, treatment which, it need hardly be said, is not infrequently followed by disastrous results.

Venereal diseases of all kinds are remarkably rare among all the Indian tribes. Among the Santa Cruz and Icaiché, such diseases were practically unknown. Even among the mixed breeds of British Honduras, they are comparatively rare, notwithstanding the fact that these natives have come much in contact with people of many other races, especially of late years with Mexican *chicleros*,[8] nearly all of whom are affected with venereal disease in one form or another.

Simple fractures of the long bones are set very neatly and skillfully in the following way: The fractured limb is pulled away from the body with considerable

---

8. I.e., chicle tappers.

force in order to overcome the displacement; over the fractured bone is wound a thick layer of cotton wool; and over this are applied a number of small, round, straight sticks, completely surrounding the limb, their centers corresponding nearly to the seat of the fracture; these are kept in place by a firm binding of henequen cord. The limb, if an arm, is supported in a sling; if a leg, the patient is confined to his hammock till the fracture is firmly knit. Excellent results are secured by this method, the union being firm, and the limb nearly always uniting in good position.

Bleeding, a favorite remedy for all complaints, is especially resorted to in cases of headache and malarial fever. Usually the temporal vein, less frequently one of the veins in the front of the forearm, is opened, having been first distended with blood by tying a ligature around the upper arm. A chip of obsidian, a sharp splinter of bone, or a snake's tooth serves as a crude lancet; the use of the last causes considerable pain but is believed to have some esoteric virtue connected with it.

Decoctions made from the charred carcasses of animals at one time were much employed, certain animals being regarded as specifics for certain diseases. Thus, during an epidemic of whooping cough (*xinki se'en*), a decoction from the charred remains of the cane rat was almost exclusively given to the children to relieve the cough, though in this case, it is difficult to trace the connection between the remedy and the disease.

Many eye troubles are treated by placing a small, rough seed beneath the lower lid of the affected eye, where it remains for a day; when the seed is withdrawn, it is covered with mucus, to which the doctor points as the injurious matter, the cause of all the trouble, which he has removed.

Massage is practiced chiefly for uterine and ovarian pains by the older women, who also act as midwives; it is used also in conjunction with kneading and manual manipulation in the cure of neuralgic pains, strains, stiffness, and rheumatism.

In confinements, which usually take place either in the hammock or on the floor, the dorsal position is invariably assumed. In such cases also, massage over the uterus is performed by the midwife. If the desired results are not secured, the patient is made to vomit by thrusting a long coil of hair down her throat, while a woman of exceptional lung power is sent for to blow into her mouth, with the object of hastening delivery.

The Indians use for medicinal purposes a great variety of plants, which grow in their country; some of these are purely empirical remedies; others produce definite physiological results and are frequently used with good effect; while a few, apparently on the assumption that *similia similibus curantur*,[9] are employed because of some fancied resemblance in form to the diseased part,

---

9. "Like cures like," or the homeopathic method of treating illnesses by administering drugs that produce the same symptoms. Homeopathy gained a following in Mexico in the nineteenth century and has survived as a popular alterative medicine to the present day.

[such] as *xudub pek,* twin seeds of the size of small eggs, the milky juice of which is used as an external application for enlarged glands and for various forms of orchitis. . . .[10]

Both children and adults play many games, most of which have probably been introduced since the conquest. A favorite among these is a game known as *tak in kul,* in which a number of players stand in a row with their hands behind their backs while one, who holds a small pottery disk in his hand, stands behind the row, another standing in front. The one holding the disk places it in the hands of one of those in the line, who in turn passes it to his neighbor, so that it travels rapidly up and down the line. The player in front has to guess in whose hand the disk is at the moment of guessing. If he is right, the holder of the disk has to come in front, while the one who guessed correctly joins the line.

Chak is a sort of "knucklebones" played with pottery disks, which are tossed from the palm to the back of the hand and back again; the one who drops [the] fewest disks in a given number of double throws wins the game.

The boys make little bows (*pojoche'*) and arrows (*jul*) tipped with black wax, with which they play war and hunting games.

A seesaw made from a small tree balanced on the stump is popular, as is also a sort of merry-go-round constructed from a cross of poles fixed on top of a stump by means of a wooden pin, which rotates freely. The children sit at the extreme ends of the poles and make the contrivance rotate by kicking against the ground vigorously at intervals as they go around.

The bull roarer, made from a dry seed pod, is popular in some villages and is probably one of the few toys used by the natives before the conquest.

Cricket, baseball, marbles, kites, and spinning tops have been introduced among the Indians of British Honduras, and all have their devotees.

The Indians, who are extremely superstitious, believe that the air is full of *pixan,* or souls of the dead. They imagine that these souls are at liberty at all times to return to the earth, and that at certain seasons they are compelled to do so. They are regarded as being capable of enjoying the spirit, though not the substance, of food or drink provided for them. Some of these *pixan* the Indians believe to be friendly and some inimical to mortals.

They believe also in spirits, usually mischievous or harmful, known as *xtabay,* who often take the form of beautiful women, though they have never been human. The natives will whisper a message into the ear of a corpse, with the certainty of having it conveyed to a friend or relative in the next world. They firmly believe that the clay images of the gods upon incense burners, at one time found in considerable numbers in forests which had been uncut since the days of their ancestors, live, walk about, and dance at certain seasons.

---

10. It is unclear to what this refers. The spelling of *xudub* is not strictly Mayan and probably represents Gann's misunderstanding of the term. The term *peek'* may in some cases refer to a fever associated with dogs. Orchitis is a testicular inflammation, and one may assume that the twin seeds were believed to have curative powers because of their resemblance to human testicles.

Another belief held by the Indians is that the images of Christian saints are endowed at times with life and perform acts desired by their devotees. A celebrated wooden image, supposed to represent San Bernardo, was credited with considerable powers in this respect, and when an Indian wanted rain for his *milpa,* the return of an errant wife, or any similar blessing, he would come and pray to the image to obtain it for him.

On one occasion an Indian came, asking the saint to aid him in the recovery of pigs which he had lost, and on returning to his village, found that the pigs had arrived home before him. Next day he returned with the intention of making an offering to the saint and incidentally to the owner of the house where the image was kept. He found the poor Santo with torn clothes and many burs sticking all over him. On inquiring how this happened, he was informed that the saint had been out in the bush hunting for pigs, a quest which had given him a great deal of trouble before he could find and drive them home, and that when he got back, he was tired out, his clothes torn by thorns and covered with burs—an explanation with which the Indian was perfectly satisfied.

The men are very unwilling to dig either in ancient mounds or ruins, as they are afraid of being haunted by the *pixan* of those whose remains they may disturb; and nothing will induce them to go into caves or burial chambers in mounds. Many curious superstitions hang about the ruins found throughout the country. I was assured by an Indian at Benque Viejo[11] that he had gone on one occasion to the ruins situated near the village, and seeing a pigeon seated on a tree, raised his gun to shoot it; before he could do so, however, the pigeon turned into a cock, and this almost immediately into an eagle, which flew at him, driving him away. There is another superstition about these ruins to the effect that when the first settlers came to Benque Viejo, they wished to build the village near the ruins, where the land is very good for growing corn, but were repeatedly driven off by a little old man with a long gray beard. At last, giving up the idea, they contented themselves with the present site for the village. . . .

The Indians here under consideration occupy an intermediate position between the civilized Maya of northern Yucatán, who have lost nearly all tradition and traces of their former civilization, and the Lacandones of the Usumacinta Valley, who have probably changed but little in their customs and religious observances since the conquest.[12] Nominally they are Christians, but the longer one lives among them and the better one gets to know them, the more he realizes that their Christianity is to a great extent merely a thin veneer, and that fundamentally their religious conceptions and even their ritual and ceremonies are survivals—degenerate, much changed, and with most of their significance lost—but still survivals of those of their ancestors of pre-Columbian days. To Christianity, not as a separate religion but as a graft on that

---

11. A small town on the border of Belize and Guatemala.

12. Most current scholarship views the Lacandons as an amalgam of Yucatec Mayas and coastal Caribbean Indian groups from farther south.

which they already practiced, they seem to have taken kindly from the first; and at the present day, as will be seen, the sun god, the rain god, St. Lawrence, and Santa Clara may all be invoked in the same prayer, while the Cross is substituted in most of the ceremonies for the images of the old gods, though many of the latter are called upon by name.

The four principal religious ceremonies of the Indians are, as might be supposed, closely associated with agriculture, especially with the corn crop. The first of these ceremonies takes place at the cutting of the bush in which the corn plantation is to be made, the second at the planting of the corn, the third during its ripening, and the fourth at harvest time. Of these the third, known as the *ch'a' cháak*, which takes place during the ripening of the corn and whose object is to secure sufficient rain for that purpose, is by far the most important, and it alone will be described, as it embraces the offerings and ritual of all the other ceremonies. . . .[13]

The day previous to the ceremony, the men of the family prepared the *pib,* an oblong hole in the ground in which the various corn offerings were to be baked, while during the night the women were busy grinding corn to make *masa* (a thick paste of ground maize) and pumpkin seeds to make *sikil.* Very early in the morning of the day of the ceremony, the priest with his assistant arrived at the house of the giver. This priest called himself *men,* but was called by the owner a *cháak,* while the Chichanhá priest called himself an *aj k'iin.*

The Indians chose a site in the midst of a grove of large trees. After clearing away the undergrowth, they swept clean a circular space about 25 feet in diameter. In this they proceeded to erect two rude huts, one 12 feet, the other 6 feet square; both were thatched with *huano* leaf, and the floor of the smaller hut was covered with wild plantain leaves. In the center of the larger hut was erected a rough altar 6 by 4 feet and 4 feet 6 inches high, built of sticks bound together with *bejuco.* The central part of this altar was covered by an arch of *jabín*[14] branches with the leaves still attached.

About a dozen small calabashes in the ring supports (Maya *ch'uyub*) were placed on the altar, and three more were hung to a string passing from the side of the shed to a post a few yards away. The *masa* prepared the previous night was then brought out in four large calabashes, two of these being placed under the altar and on top of it, a large calabash of *sikil* and one of water were also placed on the altar, and a jar of *balche'* (a drink made of fermented honey in which is soaked the bark of a tree) beneath it. Beneath the suspended calabashes was placed a small table containing piles of tortillas and calabashes of *masa* and water. In carrying out this ceremony, it is essential that everything used in it be perfectly fresh and new: the leaves, sticks, *bejuco,* and *jabín* must

---

13. From this point on, I have omitted a detailed description of a *ch'a' cháak* ceremony, along with its accompanying prayers; see Gann, *The Maya Indians,* 42–48.

14. The *jabín,* or *quebracho,* is a tall tree of Mesoamerica prized for its high tannin content.

be freshly cut; and the *masa, sikil, balche'*, and even the calabashes must be freshly made.

The *masa* was taken from the large to the small shed, where the priest and several male members of the family stand around it. After flattening out a small ball of the *masa*, the priest placed it on a square of plantain leaves and poured over it a little *sikil* (a thin paste made of ground pumpkin seed and water). Then the next man flattened out a piece of *masa*, which he placed over the *sikil*, and the process was continued until a cake was formed containing 5 to 13 alternating layers of *masa* and *sikil*, and the priest traced with his forefinger a cross surrounded with holes; these were first partly filled with *balche'*, which was allowed to soak into the cake, after which they were filled completely with *sikil*, whereupon the whole cake was carefully tied up in plantain leaf, with an outer covering of palm leaf. These cakes are known as *tuti waaj*, and their number is generally gauged by the number of participants in the ceremony. When *sikil* is not available, a paste of ground black beans is used; in this case, the cakes are known as *buul y waaj* (Maya *buul*, "bean"; *waaj*, "bread").

The priest next made a deep depression in a ball of *masa* about the size of a tennis ball, which he filled with *sikil*, covering it with the *masa* so as to leave a ball of *masa* with a core of *sikil*. A number of these balls, known as *yok waaj*, were made, each wrapped in plantain leaves. When finished, all of them [were] wrapped in a large palm leaf and tied into a bundle with split palm-leaf strands. Two more *tuti waaj* were next made, and lastly all the *masa* and *sikil* left were mixed together with a few ounces of salt. After being well kneaded, this mass was divided into two portions, each of which was tied up in plantain and palm leaf coverings.

In the meantime, some members of the family had filled the *pib*, or oven, with firewood, over which they placed a layer of small blocks of stone. The priest next made a bowl of *sak ja'* (literally "white water," a drink made from ground corn and water), with which he filled the small calabashes on the altar as well as the suspended calabashes; these, he explained, were for the *tuyum pixan*, or "solitary souls."[15]

A turkey and four fowls were then placed in front of the altar, alive, while the priest lighted a black wax candle by blowing a piece of glowing wood to a flame; this candle he placed upon the altar. He next took up the turkey, around whose neck the assistant had placed a wreath of *jabín* leaves, and poured a little *balche'* down its throat, its legs being held by the assistant. While doing this, the priest murmured the following prayer:

In kubik ti' janal ki'ichpam ko'olel, ti' San Pedro, San Pablo, San Francisco.[16]

Translation: "I offer a repast to the beautiful mistress, to San Pedro, San Pablo, San Francisco."

---

15. *Tuyun* is possibly a variation of *tu juun*, meaning "single" or "solitary."

16. Originally, *In kubic ti hahnal cichpan colel, ti San Pedro, San Pablo, San Francisco.*

37

No Need for a Volapük

A Frenchman Appreciates Peninsular Charm

In 1890–91 a young Frenchman named Ludovic Chambon toured from the Yucatán Peninsula to Mexico City and beyond. Little is known about this traveler and pithy writer. Although he was ostensibly interested in archaeological ruins, his attention quickly gravitated in other directions: wherever he went, Chambon wrote about his amorous encounters with the fair women of Mexico. It is not always clear whether these accounts depict real conquests, embroider upon experience, or simply amount to nothing more than a writer's fantasies. Whatever the case, his finely detailed and appreciative account of the charms of Maya women offers a flavor and variety not found in other ethnographic writings.[1]

Upon returning from Ticul, I found the city unusually animated. Everyone was talking about the *baile de mestizas,* which was to be celebrated that same night. Anticipating this unique fiesta, I run from one side to the other in order to analyze the costumes. The men are always dressed in white. Their costume consists of pants, a shirt that floats freely over the hips, a huge straw hat, and a *jerga* (a type of sash composed of thick strips of red and white, used only in cold weather).

In regard to the Indian woman or mestiza, their costume is among the most original and picturesque. First comes the *fustán,* which is a calico petticoat that allows one to see the tiny and always naked feet. Next, and reaching to the knees, is the *huipil,* the famous *huipil,* the voluptuous *huipil,* which leaves bare those long and beautiful arms and which allows one to cast burning gazes over that broad, squared cloth. When the *huipil* is recently starched, the sight is not pleasant; it resembles a sack. But after a few hours of use, when the fabric has lost its rigidity, the body of the Maya woman, full, robust, and well formed, reveals itself at the slightest movement, at the lightest breeze. For reasons of poverty, some Indians purchase only the cheapest cloth, one so transparent that their *huipil* serves as little more than a thin veil.

---

1. The source of the following material is Ludovic Chambon, *Un Gascón en México,* trans. Rocio Alonzo (México: Consejo Nacional para la Cultura y las Artes, 1994). The original work is in French; I have rendered it into English by following Alonzo's Spanish-language version.

All of these women wear a great necklace of gold and bearing a cross suspended over their chests; on days of fiesta they place their tiny feet, without stockings, in high shoes of light blue. Such flirtation! The *rebozo* with which they cover the head and shoulders protects them from the sun and completes their wardrobe. Their beautiful black hair, divided into two braids, forms a figure eight over the nape of the neck, somewhat in the style of the Chinese.

Despite the sheerness of the *huipil,* the Indian women maintain a very dignified attitude, even though the historian of the Conquest, Cogolludo,[2] insists that "a Spanish woman dressed in Indian costume seems very lascivious." They also have the old and curious custom of carrying light objects (such as plates and small bundles) in their hand and alongside their head, which allows their naked arms to assume an enchanting position. In sum, all of these small details serve to revive lost ages. . . .

How many times on the haciendas of the interior, upon seeing the Indian beauties come proudly and majestically to the water well or the *cenote,* gracefully carrying over their hips their "Grecian urns" and covered in the folds of their *rebozo,* how many times did I think that visions of antiquity were passing before me!

The Indian woman is beautiful in form, beautiful for her dark eyes so deep and alluring, and finally for the warm reflection of her coppery skin, which accentuates the white *huipil,* the *huipil* of Mexico. Arlesians, keep your rosaries![3] Women of Spain, keep your veils![4] Women of all countries, hold on to your regional costumes! Losing them, you will lose half your charm. . . .

The most prudent thing to do is to take oneself from all these excitements: let us leave the dance and return home . . . or somewhere else. Do you see that Indian maiden sitting under that *ramón* in a pose from Récamier?[5] Well, you have to coax her along! She knows no Spanish, you know no Maya. . . . But conversation is unnecessary. In some cases, words muddle instead of advancing the story. You will see this.

You make a light "hum!" which is to say, "May I . . . ?" As a response, you receive a fleeting smile, which means, "If there is nothing more, you may." You are near to her and, delicately, and of course without harm, you pinch that coppery-hued arm while your eyes say, "Ah, what flesh! What skin! I would like to. . . ."

Disconcerted, indignant (but not excessively so), the maiden gets up and leaves, throwing out an altogether expressive gesture: "Why do you touch me?" Fortunately for you, like the wife of Lot, when the poor thing looks back . . . she

---

2. López de Cogolludo, the seventeenth-century Spanish Franciscan chronicler.

3. Women of Arles, the Provençal city of southern France.

4. Alonzo's translation of Chambon uses the word *mantilla,* which refers to a traditional Spanish veil suspended from a hair comb and reaching to the waist.

5. The *ramón* (Maya, *óox*) is a tree known for its exuberant foliage and dense shade and is a popular source of cattle fodder. The seated and beguiling Madame Récamier was the subject of a famous portrait by French revolutionary painter Jacques Louis David (1748–1825).

seems surprised to see you still, petrified under the *ramón*. . . . Follow her. At the next turn of the road, in the exquisite shadows of lovers, you may take hold of a waist that conceals no defects—because she wears no corset—and ask her, with an interrogating glance while caressing her cheek, "Is your house far away?" Without breaking loose, she continues on her way.

Meanwhile, kisses fly from those beautiful dark eyes, and with your free hand, you show her the fireflies that flitter in the darkness of the trees, and she understands what you mean to say: "The tiny fireflies do not sparkle like your beautiful dark eyes. . . ." The door of the hut closes, the hammock strains under an unaccustomed weight, and then. . . . Oh, no! Enough! I have no intention of writing an *arte de amor*.[6] All this is to say that with such experiences, one comes to see quite well the uselessness of a Volapük.[7] The gestures and expressions of the eyes are a universal language.

---

6. "The art of love," a reference to a work by the same name by the Roman poet Ovid (43–18 B.C.) It was intended as a guide to the art of romance and seduction.

7. Volapük was the world's first artificially constructed language. It was created in 1879 by the German priest and linguist Johann Martin Schleyer (1831–1912) and, like the later Esperanto, was intended as a universal tongue. Chambon wrote at the height of Volapük's popularity.

38

"Busting the Melon"

Santiago Pacheco Cruz's Account of Rural Celebrations

Santiago Pacheco Cruz (1885–1970) was a rural schoolteacher with enormous experience in the Yucatecan countryside. Born in Tinum in the state of Campeche, he studied in Mérida and taught in rural villages from 1907 to 1914. In 1915 Pacheco Cruz embraced the cause of Salvador Alvarado, the Mexican general sent to bring revolutionary change to the peninsula. Alvarado selected Pacheco Cruz to travel throughout the countryside, reporting on rural affairs and bringing news of revolutionary policy to the Maya peasantry. Pacheco Cruz later became inspector general of a new school system that included large parts of Quintana Roo and eastern Yucatán. From the 1920s onward, he wrote numerous ethnographic texts, drawing on decades of experience in rural peninsular life.

Pacheco Cruz was a man of great contradictions. An admirer of rural life, he also harbored a profound dislike for religion and religious customs. Moreover, he had a tendency to see things through rose-colored glasses, but he usually portrayed his own time of writing (the 1920s and 1930s) as a degenerate age. Although deeply sympathetic with the revolution, he was a critical observer, who warned Alvarado that campaigns against religion and Catholic iconography had little support among the masses.[1]

The following account, published in 1947, provides something that is unavailable in other sources: a detailed description of the social and leisure activities among Mayas of the haciendas and rural towns. Pacheco Cruz explores festive costumes, dances, bullfights, community celebrations, syncretic religious ceremonies, and commemorations of the Day of the Dead. I have chosen to end the book with this document as a reminder that the Mayas of rural Yucatán, despite their many hardships, managed to find a great deal of joy and humor in everyday life.

---

1. On the life of Santiago Pacheco Cruz, see Hemeroteca Pino Suárez (Mérida), *Novedades de Yucatán*, 3 March 1996; *Diccionario histórico y biográfico de la revolución mexicana*, vol. 7 (México: Instituto Nacional de Estudios Históricos de la Revolución Mexicana, 1992), 737–38; and Franco Savarino Roggero, *Pueblos y nacionalismo, del régimen oligárquico a la sociedad de masas en Yucatán, 1894–1925* (México: Instituto Nacional de Estudios Históricos de la Revolución Mexicana, 1997), 342–46.

> *Although Pacheco Cruz was an interesting man, he was a convo-*
> *luted and pretentious writer. This translation omits the original*
> *paragraph numberings. I simplified some of the complex clauses*
> *and converted his editorial "we" to first-person singular throughout.*
> *Pacheco Cruz also included in parentheses the Maya equivalents of*
> *many words and phrases; I have omitted most of these parenthetical*
> *insertions. Readers who are interested in linguistic study are advised*
> *to consult the original text.[2]*

For years a favorite pastime [was attending] the *vaquería*[3] dances, which began at night with a high-spirited opening *jarana*[4] that summoned the people. The dancers dressed themselves in *ternos*[5] with whimsical drawings bordered by hand. [Some] adorned their necks with chains, whereas others used rosaries of gold and filigree with shields made from American coins of 5, 10, or 20 dollars[6] and which ended in lovely medallions or crucifixes. They crossed the body diagonally with a broad cloth belt that ended in a bow at the side. Their hair was worn loose or in a bun tied with a ribbon, and [they wore] a straw hat adorned with narrow ribbons and a tiny mirror on the brim and fixed to the hat's crown; their white slippers had no hose. The men wore white outfits, along with *alpargatas,* or sandals.

At the beginning of the dance, the leader[7] took charge of placing the men in a line, and with a signal of his handkerchief, the girls came up to dance. After a few turns they changed places, yielding by courtesy or upon request to give up their place to others. In the middle of the dance, they played the *jarana* known as "The Little Bull" to give the dancers a chance to turn the salon into a bullring, with the woman assuming the role of the bull and the man that of bullfighter but always dancing, the man using a handkerchief as cape; and when the woman managed to get the best of him, she received applause amid shouting and laughter of the crowd. This was the most elaborate part of the fiesta, when they played songs such as "the Yucatecan *jarabe,*"[8] "the airs," "the

---

2. The source of the following material is Santiago Pacheco Cruz, *Usos, costumbres, religión y supersticiones de los mayas. Apuntes históricos con un estudio psicobiológico de la raza* (Mérida: 1947), 74-87.

3. The term *vaquería* refers to a rural Yucatecan folk dance and celebration that is loosely associated with the tending of cattle.

4. A popular dance in 3/4 or 6/8 time.

5. A *terno* was an elaborate costume consisting of a *fustán* and a brightly colored *hipil.*

6. U.S. gold coins, including the denominations to which Pacheco Cruz refers, were not discontinued until 1933. The original U.S. coins were modeled after the Spanish silver coins of the late Bourbon era.

7. *Bastonero,* because like a drum major, he carried a *bastón,* or staff.

8. The *jarabe* is any of several provincial Mexican dances involving elaborate footwork; its origins are Spanish. Its popular renderings can be heard on the outstanding recording of Maya folk musicians produced by Radio XEPET, which is run by the National Indigenous Institute in Peto.

anguiripola," "the *degollete,*" and so forth. During the dance, when someone requested a *bomba*,[9] the music stopped and the best of the dancers recited some verses to his partner, which were in turn met with applause. . . .

The decline of this dance owes to the fact that young people have taken up more modern counterparts, and as a result no longer give it the seriousness it deserves, but instead merely dance without respect to tradition. When the *vaquero* dance is repeated at noon on the day following the fiesta, they give the participants a tasty *pozole* known as *puk' k'eyem,* diluted and sweetened with honey, another tradition that has died out altogether. The woman who dances with the best footwork receives a prize, placing upon her head a hat that the owners later pay money to recover; this is called *gala,* but now has more to do with romance because it depends less on the quality of dancing and more on desiring the woman as a sweetheart, no matter how clumsy she may be. It used to be that adolescents did not participate in this dance, but now we have the scandal of seeing seven-year-old girls taking it up in front of the school, and to the great satisfaction of their parents.

Another popular custom was *k'uub pool,* or handing over the pig's head. This was a favorite pastime of pagan origins and superstitious air that would be celebrated at the end of a dance. When I was a child, I used to see these same ceremonies carried out after religious fiestas. It ran something as follows. A group of hacienda residents, for example, which is where the ritual was done, elected as "deputies" a patron or matron to appropriately carry out the fiesta; and from the home of the chief deputy, they carried out the head in procession to the main house.[10] Over a table they would place the barbecued pig's head, adorning it with paper streamers or multicolored ribbons hung from the side, cigarettes, wheat bread, dried ears of corn, candies, small bottles of liquor, perhaps even silver coins put in the eyes; and along the edge of the table [they would place] many other objects and narrow ribbons that *vaqueras* would take hold of during the procession.

At noon on the dot the ceremony would begin under the supervision of the *chik*[11] and his wife, as the supposed owners of the animal, and amid the sounds of special music and ceaselessly dancing in time, they would go along, the accompanying dancers each clutching a ribbon. That would cause a phenomenal scandal, and even without mentioning the mournful songs, the dance steps, the gestures, the capers, and the other clownings of the *chik,* who went with his head and body painted and only his private parts covered; he wore horns and a tail in imitation of the devil. He wore bird feathers as a hat. His wife was also crudely dressed and painted and imitated him in all things, carrying in

---

9. *Bombas* are short, four-line poems, usually witty or risqué, that are used to observe a brief pause in the dancing. Here is an example: "A Yucatecan fell/ from the top of a church/ but he broke no bones/ because he landed on his head."

10. I.e., the house of the hacienda's owner.

11. Maya for "clown" or "buffoon."

one hand a small gourd with which to solicit alms and in the other a bit of corn, which supposedly enticed the pig.

On reaching his destination, the *chik* announced in Maya that the moment had come to hand over the pig's head to next year's deputies. The leader of the procession read an invocation to the gods in Maya, and afterwards the *chik* concluded matters by sprinkling everyone with *balche'* as the benediction that formalizes the new deputies. Finally, they would play "The Little Bull" or some other *jarana* that all danced wildly, carrying the head with the same formality to the house of its new patron, where they cut it up to give to those present. This ceremony has lost much of its original flavor, and I would not be wrong in saying that it is forgotten.

In 1930 in the town of Nohcacab, I witnessed one of these ceremonies, already in frank decadence because the old ritual had not been observed. What I saw was the following. At four in the afternoon, rockets and music announced that the procession was leaving the house where they had set up a table, three pitchers decorated with multicolored paper, wheat bread, cigarettes, and nothing more. It seemed that they were celebrating the *k'uub pool* ceremony, but because I did not see the main object, I asked, "Where's the head they'll be handing over?" "In the pitchers, sir," responded one of the old women guarding the table. "The pig's meat has been minced into pieces." How odd, I thought, as if they had before them two succulent plates of tidbits but without the tidbits! When I had made certain of what they had said, I felt a great loss and a horrible sense of deception on seeing the adulteration of that ceremony, and I was so upset that I could no longer remain, leaving to watch the rest from the street. Soon afterward they carried the pitchers with music, much in the style of a political demonstration, to a dance hall, where the men with the precious cargo began to dance in time around a long table; all the men added a small contribution, and with each change of music, the steps were reversed. And when there were no more contributions to be given, the dance ended; the entire time the women did not take part. There was no *chik* or election, no invocation or anything else. They did everything brusquely and with a certain disrespectful air.

I should also mention *baxal wakax,* or the game of bulls. This is a favorite pastime that is still kept up in some villages, except in the region of Santa Cruz, where it was never known. It consists of amateurs fighting young bulls, although without all the rules of the true sport. They constructed the so-called arena with poles and thatch, even interrupting traffic through the town in the process. At times they even battled with ferocious bulls, which were led through the town by horsemen or cowboys. Tying the bull to a pole in the center of this improvised ring in order to keep it in one place, they fought with cloths, handkerchiefs, hats, and so forth, usually managing to avoid being gored; but there were those who, in carrying out a dare, were knocked down and injured. The whole business was truly entertaining. It reached its apogee

in the 1890s and owed its decline to the establishment of professional bullfights that charged admission, affairs that had real *toreros* in special costume
who also took part in special bullrings. In towns without rings, they build them
out of wood planks, imitating the circular form of the Roman circus.

Those wooden rings have an upper area and are built from wood and
thatch and can be dangerous; there have already been several cases of such
arenas collapsing and causing injuries. They decorate them with banners and
large strips of multicolored paper, and there are places where they fight as
many as 25 bulls before a public thrilled by what I can only call barbarous
entertainment. What worthwhile lesson can be gained from the bullfight?
None. And to be certain, there are those passionate aficionados who pay no
attention to the steep admission price and who prefer it to a good book. And
there are those who travel regardless of the distance or the cost in order to
attend a bullfight. As if this wasn't bad enough, others will hire out a special
airplane merely to travel to a single fight, as did certain young fanatics from
Chetumal and Havana. Fortunately, not all the nations of the world have
accepted this savagery, which they see as inhuman and barbarous; I personally
oppose such entertainment. . . .[12]

I should also mention *pa p'úul,* or breaking the pitcher, pitchers, or piñata,
something which I have described elsewhere as "pitcher" or *p'úul.* This custom is disappearing, now replaced by a watermelon that is set up and then
shattered by blows from the fist. They call this "busting the melon" (*ts'oop
sandía*), and it also appears to be passing into history.

Then there was the *kuuch,* or burden. This entertainment, apparently of
superstitious origins, was usually celebrated during May in connection with
novenas to the Cross. A group of townsfolk responsible for celebrating the last
night of the novena carried out this custom, honoring the Cross and praying for
the health of both the local people and the crops. After [saying] a rosary, they
brought the image to the house of the group's leader, where a dance was held.
This man had the obligation to cover the costs, including food for all the participants—in effect, he carried all of the "burden," and hence the name. From
the end of the celebration until daybreak, they placed the Cross in the taberna-
cle and elected members for the group who would do the same thing the following year. In some eastern villages, they still keep up these customs, with no
lack of alcohol or of victims who will never see the ceremony's end.

Jats' pach, or a dance of *vaqueras,*[13] was celebrated on the last night of their
fiestas. This custom seems to be the property of villages in eastern Yucatán,
where I have had the opportunity to attend. The same is true of the *nona,* or
midnight serenade by full orchestra, raising an absolute uproar as the sponsors

---

12. Here I have omitted two largely rhetorical paragraphs on bullfighting, which Pacheco Cruz
had reproduced from his 1921 article in *La revista de Yucatán.*

13. I.e., a dance of only the women.

parade merrily through the streets with loud fireworks that wake up everyone. Both customs are gradually being forgotten for lack of frequent use.

Janal pixan, food of the spirits or meal of the dead, is a practice still observed in the present day. In the modern-day Maya communities of the Santa Cruz region, they are accustomed to hanging torches or lit candles at intervals from the entrance of the property to the house. These illuminate the path that the spirits of the dead are to follow in returning to the grave and keep them from being harmed by demons. I have been able to observe this ceremony or superstitious belief, which, guarded by ignorance, still prevails. In contrast, the natives who live in more progressive villages observe these days using other practices that I have described elsewhere. . . .[14]

I remember that when [I was] only a boy during the season of the Dead, I was accustomed to tagging along with the prayer chanters, hoping to pick up a bit of the alms they received when they went from house to house praying. On the hacienda where I spent that delightful season, the esoteric ceremony known as *janal pixan,* or "food of the souls," was observed with great ceremony. Greedy child that I was, I thought nothing of going out with the other *wíinikitos,*[15] Indian children who went from house to house in front of the chanters. Children both great and small carried on their shoulder their classic henequen sacks,[16] others their satchels, and still others mere sacks, in order to feed the chanters with the traditional corn bread baked in the ground or else the same corn bread cooked with beans inside. These breads were specially baked for the ceremony. The procession began at 3:00 P.M. in order to finish before nightfall after passing before all or most of the houses on the hacienda.

In those days I would dress in a shirt of *juntich',* or common cloth. My hat was made from straw, completely frayed around the edges by use; I also wore a chain with an all-important talisman, with its coin piece[17] that my grandmother had bought at the fair at Halachó, along with my sandals, little more than a piece of leather tied with a twisted rough string of henequen. In brief, I was a half-wild, a demon, but certainly in keeping with the spirit of the time. The houses of the hacienda were wattle and daub over wood poles, with the corresponding door of heavy vines and a guano roofing. They had no rooms or divisions, not even in the patio, because it seemed that everyone lived in common. Everyone shared the responsibility of participating in the prayers in order to be entitled to the ceremonial dinner. . . .

Fastened to the wall on one end of the oval-shaped homes would be a

---

14. Pacheco Cruz extracted the following eight paragraphs from his article "*Janal Pixan* in the Final Decade of the Nineteenth Century," published in the December 1924 issue of *Boletín de Universidad Nacional del Sureste.* I have omitted the quotation marks that set these paragraphs apart from the main text.

15. A Maya-Spanish term meaning "little people."

16. Here Pacheco Cruz uses the peninsular term *jabuco,* known in Maya as *paw.*

17. Pacheco Cruz uses the term *dinero en cruz,* apparently referring to a coin that formed the intersection of the three threads of the rosary.

wooden table, which they used as an altar. Upon it they placed a green cross with a sky blue ribbon, along with various symbols painted on the wood; various ceramic objects; to the side, various engravings with a multitude of wildflowers, including rue, basil, *xp'ujuk,* and others, whose rich scents permeated the air. To illuminate the altar they used a wealth of candles in combination with box lamps made with oil and cotton wicks. Beyond this, there were other enormous clay pots with assorted foods; tasty pieces of yucca with a bit of honey; bits of *camote;* jícama; *pibil nal,* or earth-baked corn bread; gourds of *pozole* suspended from the rafters; fresh *atole* and so forth; some *pibil* with lots of chile; various small cases of cigarettes to distribute after the prayer; two pumpkins containing a drink known as *balche'* or *pitarrilla,* which, when taken in quantity, produces the same effect as alcohol; *taburetes* and two *jekeb che'ob,* or armchairs, over a guano mat placed in front of the altar.

There were also various stools, chairs, and so forth for those attending, along with an incense commonly used to perfume the altar and surrounding area. This was what one was to find in the interior; the exterior decorations were even more extravagant. There the spirit found room to breath; one could delight just as much in the scenes of the patio as in the interior of the kitchen and underneath the bower. This is what would happen. In the kitchen there would be three or four girls of the house, strong and sassy and dressed in regional costume; these ground the *nixtamal*[18] to make the dough for tortillas. . . . [T]hey pinned back part of their *huipil* at the hips to avoid damaging it as they worked. The distinctive hair arrangement ended in the classic bun or knot made with the hair at the nape and tied with brightly colored ribbons. They would skillfully work the grinding stone over the metate, and in a second the corn was ground. . . .

[In the patio] you could see the women, each with her distinct responsibilities. I refer to the married and older women, not to the elderly. In one of those thick *ramonales*[19] (*oxo'ob*) would be a group of girls charged with patting out the dough into tortillas; sometimes the girls of the house helped in this task, but because it was not as difficult as the grinding, it was usually reserved for the older women. Somewhat removed and stationed beside a griddle over the fire, a young girl busied herself with fanning or reviving the flame, whereas beside all who patted out tortillas stood a large gourd filled with water, which they used to periodically moisten the dough and to wet down and soften the banana leaf they used for pressing the tortilla.

A bit farther away, beneath the shade of a bitter orange tree, two or three women tended the turkeys and chickens that formed the marrow of the *pib* that they make so well. After forming the breads in a circular mold, they cover them with banana leaves until the moment of burial. Toward the rear of the property,

18. *Masa,* or uncooked cornmeal; in Maya, *k'u'um.*
19. I.e., a grove of *ramón* trees.

the men would dig a pit where, heated with stones and much firewood, they left the breads to bake underground. Both sexes wore little more than the clothes of Adam, suffering the full force of the sun, to which they were accustomed. To one side of the ceremony stood heaps of firewood, stones, and oak leaves, which complemented the operation. Under the bower, truly touching scenes took place: there were elderly men and women smoking cornhusk cigarettes and chatting merrily, waxing nostalgic over the *úuchben*,[20] a past that put them in a religious mood, reflecting in their emaciated faces the marks of pain it caused them to remember their ancestors.

Some remained squatting, others sat on the stools, whereas the old women kept to their armchairs, all awaiting the traditional and long-anticipated hour of the *pixano'ob*, or souls, in order to divide up the food. At noon they performed the burial, after which they would rest a while to recover their strength; as the food cooked they talked without forgetting the *balche'*, which at times even the women take to calm their stomachs. At 3:00 P.M., more or less, they proceeded to take out *jóok'saj*. For this, they brought out tables on which to place the hot bread, peeling away the leaves to carry them to the altars as *janal pixan*, or food of the spirits. Once the feast was set up, they entertained the spirits with prayers and songs, much as the *trovadores*[21] do today when contracted to accompany a dinner. In reality, you have to hear these prayers: an amalgam that I could barely understand because once they began to speak, it was all in the Maya language, or Greek to me.[22] When the prayers ended and after the familiar and ceremonial exchanges of respect—performed in conjunction with the corresponding *tsuuts k'abo'ob*, or kissing of the hands, which the youngsters do with respect to their elders—came the division, giving to each participant a generous helping as a gift for having honored the house with their presence. Afterwards, all went away and the house remained once more with its occupants wrapped in a funereal silence. . . .

Another custom was *ch'uuk*, meaning "to spy." This was a method for nighttime hunting that can still be found today. When farmers find tracks of a four-legged animal in their *milpas*, they set up a blind near the place where the animal is believed to enter, something that they usually do at night by the light of a full moon. Indeed, only in the most urgent cases will they go out using special lamps that allow them to see their quarry. This system carries no risks because they go accompanied by nothing more than their dogs, and sometimes not even these.

To determine the hours of the day, the natives employ a solar clock,

---

20. I.e., the *úuchben máako'ob*, or the ancient Mayas.

21. The *trovadores* are trios of singer-guitarists known for their melancholy and nostalgic style of music.

22. This was an odd comment because Pacheco Cruz himself spoke Maya. Their prayers probably contained elements of Spanish and archaic Maya and were spoken rapidly and perhaps even mumbled.

whereby they plot the course of the sun, and at night, of the moon (if there is one). They have done this since before the conquest and, in fact, a good deal afterward; they had no knowledge of the invention of the clock. The Franciscans themselves had to make use of sundials, something that I have seen intact as late as 25 November 1830, in the ruins of the convent in Mama in the Ticul district. . . .[23]

To the present day, the natives are completely uninterested in the use of the clock because they consider it a luxury item and, despite all advances, continue to tell time by the path of the sun. In fact, there are some hamlets in the Maya region where they have never heard of nor need a clock, something that I was able to determine during my visits with them. When I asked them the time, they would look up to see the position of the sun. Their answers, based on this calculation, almost always corresponded with the hour of my own watch. *Ba'ax k'iinil t-ulech?* one says, or "What time is it?" The reply is, *Bey yanil k'iina',* or "That's where the sun is." They will probably continue this traditional practice for centuries to come.

[There is little interest in the] *k'iin k'aaba',* meaning onomastic or saint's day. They waste no time in such matters, where other people squander money, often with tragic consequences.[24] They neither know how to celebrate their saint's day, nor feel any need to do so. The one celebration they did follow was the carnival, something they observed with all due ritual and ingenuity, including the dances punctuated with genuflections, grimaces, clownish antics, and so forth. These dances inspired revelry and ended in the burning of an effigy known as "John of the Carnival." However, they have lost much of their original flavor. Everything has been adulterated, even the masquerades with their unusual and devilish dances. Each day, it seems, they fall deeper into decline, to the point of leaving no trace of their former selves. Current carnivals lack the splendor of years past. Villagers no longer construct the famous allegorical floats, which were the events' heart and soul, but rather confine themselves to dances, which usually degenerate into drunken benders. But the carnivals that were celebrated 30 or 40 years ago were authentic fiestas where the spirit expressed itself and reveled in its own playfulness and undisguised joy.

Beyond these diversions, the natives of Yucatán also had a predilection for sports, although without the technique today learned in schools. They played *polokpok,* or a ball game; *lolomche',* or canes; *ets'ya',* or hands; *kuuch lu'um che', oklombat,* and *buul,* which they played using lima beans much like dice. All the children took to these games as a way of avoiding idleness and vagrancy, but nowadays it horrifies one to see how native children grow up.

---

23. I have omitted the author's detailed description of the Franciscan sundial.

24. A supporter of progressive revolutionary factions, Pacheco Cruz opposed many features of traditional folk Catholicism, particularly those that appeared to be wasteful and inefficient, such as the elaborate celebrations for saints' days.

Conclusion

Yucatec Mayas in the Modern Day

Virtually all of the ethnographic writings in this book are based on observations made between 1800 and 1900. After such a detailed exploration of the events and culture of the nineteenth century, it is worth taking a moment to follow events to the present day. Maya-speaking peoples have by no means disappeared, and the agriculturally based Maya lifestyle continues in many parts of southeastern Mexico. Their survival from the beginning to the end of the twentieth century has been a story of struggle, loss, persistence, adaptation, and triumph.

The Mexican Revolution, that terrible epic of national catastrophe and rebirth, came late to the Yucatán Peninsula. High international demand for henequen helped insulate the region from the economic pressures that afflicted other parts of the nation during the first decade of the twentieth century. Sporadic rural violence did occur in the region between 1910 and 1915, but it failed to assume the coherence or intensity of the *zapatista* movement in Morelos or of the widespread lower-class mobilizations in the state of Chihuahua. Some of the early revolutionary violence in Yucatán was apparently sparked by elite groups rallying their economic dependents in an effort to gain momentary political advantage.

Southeasterners began to experience serious conflict only when revolutionary "first chief" Venustiano Carranza sent an occupying force under Gen. Salvador Alvarado to bring Yucatecans into line with national goals and authority. During his tenure as military governor (1915–19), Alvarado outlawed debt peonage, a linchpin of the hacienda system, but he left much of the remaining structure in place. Like Juan Perón in Argentina, he simply created a state purchasing monopoly to finance reform and development.

Alvarado's successor, the far more radical (and native Yucatecan) Felipe Carrillo Puerto (1922–24), tried to mold a base of political support among the rural Mayas. Carrillo Puerto attempted serious land reform, but his poorly armed and disorganized militias proved little help against a wave of organized counterrevolutionary repression, which claimed the radical governor's life in 1924. Real change, however, occurred during the next two decades. The revolution destroyed the great henequen haciendas, whose days were probably numbered anyway because of declining world markets and increasing foreign competition. In the 1930s the land was finally divided and distributed as *ejidos,* or collective organizations that resembled the corporate villages of the colonial era.

Yucatán's henequen *ejidos* are cloaked in the same ambiguity that masks land reforms in other parts of Mexico. On one hand, the revolutionary system brought hope and dignity to a generation of rural Mayas, gains that boosted their resistance to servitude. On the other hand, virtually all studies conclude that former peons gradually became servants to a government bureaucracy.

Until the 1950s fiber processing remained in the hands of former *hacendados;* the subsequent state-owned Cordemex processing plant proved to be no less manipulative. State control minimized individual incentives. The state-managed cordage industry was finally allowed to die a natural death in the 1990s. The former processing plant is being converted into a series of shopping malls.

The *ejidos* have followed a similar path. *Ejido* privatization from 1992 onward has resulted in winners, who have made successful transitions to private entrepreneurs, often working their orchards while maintaining day jobs, such as teacher; and in losers, who have had to sell or rent their land, or make ends meet by pedaling three-wheeled rural rickshaws known as *trici-taxis*. Rural communities in southern Campeche, such as Xpujil, remain some of the poorest and most isolated in the nation.

In the region of the Speaking Cross, tourism has replaced militarism. Resorts such as Cancún and Xcaret draw villagers by the thousands to serve as construction workers and groundskeepers. Tourism revenues, however, do not help the isolated and impoverished communities that still revere the cross, places such as Señor, Tixcacal Guardia, and Chum Pon. Former *ejidatarios* in areas without tourist attractions or alternative crops, such as citrus, have migrated in large numbers to the United States.

In other respects, the post–Carrillo Puerto years have been kind to the Mayas. The ersatz sentimentality of early revolutionary indigenism gradually gave way to increased knowledge of, and respect for, Maya culture. Over time the revolutionary programs have tended to lift, at least partially, the colonial stigma placed on Maya-speaking peoples. Rural social programs, undreamed of in the profoundly racist and laissez-faire nineteenth century, have improved some of the worst conditions. In the 1970s, Maya-language education was introduced in the first six years of primary school, a praiseworthy program still operating today. Maya-language radio programs can be heard on Radio XEPET, which is run by the National Indigenous Institute in Peto.

In cities, small towns, and villages, people of Maya descent are increasingly participating in politics and professional life. Enhanced access to education and careers has created a special group in Yucatán, as it has elsewhere in Mexico: a strata of indigenous (and at times indigenist) intellectuals, who retain their original language and their feel for the rural milieu, but who now have the ability to articulate cultural statements and formulate political positions. This has not resulted in demands for political independence; it has, however, boosted the self-esteem of Yucatán's rural people, helped to preserve an important cultural component of the Western Hemisphere, and provided a heritage and continuity for rural inhabitants faced with an often painful transition to urban life.

Historical writing has also adopted a more reasoned view of the Yucatec Mayas. No longer dismissed as atavistic barbarians or passive "political cattle," the rural inhabitants of southeastern Mexico are increasingly viewed as active participants in the social, economic, and political life of Mexico. This trend holds true for historical commentaries on both the colonial and the modern eras.

Perhaps the most remarkable achievement has been to retain and system-atize the Yucatec Maya language. Many scholars, even the most sympathetic, have dismissed Maya as a dying language. In 1913, for example, amateur Maya scholar Santiago Pacheco Cruz (author of this book's final entry) wrote, "The Maya language will disappear, that fact we do not doubt, but for all the cen-turies it will retain its great historical value."[1]

Viewed from the city, this prophecy seems to have been accurate: urban Mexicans today seldom learn indigenous tongues, which they regard as irrele-vant at best and the language of losers at worst. In reality, however, Pacheco Cruz's words have yet to be fulfilled. The number of Yucatec Maya speakers has actually increased during the past five decades. The language's persistence is partly due to improved rural living conditions and decreased infant mortality rates from 1940 onward. The survival of Maya, however, is mainly due to con-scious initiatives. Beginning with Alfredo Barrera Vázquez in the 1930s, pas-sionately committed Maya speakers have codified its grammar, spelling, and vocabulary. Printed texts of poetry, folklore, religion, local history, and peda-gogical material are now available, as well as public and private classes for would-be *mayeros,* or followers of the Maya agriculturally based lifestyle.

According to Mexico's National Institute for Statistics, Geography, and Information (INEGI), the number of Maya speakers has grown considerably since the 1950s. Today it ranks as the second-largest indigenous language in Mexico (after Nahuatl, which is actually fragmented into several local dialects). An estimated 700,000 people know Maya, the majority of whom are bilingual in Spanish.[2] Maya has managed to survive partly through continued evolution and has incorporated more Spanish (and English) words than ever before. Whether this extremely ancient tongue can persist in the face of Mexico's cur-rent social and economic changes remains to be seen.

Whatever the future may bring, I hope that this collection has provided some insight into the lives of a people whose nineteenth-century travails played such a dramatic role in the history of the Mexican and Central American nations. For them and for their heirs, I offer a saying from rural Yucatán: *Bis u yutsil bej, bik xi'ikech ich k'i'ixil;* "Go down a good road, not through the briars."

---

1. Santiago Pacheco Cruz, *Compendio del idioma maya: Modelo "Pacheco Cruz"* (Mérida: Imprenta Constitucionalista, 1920; orig. 1913), 119.

2. Instituto Nacional de Estadística, Geografía, e Informática, *Estadísticas históricas de México,* I (Mexico City: INEGI, 1994), 139. The exact number of Nahuatl or Mexicano speakers ages five years and older is listed as 1,197,328; Maya is second at 713,620; Zapotec runs third at 403,457.

Glossary

Word origins: E = English; G = Greek; M = Maya; N = Nahuatl; S = Spanish; T = Taino.

aak' (M) Literally, "tongue." Also refers to vines, which are used to bind the pole frames of Maya huts.

abogado defensor de indios (S) Indian Defense Attorney, who represented the Mayas in the law courts during the years 1864–67.

adelantado (S) Literally, "trailblazer." An explorer or conquistador.

aguada (S) A pond or small lake that is common in southern Yucatán, Campeche, and Quintana Roo.

aguardiente (S) A crude form of rum common in rural southern Mexico.

aj bolon pixan (M) A patron saint.

aj k'iin (M) A priest.

ajua kaan (M) Literally, "serpent king." The supernatural being believed to be the protector of snakes.

albañil (S) A mason.

alcabala (S) A regional import/export duty.

alcalde (S) A mayor or head official of a town. Also refers to a third-tier official on the *república de indígenas.*

almud (S) A Spanish weight measure equal to 3.5 kilograms.

alpargata (S) A sandal.

anguiripola (S) A form of *jarana,* or popular dance. Also known as *angaripola.*

anís (S) A sweetened, anise-flavored liquor.

anisado (S) A variation of *anís.*

aniseed (S) A variation of *anís.*

arancel (S) A schedule of fees for clerical services established in the late colonial period.

arbitrio (S) A municipal sales or property tax.

arras (S) The groom's equivalent of a dowry given to the bride at the wedding.

arroba (S) A Spanish weight measure equal to twenty-five pounds. Also refers to a Spanish liquid measure equal to 2.6 to 3.6 gallons.

atole (N) A drink made of dried ground cornmeal dissolved in hot water.

avanzada (S) A military term that refers to a vanguard position outside a larger settlement or fortification.

ayuntamiento (S) A Hispanic city council.

bachiller (S) A person who holds an educational degree beyond the level of *primeras letras* (basic education) and below the level of *licenciatura* (four-year completion).

baile (S) A dance.

balam (M) A field god. Also called *yumstil.*

balche' (M) A beerlike beverage popular in rural villages.

batab (M) A village headman or *cacique*.

baxal wakax (M) Bullfighting.

bejuco (S) A vine.

bomba (S) A witty, often risqué, four-line poem used to punctuate popular dances known as *jaranas*.

bomi p'óok (M) A straw hat made of fine leaves.

bóoch' (M) *See* **rebozo**.

bozal (S) A black slave born in Africa.

bungay (E) A nineteenth-century Belizean term for a small boat used for river navigation.

buul (M) A bean or beans. Also refers to a game played with lima beans used as dice.

cabildo (S) A town council. Also refers to the building where the council held its meetings.

cacique (S, from Arawak) *See* **batab**.

calesa (S) A small, low-wheeled carriage.

camote (N) A root crop similar to a sweet potato.

cantón (S) A military outpost or canton.

carbonero (S) In normal usage, a charcoal maker. Among the rebels of Chan Santa Cruz, someone who is responsible for guarding the community's supply of gunpowder.

carga (S) A Spanish weight measure equal to forty-five pounds.

casa real (S) A community building used for ceremonial functions and for lodging travelers. After Mexican independence, the *casa real* was more commonly referred to as the *casa constitorial*.

castillo (S) Literally, "castle." In nineteenth-century Mérida, a building that was the site of the grain market.

caudillo (S) A military/political leader or chief.

cenote (S, from M, *ts'ono'ot*) A limestone sinkhole.

cha' (M) Chicle, or the sap from the *chicozapote,* tree, used as the basis for chewing gum.

cháak (M) One of the four rain gods.

cháamcham (M) A pastry made of corn and meat or corn and beans.

chak (M) A game played by tossing pottery disks from the palm to the back of the hand.

chan yum tupilo'ob (M) Literally, "small sir sheriffs." Used as a term of respect for a lesser chief among the Maya rebels and *pacíficos*.

chichem (M) A tree with caustic sap.

chiclero (S) A chicle tapper.

chicozapote (N/S) The sapodilla tree, from which chicle is derived.

chik (M) A clown, specifically someone who plays the role of buffoon in a rural celebration involving the ceremonial gift of a pig's head. *See also* **k'uub pool**.

chile (S) A chile or pepper.

chokwil (M) A fever.

chultun (M) An artificial, underground receptacle used for storing rainwater.

chúuj (M) A gourd used to carry water.

ch'a' cháak (M) A rain ceremony.

ch'il (M) A corn crib.

ch'uuk (M) Literally, "to spy." Also refers to hunting animals from a blind.

ch'uyub (M) A gourd cup.

coa (T) A short, hook-bladed machete. The term may be an adaptation of the Spanish word *corva,* or "a curved form."

comandante (S) A commander.

comandante de armas (S) A military commander.

compadre (S) Literally, a close friend or relative who pledges himself to care for one's child in the event of one's death; figuratively, a close friend.

copal (S) Incense produced from the resin of a tropical tree. Also refers to this tree.

corregidor (S) In early national Guatemala, a district official or governor.

cuartel (S) Barracks.

cuartilla (S) A liquid measure equal to approximately .188 liters, which was often contained in a hip flask.

cura (S) A village pastor.

degollete (S) A folk dance that culminated in the decapitation of a turkey.

doctrina (S) Basic catechism lessons.

eex (M) Cotton drawers or trousers worn by Maya peasants.

ejidatario (S) A member of a government-sponsored agricultural cooperative created in the wake of the Mexican Revolution.

ejido (S) A village communal land. After 1920, a government-sponsored agricultural cooperative.

encomendero (S) In the colonial era, the receiver of Indian tribute, or *encomienda.*

escopeta (S) A shotgun.

escribano (S) A scribe. An official position on the *república de indígenas.*

ets'ya' (M) A game played with the hands.

fianza (S) The bonding of executors by a third party.

fiscal de doctrina (S) Maya church assistant responsible for overseeing the teaching of catechism to Indian children.

frijol (S) A bean.

fustán (S) The lace petticoat worn under a *hipil.*

fustic (S) A wood used for the extraction of yellow dyes.

gala (S) In rural Yucatán, a women's dance competition based on elaborate footwork.

gobernador (S) Among the Mayas of the Petén in Guatemala, the equivalent of *batab.* Although used at times in colonial Yucatán, this term became relatively rare by the nineteenth century.

guarache (N) A sandal.

habanero (S) An extremely hot (spicy) chile pepper.

habuco (S) A sack or bag, often made of henequen fiber.

hacendado (S) The owner of a hacienda.

hacienda (S) A commercial estate with resident workers.

hidalgo (S) Originally a Spanish nobleman. The title was subsequently granted to Mayas who had cooperated during the conquest of Yucatán. The title became hereditary but had declined in importance by the beginning of the nineteenth century. The term should not be confused with *indio hidalgo.*

hipil (N) A sleeveless blouse commonly worn by Maya women. Also spelled *huipil*.

h-men (M) A Maya shaman.

huano (N) A palm leaf used to thatch huts. Also the tree that produces this leaf.

iik (M) *See* **chile**.

indios hidalgos (S) An honorific title conferred upon Maya peasants who performed ancillary services during the Caste War.

jabín (S) A tall tree prized for its high tannin content.

janal pixan (M) Literally, "food of the dead." A ceremony associated with the Day of the Dead, on which offerings of food and drink are provided for consumption by dead ancestors.

jarabe (S) Any of several provincial Mexican dances involving elaborate footwork.

jarana (S) A popular dance performed in 3/4 or 6/8 time, often punctuated by witty four-line poems known as *bombas*.

jats' pach (M) A rural dance performed by women, which is part of a public celebration known as a *vaquería*.

jefatura político (S) A district comprising several municipalities governed by a *jefe político*.

jefe político (S) In nineteenth-century Mexico, a politically appointed administrator of a district. The office was abolished after the Mexican Revolution in 1910.

jekeb che' (M) An armchair.

jerga (S) A sash of thick cloth.

jóok'saj (M) To take out or withdraw.

jornalero (S) A temporary worker on an estate.

jul (M) An arrow.

juntich' (M) A coarse cotton textile.

kaltal (M) Drunkenness.

kanchikin (M) A splenic enlargement.

kanlajun tas waaj (M) Literally "fourteen tortillas." A special form of bread associated with the *tich'* ceremony.

keex (M) Literally, "change." A ceremony used to save a dying person by placating Death with offerings of food and drink. In modern parlance, *keex* often refers to a married woman's lover.

kisin boox (M) Literally, "black devil." A term for blacks.

koché (M/S) A sedan transportation service. The term is probably an adaptation of the Spanish word *coche,* or "car."

koj kaan (M) Literally, "serpent's tooth." A healing process that involves bleeding with a serpent's tooth or hollow fish bone.

kool (M) A *milpa,* or cornfield.

kuspach (M) A Maya runner or porter.

kuuch (M) Literally, "burden." A rural ceremony in which the sponsor assumes the "burden" for offerings to propitiate the gods.

kuuch lu'um che' (M) An unidentified game for Maya children.

kuum (M) An earthen pot.

k'áaj (M) A corn-based drink similar to *pozole*.

k'áak' (M) A fire or bonfire. Smallpox.

k'áan (M) A hammock.

k'áanche' (M) A low wooden bench.

k'eyem (M) *See* **pozole**.

k'íilkabankil (M) A sweat treatment used to cure malaria.

k'iin k'aaba' (M) Literally, "name day." A birthday.

k'íiwik (M) A plaza or market.

k'óoben (M) The three-stone hearth of a Maya hut.

k'óol (M) Soup or broth.

k'uub pool (M) Literally, "handing over the head." A Maya celebration that involves the ceremonial giving or entrusting of a pig's head.

k'uuch (M) To spin (e.g., cloth).

k'u'um (M) *See* **nixtamal**.

legua (S) A league. A distance measure equal to 2.4 to 4.6 miles.

ligeros (S) Lightly armed soldiers responsible for carrying provisions and tending the wounded.

lolomche' (M) A game played with canes.

loobche' (M) *See* **coa**.

lunero (S) Resident worker on a hacienda.

ma'alob (M) Good.

macewal (M, from N) Common rural term for an indigenous peasant.

maestro de capilla (S) Maya church assistant responsible for the cleaning and upkeep of the church.

majagua (S) The linden tree, whose vines are used for weaving footwear.

makab aak' (M) A door made of woven vines, which is common in Maya huts.

masa (S) *See* **nixtamal**.

mayero (M/S) A follower of the Maya rural lifestyle.

mayordomo (S) The manager of a hacienda.

mecapal (S) A form of apron worn by Maya laborers.

mecate (N) A unit of land measuring approximately four hundred square meters, or twenty meters on each side.

medio (S) One-half of a *real*.

men (M) See *h-men*.

mestizo (S) A person with a mixture of Spanish and Indian blood. Later in the nineteenth century, the term *mestiza* became a euphemism for Maya women.

metate (N) A flat stone used for grinding corn.

milpa (S) A cornfield.

milpa caña (S) A cornfield that still contains the dry stalks from the previous year.

milpa rosa (S) Overgrown fallow land.

mirmecófagos didáctilos (G) The two-toed anteater.

mitote (N) A Maya drum made from a hollowed-out tree trunk.

mojonero (S) *See* **multun**.

mulatto (S) A person with a mixture of Spanish and black (African) blood.

multun (M) A stone marker used to designate property boundaries.

nixtamal (N) Cooked and ground cornmeal to be shaped into tortillas.

noj kalam (M) *See* **nojoch yum taat**.

nojoch yum taat (M) Literally, "great sir father." A term of respect for the head chief among Maya rebels and *pacíficos*.

nona (S) A midnight serenade with full orchestra associated with a *vaquería*.

oklombat (M) An unidentified game for Maya children.

óox (M) *See* **ramón**.

oxo'ob (M) *See* **ramonal**.

pabajtun (M) *See* **cháak**.

pacíficos (S) The inhabitants of several communities in the southern and northeastern Yucatán Peninsula. The *pacíficos* swore loyalty to the Mexican government in exchange for tax exemptions and virtual autonomy.

pacíficos del sur (S) *Pacíficos* in southern Campeche.

pago (S) A tax.

palma real (S) The royal palm.

pa p'úul (M) Literally, "break the pitcher." A type of *piñata* ceremony in which participants shatter a pitcher filled with treats.

pardo (S) A person with a mixture of black (African) and Indian blood.

partido (S) An administrative unit consisting of a head town and surrounding smaller communities.

peseta (S) *See* **peso**.

peso (S) A coin worth eight *reales*.

petate (N) A straw mat used for covering the earthen floor of a hut.

peten aak' (M) Literally, "island of vines." A shelf or storage container suspended by vines from the roof of a hut.

pib, pibil (M) Any of a variety of foods baked in an underground oven. Also refers to the oven.

pibil k'éek'en (M) Pork baked in an underground oven.

pibil nal (M) Corn baked in an underground oven.

pibil xkaax (M) Chicken baked in an underground oven.

piik (M) *See* **fustán**.

pimpim waaj (M) A thick form of tortilla.

pinole (N) A beverage made of toasted ground corn.

pitarrilla (S) A fermented beverage made from tree bark

pixan (M) A soul or spirit.

pojoche' (M) A bow for shooting arrows.

pok jaachbil waaj (M) A soft, thin tortilla.

polokpok (M) A ball game.

pom (M) *See* **copal**.

pozole (N) A beverage made from freshly boiled corn.

puk' k'eyem (M) *See* **pozole**.

pul ya'aj (M) A witch.

ramón (S) A large tropical tree with dense foliage.

ramonal (S) A grove of *ramón* trees.

rancho (S) A commercial estate, usually smaller and less capitalized than a hacienda.

real (S) A coin worth one-eighth of a peso.

rebozo (S) A shawl worn by Mexican women of the nineteenth century, which is still common among rural women today.

regidor (S) Literally, "ruler" or "representative". A fourth-tier official on the *república de indígenas*.

república de indígenas (S) A Maya town council.

sa' (M) *See* **atole**.

saastun (M) Literally, "clear stone." A device used by Maya *h-men* for healing and divination.

sakal (M) To weave.

sak ja' (M) A corn-based beverage similar to *atole*.

sak pet waaj (M) A hard, thick tortilla.

sanjuanista (S) A member of a Yucatecan liberal political club in the years immediately preceding Mexican independence in 1821.

Santo Kaaj (M) Another name for the town of Chan Santa Cruz, which today is called Felipe Carrillo Puerto.

sargento (S) A sergeant.

sarsaparilla (S) A tropical root used for flavoring beverages, particularly root beer.

sicte' (M) *See* **cha'**.

sikil (M) A pumpkin seed or seeds or the paste made from them.

sitio (S) A small, undeveloped parcel of land used for raising cattle, beekeeping, or farming.

solar (S) An urban lot.

subdelegado (S) A *partido* official charged with tax collection and general administration. The position was created during the eighteenth century. Most of its responsibilities were gradually transferred to the *jefe político* after 1835.

sublevados bravos (S) The rebels of Chan Santa Cruz.

sublevados pacíficos (S) *See* **pacíficos**.

taburete (S) A footstool or ottoman.

tak in kul (M) Literally, "I want to sit." A game in which one of the players has to guess which of the others is holding a clay disk.

tamal, tamale (N) A mixture of *nixtamal* and lard wrapped in a corn husk or banana leaf and steamed. It often contains a savory filling.

taman (M) Cotton.

tankasche' (M) A type of tree whose bark is used for making crosses believed to have medicinal value.

tankul (M) A variation of *tunk'ul*.

tapezco (S) A spit.

tasita (M/S) Probably a Spanish variation of the Maya term *tas che'*, or a latticework made of sticks and vines.

tatich (M) A grandfather. Also refers to the leader of Chan Santa Cruz and to the person who interprets what the Speaking Cross says.

teniente (S) A lieutenant. Also refers to the second-highest official on the *república de indígenas*.

terno (S) An elaborate form of *hipil* and *fustán*.

testamentaría (S) The legal process of executing a will.

tich' (M) A Maya field ceremony.

tóok pom (M) Literally, "the burning of incense." A component of Maya field ceremonies.

torero (S) A bullfighter.

tortilla (S) A thin round cake of cornmeal.

totoposte (S) A type of hardtack made of cornmeal.

trici-taxi (S) A three-wheeled, pedal-powered rickshaw.

trovador (S) A trio of singers or troubadours.

tsuuts k'abo'ob (M) Literally, "kiss the hands." A ceremony once associated with the Day of the Dead, in which young people show deference to their elders.

ts'ono'ot (M) *See* **cenote**.

ts'oop sandía (M/S) Literally, "bust the melon." A rural ceremony that involved shattering a watermelon with one's fist.

tunk'ul (M) A drum made from a hollow log.

tuti waaj (M) A cornmeal cake or cakes used as offerings in Maya rain ceremonies.

tuup (M) A large golden earring or earrings.

tuyum pixan (M) Solitary souls believed to require special propitiation during Day of the Dead ceremonies. The term *tuyum* is of uncertain origin but may be an adaptation of *tu'ub*, "to forget."

úuchben máako'ob (M) Literally, "the ancient people." Refers to the pre-conquest Mayas.

u'ul (M) Pottery.

vaquería (S) A rural Yucatecan folk dance celebration that is loosely associated with the tending of cattle

vaquero (S) A tender of cattle. A cowboy.

vara (S) A distance measure equal to approximately .835 meter.

vecino (S) A non-Maya resident of a town.

waaj (M) A tortilla or tortillas.

wíinikito (M/S) Literally, "little men." An affectionate term for children.

xakal (M) A small circular blister.

xamach (M) A clay or iron griddle used for cooking tortillas.

xanab k'éewel (M) Literally, "leather shoe." Refers to a type of shoe worn in folk dances, as well as to the type of dance itself.

xani p'óok (M) A straw hat made of coarse leaves.

xinki se'en (M) Whooping cough.

xkan muk'uy (M) Anemia.

xkantumbub (M) An herbal medicine.

xkuleex (M) Short cotton drawers or underpants.

xp'ujuk (M) A wildflower.

xtabay (M) A mythical creature believed to transform itself into a beautiful woman in order to lure men to their doom.

xudub pek (M) A pod of twin seeds used for medicinal purposes.

xúux (M) A wicker basket.

yáax ja' (M) Literally, "first water." A popular term for *aguardiente,* or rum.

yerbatero (S) Someone who cures by using herbs.

yok waaj (M) A ball or balls of cornmeal dough cooked in banana leaves and used as ceremonial offerings.

yumil k'áax (M) *See* **balam**.

yumkimil (M) Death or the Grim Reaper.

yumxcrib (M) *See* **escribano**.

yupte (M) *See* **hipil**.

yuum (M) A master.

zapatista (S) A member of the Zapata National Liberation Army, or EZLN, which launched a rebellion on 1 January 1994 in the state of Chiapas.

zapote (N) A fruit common in tropical Mexico. Also refers to the tree that produces this fruit.

Bibliographical Essay

In 1943 Howard F. Cline produced the first comprehensive bibliography on the ethnohistory of the Yucatán area, a work that proved to be the starting point for many a reader and researcher. A lot has transpired since then. The Maya peoples of Yucatán, Guatemala, and Belize have long inspired the attention of scholars. In the United States alone, the last twenty years have generated a wealth of studies, and new dissertations continue to appear under a variety of disciplinary headings. The Universidad Autónoma de Yucatán's Facultad de Antropología and other research institutes throughout Mexico have also created an impressive collection of studies on the Maya peoples, their history, and their culture and language.

This essay provides an overview of published ethnographic materials, (mostly academic) in both Spanish and English. It also provides something that was virtually impossible in Cline's day: a survey of the vast collection of primary materials now available in historical archives in Yucatán, Mexico City, Campeche, Belize, Guatemala, and the United States. Unfortunately, because of the scope of this subject, I must exclude related studies on the Maya peoples of Chiapas and the regions of Guatemala outside of the Yucatán-influenced Petén. Nevertheless, the reader will have the resources to begin any serious investigation into the history and culture of the Yucatec Mayas.

Here as elsewhere, ethnography began with the conquistadors. Among the first Spaniards to reach the Yucatán Peninsula was Bernal Díaz, the soldier who fought with Hernán Cortés in Tenochtitlán; see Díaz's *Conquest of New Spain* (Harmondsworth, England: Penguin, 1963). Díaz's ethnographic observations regarding the Mayas, however, are fairly limited. The earliest published ethnographic writings come from the Franciscan missionaries, two of which are particularly important. Diego de Landa's *Relación de las cosas de Yucatán* (Madrid: Hermanos García Noblejas, 1985) provides the earliest systematic account of the Yucatec Mayas and continues to hold great relevance for modern researchers. In the mid-1600s another Franciscan, López de Cogolludo, produced his own comprehensive, three-volume account of contact, conquest, and colonization: *Historia de Yucatán* (Campeche: Comisión de la Historia de Campeche, 1954).

Interest in the Yucatán flourished among patricians during the nineteenth century. In the early years of the Caste War, Campeche-born Justo Sierra O'Reilly began a history of the peninsula to explain the conflict; although never completed, *Los indios de Yucatán* remains an invaluable source for late colonial history and independence. The most important patrician history of the Caste War is Serapio Baqueiro's *Ensayo histórico sobre las revoluciones de Yucatán,* 3 vols. (Mérida: Manuel Heredia Argüelles, 1879). Eligio Ancona, a journalist and one-time governor of Yucatán, produced his own four-volume

Historia de Yucatán in 1881 (Mérida: Gobierno del Estado de Yucatán, reprinted 1917). A late-nineteenth-century author named Francisco Molina Solís produced several patrician histories; the most valuable of these is *Historia de Yucatán durante la dominación española,* 3 vols. (Mérida: Imprenta de la Lotería del Estado, 1903–14).

For a counterweight to Yucatecan self-perceptions, the reader should consult two travelogues by gentleman-archaeologist John Lloyd Stephens: *Incidents of Travel in Central America, Chiapas, and Yucatan,* 2 vols. (New York: Dover Publications, Inc., 1969; orig. 1841); and *Incidents of Travel in Yucatan,* 2 vols. (New York: Dover Publications Inc., 1963; orig. 1841). These four volumes are so well known that I have made no attempt to excerpt them in this book. For additional information on nineteenth-century travelers' accounts, the reader should consult the Cline bibliography, which appeared as an appendix in Alfonso Villa Rojas, *The Maya of East-Central Quintana Roo* (Washington, D.C.: Carnegie Institution, 1943), pp. 165–82. (This larger work will be discussed later in this essay.)

Serious academic study of colonial society and the Yucatec Mayas is almost entirely a product of the twentieth century. Research began with the work of two men, Ralph Roys and Robert Chamberlain. Roys's *The Titles of Ebtun* (Washington, D.C.: Carnegie Institution, 1939) reproduced and translated a series of Maya *república* documents from a village immediately west of Valladolid. Chamberlain's *The Conquest and Colonization of Yucatan, 1517–1557* (Washington, D.C.: Carnegie Institution, 1948) was the first English-language treatment of its subject and the first to attempt to reconstruct events using documents from the Archivo General de las Indias in Spain. A somewhat later Roys work, *The Indian Background of Colonial Yucatan* (Norman: University of Oklahoma Press, 1972) sketched the basic contours of Maya social organization before 1821.

Since 1980, however, several studies have emerged that radically clarify the Roys/Chamberlain vision. Valuable information on demography and patterns of colonization appear in Peter Gerhard's *The Southeast Frontier of New Spain,* rev. ed. (Norman: University of Oklahoma Press, 1993). Two other studies reexamine the conquest of the Yucatec Mayas. Inga Clendinnen's *Ambivalent Conquests* (Cambridge: Cambridge University Press, 1987) attempts to penetrate the cultural assumptions that conditioned the perceptions of Spaniards and Mayas. Matthew Restall's *Maya Conquistador* (Boston: Beacon Hill, 1998) follows the conquest and its initial impact through the vantage point of Maya-language documents.

During the past fifteen years, numerous studies on the construction of colonial society have been published. The first of these is Nancy M. Farriss's *The Maya under Colonial Rule* (Princeton, N.J.: Princeton University Press, 1983), a three-hundred-year overview of Maya history that stresses the continuity of what the author refers to as "core culture." Robert W. Patch's *Maya and*

Spaniard in Yucatán (Stanford: Stanford University Press, 1993) offers a more materialistic and economic reading of colonial Yucatecan history. In *The Maya World* (Stanford: Stanford University Press, 1997), Matthew Restall reexamines the period through the illuminating prism of Maya-language documents from the indigenous town councils. Sergio Quezada's *Los pies de la república* (Mexico City: CIESAS/INI, 1997) provides its own overview of the pre-Bourbon colonial period and includes a large number of translated primary documents. Those who are interested in the 1761 rebellion of the Maya messiah Jacinto Canek should consult Robert W. Patch's "Culture, Community, and 'Rebellion' in the Yucatec Maya Uprising of 1761," in Susan Schroeder, ed., *Native Resistance and the Pax Colonial in New Spain* (Lincoln: University of Nebraska Press, 1998).

The nineteenth century has received far less scholarly attention, and until recently most of it has focused on either the century's transcendent event—the Caste War—or on the emergence of the later henequen economy. Several nineteenth-century patricians wrote valuable histories of the period, as stated previously.

The groundwork for virtually all modern studies of nineteenth-century Yucatán has been Howard F. Cline's unpublished Ph.D. dissertation, "Regionalism and Society in Yucatan, 1825–1847" (Cambridge: Harvard University Press, 1947). Most scholars of nineteenth-century Yucatán, however, have probably entered the subject through Nelson Reed's *The Caste War of Yucatan* (Stanford: Stanford University Press, 1964). Reed resurrected the subject by reversing the roles of heroes and villains, while adding anthropological perspectives and materials culled from the Archives of Belize.

Shortly after Reed's work appeared, two Spanish-language volumes were published. The first and lesser satisfying is Ramón Berzuna Pinto's *Guerra social en Yucatán* (Mexico City: Costa-Amic, 1965), which is mostly a rehash of patrician histories. The second volume, which is better documented, more original, and more ambitious, is Moisés González Navarro's *Raza y tierra* (Mexico City: Colegio de México, 1970). This latter work, however, focuses on macroeconomic information and relies heavily on published laws and decrees. The penultimate chapter of Leticia Reina's *Las rebeliones campesinas en México* (Mexico City: Siglo Ventiuno, 1980) offers a summary of the Caste War, plus an intriguing selection of documents drawn from Mexico's Defense Archives.

Several works from Yucatecan scholars document features of the early national period in southeastern Mexico. Pedro Bracamonte y Sosa's *Amos y sirvientes* (Mérida: Universidad Autónoma de Yucatán, 1993) explores the critical issue of hacienda life. In *Liberalismo en tierras del caminante* (Zamora, Michoacán: Colegio de Michoacán, 1994), Arturo Güémez Pineda analyzes land tenure as a factor in the emergence of the Caste War, although to the exclusion of all other issues.

The Caste War has been the subject of many recent studies. Terry Rugeley's

Yucatán's Maya Peasantry and the Origins of the Caste War, 1800–1847 (Austin: University of Texas Press, 1996) offers a social history of the period, reconstructing the people and problems of the era through primary documents. Another work by the same author, *Of Wonders and Wise Men: Religion and Popular Cultures in Southeast Mexico* (Austin: University of Texas Press, 2000), explores cultural components, both Mayan and Hispanic, of the years 1800–76. A special issue of *The Americas* (53, no. 4, April 1997) includes essays on pre-war political violence, the Speaking Cross, the *pacífico* communities of southern Campeche, and the manipulation of Caste War memories during the years of Lázaro Cárdenas. Don E. Dumond's massive *The Machete and the Cross* (Lincoln: University of Nebraska Press, 1997) explores the Caste War from its origin to the early twentieth century, although often from limited source material. Dumond's principal contribution is his exploration of the alliances and rivalries of Maya war leaders in the Chan Santa Cruz and southern Campeche regions, drawn largely from materials located in the Archives of Belize.

Social and political sequels of the conflict have their own growing literature. Readers who are interested in the final days of the independent Maya groups should consult Felipe Nery Avila Zapata's *El general May* (Chetumal, Quintana Roo: Gobierno del Estado de Quintana Roo, 1974) for a close look at the last leader for one group. For a collection of translated Maya correspondence from rebel leaders, see Fidelio Quintal Martín, *Correspondencia de la Guerra de Castas* (Mérida: Universidad Autónoma de Yucatán, 1992). Teresa Ramayo Lanz's *Los mayas pacíficos de Campeche* (Campeche: Universidad Autónoma de Campeche, 1996) explores the largely autonomous communities of the south. *Guerra de Castas: Actores postergados* (Mérida: Unicornio, 1997), edited by Genny M. Negroe Sierra and coordinated with the sesquicentennial of that conflict, contains five essays related to the violent history of nineteenth-century Yucatán. A recent reexamination of the rebel Maya society of Chan Santa Cruz is found in Lorena Careaga Viliesid's *Hierofanía combatiente* (Chetumal, Quintana Roo: Universidad de Quintana Roo, 1998). For the story of the gradual incorporation of southeastern Yucatán into Mexico's political and economic spheres, see Antonio Higuera Bonfil's *Quintana Roo entre tiempos* (Chetumal, Quintana Roo: Universidad de Quintana Roo, 1997) and Carlos Macías Richard's, *Nueva frontera mexicana* (Chetumal, Quintana Roo: Universidad de Quintana Roo, 1997).

The Mexican Revolution arrived late in southeastern Mexico, but it nevertheless was a critical moment in the region's ethnohistory. Gilbert M. Joseph's *Revolution from Without* (Cambridge: Cambridge University Press, 1982) is the first English-language examination of the attempts at revolutionary reform and mobilization in Yucatán, including Salvador Alvarado's liberation of indebted Maya peons and Felipe Carrillo Puerto's attempts to organize a Maya support base for his Socialist vision. Allen Wells, in *Yucatán's Gilded Age* (Albuquerque: University of New Mexico Press, 1985), provides a social history of the peninsula's rural world during the late nineteenth century. Allen Wells and Gilbert M. Joseph, in *Summer of Discontent, Seasons of Upheaval* (Stanford: Stanford University Press, 1996), connect the politics and social formations of the time, including hacienda life and rural *caciquismo,* to larger national structures. Ben Fallaw's *Cárdenes Compromised* (Durham, N.C.: Duke University Press, in press) explores Yucatán's rural politics from 1924 through 1940. Franco Roggero Savarino's *Pueblos y nacionalismo* (Mexico City: Instituto Nacional de Estudios Históricos de la Revolución Mexicana, 1997) reviews mainly urban politics but also includes information on haciendas and on attempts to recruit revolutionary support among rural Mayas.

Yucatán's *ejido* system, which is rapidly disappearing at the time of this writing, constituted one of the most important institutions in the lives of modern-day Mayas. The successes and more evident failures of the southeastern *ejidos* have attracted an important body of scholarship, much of it coming from sociologists and economists. Literature on the Yucatecan *ejido* system, however, has been overwhelmingly critical. One of the most thorough studies of its problems is Otón Baños Ramírez's *Yucatán: Ejidos sin campesinos* (Mérida: Universidad Autónoma de Yucatán, 1989). This same author's subsequent *Neoliberalism, reorganización y subsistencia rural: El caso de la zona henequenera de Yucatán, 1980–1992* (Mérida: Universidad Autónoma de Yucatán, 1996) follows the story through the dismantling of the *ejido* system under presidents Miguel de la Madrid and Carlos Salinas de Gortari. The principal English-language study is *Agrarian Reform and Public Enterprise in Mexico* (Tuscaloosa: University of Alabama Press, 1987), by Jeffrey T. Brannon and Eric N. Baklanoff. All of these studies tend to focus on underproductivity and the limitations that state control places on worker initiative. Esteban Krotz's *Cambio cultural y resocialización en Yucatán* (Mérida: Universidad Autónoma de Yucatán, 1997) contains eleven essays that document present-day Mayas' attempts to deal with the collapse of rural life, the increasing presence of the state, the rise of religious pluralism, and other national and international pressures.

Although its economic reforms were thwarted, and thus proved disappointing in practice, the revolution had a profound impact on the region's intellectual climate. The late revolutionary period (1920–40) witnessed the first systematic study of the region and its peoples and produced the most important body of ethnographic writings, thanks to the Carnegie Project. During this time, anthropological giants walked the earth; their writings are in a class by themselves. The three main products of the Carnegie Project were Robert Redfield and Alfonso Villa Rojas, *Chan Kom: A Maya Village* (Chicago: University of Chicago Press, 1934); Villa Rojas, *The Maya of East-Central Quintana Roo* (Washington, D.C.: Carnegie Institution, 1943); and Redfield's grand synthetic statement, *The Folk Culture of Yucatan* (Chicago: University of Chicago Press, 1940). Also of interest is Redfield's return to Chan Kom and his revision of his own theories: *A Village That Chose Progress* (Chicago: University of Chicago

Press, 1950). An important but overlooked product of the Carnegie Project is the folklore collection by Margaret Park Redfield, *The Folk Literature of a Yucatecan Town* (Washington, D.C.: Carnegie Institution, 1935). Scholars should also consult Howard F. Cline's bibliography on pre-1943 ethnographic sources, which is included as an appendix to the Villa Rojas work cited above.

Ethnographic writing from the post–Carnegie Project to the present is particularly rich, thanks to the research of the many anthropologists who have worked on the Yucatán Peninsula. Richard Thompson's *Winds of Tomorrow* (Chicago: University of Chicago Press, 1974) studies the town of Ticul. Irwin Press's *Tradition and Adaptation* (Westport, Conn.: Greenwood Press, 1975) considers cultural blending in the village of Pustunich. Mary Elmendorf's *Nine Maya Women* (New York: Schenkman Publishing Co., 1976) might be considered an alternative to the vision of Redfield and Villa Rojas because the author restricts her study to the *women* of Chan Kom. Carlos Kirk's *Haciendas en Yucatán* (Mexico City: Instituto Nacional Indigenista, 1982), which has never been translated into English, documents the hardships and bureaucratic red tape on a henequen *ejido*. Margarita Rosales González's *Oxkutzcab, Yucatán, 1900–1960* (Mexico City: Instituto Nacional de Antropología e Historia, 1988) traces the region's development as a citrus producer. A closely related study is Carmen Morales Valderrama's *Ocupación y sobrevivencia campesina en la zona citrícola de Yucatán* (Mexico City: Instituto Nacional de Antropología e Historia, 1987).

Anthropology among the Yucatec Mayas continued to thrive in the 1990s. Yet another study of southeastern Mexico's most scrutinized village appears in Alicia Re Cruz's *Two Milpas of Chan Kom* (Albany: State University of New York Press, 1996), which explores the cultural effects of transferring much of the town's labor force to Cancún. Quetzil E. Castañeda's *In the Museum of Maya Culture* (Minneapolis: University of Minnesota Press, 1996) examines contemporary politics and racial attitudes; the author's postmodernist vocabulary will more often baffle than enlighten the reader, but the book's occasional wry humor adds life. A more recent contribution, *Mayan People within and beyond Boundaries* (Amsterdam: Harwood Academic Publishers, 1999), by Peter Hervik, analyzes the modes of rural self-definition, as well as the problems that arise when one culture writes about another.

Few studies of the Petén or its Maya-speaking inhabitants are available, although for historical depth three works stand out. For the early colonial period, Grant D. Jones's *Maya Resistance to Spanish Rule* (Albuquerque: University of New Mexico Press, 1989) is the key work; a successor volume, *The Conquest of the Last Maya Kingdom* (Stanford: Stanford University Press, 1998) explores the 1697 conquest and its immediate aftermath. For the eighteenth- through twentieth-century picture, see Norman B. Schwartz, *Forest Society* (Philadelphia: University of Pennsylvania Press, 1990).

Maya society in Belize has received even less attention. Some information appears in the Caste War studies by Nelson Reed and Don Dumond. Readers who are interested in local memory and personal narrative should consult Alfonso Ambrosio Tsul's *After One Hundred Years* (Maya Institute of Belize, 1993), an account of his family's flight from the Caste War and its eventual resettlement in the Cayo district of Belize.

Southeastern Mexico enjoys a vast and inventive body of folklore that stems from both Maya and Spanish roots, all filtered through the historical experiences of the past few centuries. Bits and pieces appear in the Franciscan chronicles. Daniel Brinton collected beliefs and folk narratives in his "Folklore of Yucatan" (*Folklore Journal* 1, 1883). Manuel Rejón García's *Supersticiones y leyendas mayas* (Mérida: 1905) is one of the earliest known patrician writings on the topic. Margaret Park Redfield's *The Folk Literature of a Yucatecan Town* (Washington, D.C.: Carnegie Institution, 1935), a compilation drawn from the town of Dzitás, constitutes the first serious attempt at collection and remains a classic in the field. Equally important is Allan F. Burns's *An Epoch of Miracles* (Austin: University of Texas Press, 1983). A collection gathered by Cuban-born anthropologist Manuel Andrade has been transcribed in both Maya and Spanish by Hilaria Máas Collí in *Cuentos mayas yucatecos,* 2 vols. (Mérida: Universidad Autónoma de Yucatán, 1991). The thirty-five-volume Spanish-Maya series entitled *Colección letras mayas contemporáneas* (Tlahuapan, Puebla: INI/SEDESOL, 1994) is an invaluable source of narratives, songs, prayers, local history, and other assorted lore. For a review of additional sources on folklore, see "Geography, Misery, Agency, Remedy: The Unwritten Almanac of Folk Knowledge," in Terry Rugeley's *Of Wonders and Wise Men,* pp. 1–37.

Since 1900 many scholars have tackled the Maya language, and thanks to their efforts, we have extensive research into grammar, vocabulary, and assorted nuances. The earliest English-language analysis in this century was Alfred M. Tozzer's *A Maya Grammar* (New York: Dover Publications, Inc., 1977; orig. 1921). One of the best grammatical studies of the Maya language is Alfredo Barrera Vázquez's "La lengua maya de Yucatán," which was included in volume 6 of the *Enciclopedia yucatanense* (Mexico City: Gobierno de Yucatán, 1946), pp. 205–62. Historical scholars will find Barrera Vázquez's monumental *Diccionario Maya Cordemex* (Mérida: Cordemex, 1980) an indispensable reference work, although its sheer size and its collection of vocabularies from radically different time periods may make it too unwieldy for modern-day Maya conversation. A less comprehensive but more serviceable volume is the *Diccionario básico español-maya, maya-español,* by Ramón Bastarrachea et al. (Mérida: Maldonado Editores, 1992). Although this dictionary could be considerably expanded and revised, it reflects contemporary speech better than does the encyclopedic work by Barrera Vázquez. Gary Bevington's recent *Maya for Travelers and Students* (Austin: University of Texas Press, 1995) offers a brief introduction to the language, as well as a useful Maya-Spanish-English vocabulary. For a more detailed grammatical analysis of the language's most difficult component, see Glenn Ayres's and Barbara Pfeiler's *Los verbos mayas* (Mérida: Universidad Autónoma de Yucatán, 1997). Many of the subtleties of Maya are explored in David and Alejandra Bolles's *A Grammar of the Yucatecan Maya Language* (Lee, N.H.: typescript, 1985). Victoria Bricker, Eleuterio Poot Yah, and Ofelia Dzul de Poot have compiled a comprehensive dictionary and grammar entitled *A Dictionary of the Maya Language As Spoken in Hocabá, Yucatán* (Salt Lake City: University of Utah Press, 1998).

Readers who are interested in diverse aspects of the Yucatec Mayas' historical experience should consult a number of edited works. Grant D. Jones's *Anthropology and History in Yucatán* (Austin: University of Texas Press, 1977) offers a variety of essays on the Mayas from the colonial period to the present day. *Yucatán: A World Apart* (Tuscaloosa: University of Alabama Press, 1980), edited by Edward H. Moseley and Edward D. Terry, is a broad collection of essays on geography, culture, history, literature, and regional political issues. Jeffrey T. Brannon's and Gilbert M. Joseph's *Land, Labor, & Capital in Modern Yucatán* (Tuscaloosa: University of Alabama Press, 1991) contains useful studies on land, resistance, and political economy. Readers should also consult Otón Baños Ramírez, ed., *Liberalismo, actores y política en Yucatán* (Mérida: Universidad Autónoma de Yucatán, 1995) for essays concerning the role of nineteenth- and early-twentieth-century liberalism in Yucatán.

Archives offer a wealth of primary source material. Collections of historical documents are far more organized and accessible than in Howard Cline's day. Their systematic exploration, more than anything else, has led to reevaluations of not only the Mayas but also the history of the region. The most extensive collection of documents on the Yucatec Mayas is housed in the Archivo General del Estado de Yucatán (AGEY), located in Mérida. One of the largest repositories of historical papers in Mexico, the AGEY contains vast amounts of information on land, labor, taxes, migration, and the innumerable legal quarrels initiated by or against Mayas. A detailed breakdown of its holdings is impossible here. The AGEY will continue to be a key resource for Maya scholars and historians of southeastern Mexico.

The Archivo Notarial del Estado de Yucatán (ANEY) in Mérida documents the legal and economic life of the Mayas. The main documents filed here are wills, registers of sale, loans and mortgages, debt repayments, powers of attorney, bail bonds, commercial contracts, and claims for public lands. All of these documents involve Yucatec Mayas, and some, particularly those dated before Mexican independence (1821), are written in Maya. Most of the ANEY's nineteenth-century holdings have been transferred to the AGEY, but some of that material remains, particularly the protocols of towns outside of Mérida.

The Centro de Apoyo a la Investigación Histórica de Yucatán (CAIHY), also located in Mérida, contains books, manuscripts, imprints, and proclamations, many of which provide unparalleled access to the lives and perceptions of the Yucatec Mayas. The CAIHY is the principal repository of the Maya-language correspondence of the Caste War. It also provides one of the strongest reading and research libraries for scholars working in Mérida. The CAIHY's sister institution, the Hemeroteca José María Pino Suárez, is located in the same building and offers an unrivaled collection of newspapers and literary and political journals from the nineteenth and twentieth centuries.

After the state, the Catholic Church was the largest single generator and archiver of documents dealing with the Mayas. The Archivo Histórico de la Arquidiócesis de Yucatán (AHAY), located on the second floor of the Mérida cathedral, contains hundreds of boxes of church history, much of it relating to daily affairs in the rural villages: parish management, *cofradías* (lay religious brotherhoods), marriage dispensations, complaints, investigations, loans, Caste War turmoil, and other topics that affected church life. The ground floor of the same cathedral houses the Archivo Histórico del Arzobispado, which contains baptism, marriage, and burial records for towns and villages throughout Yucatán, dating from the colonial period to the present day, and which offers outstanding materials for social and demographic study.

Several collections in Mexico City are also useful in the study of Maya history and culture. The Archivo General de la Nación de México, particularly the collection known as Bienes Nacionales, includes a substantial body of material on daily life in nineteenth-century Yucatán, much of it Maya related. Information on the Caste War rebels, as well as the Maya noncombatants, may be found among the papers of the Archivo Histórico de la Defensa de la Nación. A selection of these has been reprinted verbatim by Letitia Reina in *Las rebeliones campesinas en México*. Readers who are interested in post-1876 Yucatán and lingering Caste War hostilities should consult the Archivo Porfirio Díaz, located in the Universidad Iberoamericana.

The lives and history of the nineteenth-century Mayas also found their way into archives outside of Mérida and Mexico City. The Archives of Belize (formerly the Archives of British Honduras), located in Belmopan, contain a wealth of information regarding the rebel society of Chan Santa Cruz, the *pacíficos del sur*, and the Mayas and Hispanics who fled to Belize to escape the violence of the Caste War. In Campeche, Mérida's sister city and sometimes rival, the Archivo Parroquial del Obispado de Campeche (APOC) offers a well-organized collection of baptism, marriage, and burial records (many of which are Mayan) for Campeche city and state. The APOC also contains important demographic information on the *mayas pacíficos*, who received occasional visits from the priests of Campeche.

The Archivo General del Estado de Campeche contains far less Maya-related material than its Yucatecan counterpart but merits attention. Its newspaper collection provides exceptionally strong information on the Caste War in the state of Campeche. The war and its aftermath also affected the Petén, the northernmost district of Guatemala. The papers of Guatemala City's Archivo General de Centroamérica often reveal aspects of the Caste War and of Maya-Hispanic relations that are not available in the Yucatecan collections.

Researchers working in the United States have many resources at their disposal. The most important of these is probably the Special Collections of the University of Texas at Arlington (UTA). This archive includes hacienda papers of the influential Peón family, as well as the partial correspondence of José Salazar Ilarregui, the man who served as imperial commissar during the brief years of the French Empire in Mexico. UTA also includes microfilmed copies of much of the material in the AGEY, ANEY, and AHAY and of newspapers from Mérida and Campeche, all of which are available through interlibrary loan. A detailed list of UTA's considerable Yucatán-related holdings appears in Maritza Arrigunaga Coello, *Catalogue of Yucatecan Documents and Newspapers on Microfilm in the University of Texas at Arlington Library* (Arlington: University of Texas at Arlington Press, 1983).

A substantial portion of the CAIHY's collection of imprints and manuscripts can be accessed through the microfilm collection of the University of Alabama at Tuscaloosa; for details, consult Marie Ballow Bingham, *A Catalogue of the Yucatán Collection on Microfilm in the University of Alabama Libraries* (Tuscaloosa: University of Alabama Press, 1972). The Nettie Lee Benson Library of the University of Texas in Austin includes a small corpus related to Yucatán. The Latin American Collection of Tulane University in New Orleans contains Maya- and Yucatán-related material from the colonial era to the nineteenth century, with a significant portion covering the early nineteenth century. Although not as significant as the previously mentioned archives, the Clements Library of the University of Michigan includes four boxes of papers related to Yucatán and the Caste War. Although it is not focused on Yucatán or southeastern Mexico, the Bancroft Library of the University of California in Berkeley, includes microfilmed copies of the British Foreign Office records, much of which supplements and clarifies materials located in the Archives of Belize.

The corpus of Maya ethnohistorical and ethnographic material has vastly grown since the days of Howard Cline's bibliography. Although several misconceptions have been corrected, older works have not lost their value or charm; they now receive additional depth from scholars who invoke methods and perspectives that were unavailable to previous researchers. If the number of current Yucatán-related dissertation projects is any indication, interest in the topic has not waned. In addition to attracting Mexican scholars, Yucatán remains one of the principal destinations for U.S. graduate students in anthropology and history, as well as for investigators from Europe and Japan. Future studies will provide an even finer grained image of Maya—and Mexican and Central American—life during the tumultuous period from the Spanish Empire to the Mexican Revolution and beyond.

Index

References to illustrations are in italic type.